NEUROPSYCHOLOGY IN THE COURTROOM

NEUROPSYCHOLOGY IN THE COURTROOM

Expert Analysis of Reports and Testimony

Edited by
ROBERT L. HEILBRONNER

THE GUILFORD PRESS
New York   London

© 2008 The Guilford Press
A Division of Guilford Publications, Inc.
72 Spring Street, New York, NY 10012
www.guilford.com

Printed in the United States of America

This book is printed on acid-free paper.

Last digit is print number: 9   8   7   6   5   4   3   2   1

Library of Congress Cataloging-in-Publication Data

Neuropsychology in the courtroom : expert analysis of reports and testimony / edited by
Robert L. Heilbronner.
    p. ; cm.
Companion v. to: Forensic neuropsychology casebook. c2005.
Includes bibliographical references and index.
ISBN-13: 978-1-59385-634-2 (hardcover : alk. paper)
ISBN-10: 1-59385-634-2 (hardcover : alk. paper)
  1. Forensic neuropsychology. I. Heilbronner, Robert L. (Robert Louis) II. Forensic
neuropsychology casebook.
  [DNLM: 1. Forensic Medicine. 2. Neuropsychology. W 700 N494 2008]
  RA1147.5.N49   2008
  614'.1—dc22
                                                                    2007026807

About the Editor

Robert L. Heilbronner, PhD, ABPP, is a board-certified clinical neuropsychologist practicing in Chicago. He is the Director of the Chicago Neuropsychology Group. Dr. Heilbronner has faculty appointments at Northwestern University, Feinberg School of Medicine, and the University of Chicago Hospitals, Pritzker School of Medicine. He is a Fellow of the Division of Clinical Neuropsychology of the American Psychological Association and of the National Academy of Neuropsychology, and is an elected member of the board of directors of the American Academy of Clinical Neuropsychology. Dr. Heilbronner has published articles and book chapters, and has presented on clinical and forensic neuropsychology issues at national and international meetings. He has also testified in a number of civil, criminal, and capital cases locally and nationally.

Contributors

Ida Sue Baron, PhD, Department of Pediatrics, University of Virginia School of Medicine, Charlottesville, Virginia; private practice, Potomac, Maryland, and Reston, Virginia

Erin D. Bigler, PhD, Departments of Psychology and Neuroscience, Brigham Young University, Provo, Utah; Department of Psychiatry and the Brain Institute, University of Utah, Salt Lake City, Utah

Brian L. Brooks, PhD, British Columbia Mental Health and Addiction Services, Vancouver, British Columbia, Canada

David S. Bush, PhD, private practice, Palm Beach Gardens, Florida

Shane S. Bush, PhD, Long Island Neuropsychology, Lake Ronkonkoma, New York

Jacobus Donders, PhD, Psychology Service, Mary Free Bed Rehabilitation Hospital, Grand Rapids, Michigan

Kevin W. Greve, PhD, Department of Psychology, University of New Orleans, New Orleans, Louisiana

Robert L. Heilbronner, PhD, Chicago Neuropsychology Group and Department of Psychiatry and Behavioral Sciences, Feinberg School of Medicine, Northwestern University, Chicago, Illinois

James A. Holdnack, PhD, Harcourt Assessment, Inc., Bear, Delaware

Grant L. Iverson, PhD, British Columbia Mental Health and Addiction Services and Department of Psychiatry, University of British Columbia, Vancouver, British Columbia, Canada

Michael McCrea, PhD, Neuroscience Center, Waukesha Memorial Hospital, Waukesha, Wisconsin

Wiley Mittenberg, PhD, Center for Psychological Studies, Nova Southeastern University, Fort Lauderdale, Florida

Joel E. Morgan, PhD, private practice, Madison, New Jersey

Howard Oakes, PsyD, Department of Psychology, Hartford Hospital, Hartford, Connecticut

Wilfred G. van Gorp, PhD, Neuropsychological Assessment Service, Columbia Presbyterian Medical Center, New York, New York

Karen Wills, PhD, Department of Psychology, Children's Hospitals and Clinics of Minnesota, Minneapolis, Minnesota

Preface

In 2005, I edited *Forensic Neuropsychology Casebook*, a text that offered personal insights into the intricacies of conducting forensic neuropsychological assessments and serving as an expert witness in civil and criminal matters. Each author was asked to reflect on the process of clinical decision making in a particular forensic case in which he or she was involved. The process of editing that casebook led to the current text, which seeks to expand upon the previous efforts by providing insight into the minds of neuropsychologists as they analyze and critique the reports and testimony of opposing experts. The current authors were asked to analyze a report or testimony of another neuropsychological expert and to provide constructive criticism much like they would do in a situation in which they are serving as a consultant to an attorney who is about to cross-examine the opposing expert.

Very little has been written about the phenomenological experience of the clinical neuropsychologist working in a forensic context. This text, a useful companion to *Forensic Neuropsychology Casebook*, again uses the case-study approach to gain insight into the mind of the forensic neuropsychologist. It provides a forum for the reader to begin to understand the thought process of the neuropsychologist as he or she ventures into the forensic arena. Topics were chosen to reflect the current scope of forensic neuropsychology practice. A broad array of conditions (e.g., traumatic brain injury, multiple chemical sensitivity, and electrical injury) are included, written from the perspectives of adult and pediatric experts. In choosing the present complement of authors, I wanted to make sure that there was a broad enough representation of individuals experienced in managing the different kinds of issues that neuropsychologists are often asked to address in forensic cases. Readers familiar with forensic neuropsy-chological research, attendees of continuing professional education pro-grams, and those experienced in forensic practice should recognize the names of many of the authors included in this volume. All of them bring to their topics a vast array of knowledge and experience obtained through their own research or clinical practice.

Each chapter followed a recommended format, although authors were allowed a fair degree of artistic freedom to write as they wished. They were asked to identify the approach they customarily take when reviewing/ critiquing reports and depositions; describe the background of a particular case on which they consulted; analyze and comment on the interpretations and opinions of the opposing expert as if they were providing consultation to an attorney who was about to cross-examine that expert. Finally, they were asked to comment on what they learned from their involvement in that particular case and what kind of knowledge others might be able to gain from their insights and perspectives. I gratefully acknowledge the con-tribution and time commitment each of the authors has made in preparing this book.

Once again, I am very grateful to the staff at The Guilford Press for their ongoing suggestions and support. Thanks to my colleagues in Chicago and elsewhere who continue to provide peer consultation in some of the more difficult forensic cases in which I have been asked to serve as an expert. My children remain a constant source of pride and satisfaction for me and have always been supportive of my professional pursuits. Again, my wife, Diane, deserves special recognition for her unwavering support throughout all aspects of our life together.

Contents

PART II. FORENSIC CASE ANALYSIS FROM OPPOSING PERSPECTIVES

PART III. SPECIAL TOPICS

NEUROPSYCHOLOGY IN THE COURTROOM

Part I
Case Analyses

1

Traumatic Brain Injury

Do You See What I See?

Jacobus Donders

TRAUMATIC BRAIN INJURY

Traumatic brain injury (TBI) occurs when there is an acute, external force to the head, which may result in transient alteration of consciousness and/or compromise of brain matter. It is one of the most common acquired neurological conditions, but the vast majority (> 80%) of all cases of TBI can be classified as mild in the sense that they are associated with no or minimal (< 30 minutes) loss of consciousness, limited (< 1 day) posttraumatic amnesia, and no acute intracranial findings on computed tomography (CT) or magnetic resonance imaging (MRI) of the brain. Recent literature reviews suggest that mild, uncomplicated TBI is rarely associated with persistent neuropsychological sequelae (Iverson, 2005; Schretlen & Shapiro, 2003). Yet, cases of mild TBI are encountered increasingly in the medical–legal arena pertaining to personal injury claims in civil court.

In this chapter, I review a case from my own practice that involved a claim of neurobehavioral impairment, more than 1 year after mild TBI. I had done the original neuropsychological evaluation of the plaintiff, which was subsequently critiqued by a different psychologist who was involved with his treatment, and I was then asked to comment on that other psychologist's review. There was additional follow-up after the plaintiff psychologist was deposed by the attorney who had retained me. Eventually, the case was settled out of court before my scheduled deposition was taken. Some of the specific identifying information in this case description has been altered to protect privacy, but the psychometric test results and quotations are identical to the original texts.

PROFESSIONAL APPROACH

Neuropsychological independent medical–legal evaluations (IMEs) make up about 15% of my practice at a private, not-for-profit rehabilitation hospital, and the majority (> 70%) of these involve cases of TBI. I never advertised to seek these kinds of referrals, nor did I make any attempts to cultivate them. It is probably most accurate to say that the referrals found me because I had been practicing in the local community for several years and was doing quite a few clinical neuropsychological evaluations in the context of rehabilitation. Some of those cases eventually involved claims of long-term impairment or disability, leading to legal procedures where I was typically called to testify in depositions as a treating doctor or fact witness. Gradually, I started getting referrals directly from attorneys who had cross-examined me during such processes. Currently, the vast majority (> 90%) of these IME referrals come from representatives of the defense—typically either an attorney defending a person who is being sued as being at fault in a motor vehicle accident and therefore potentially responsible for the plaintiff's subjective symptoms or an insurance company that is questioning the causal relationship between an accident and the plaintiff's ongoing subjective complaints.

I typically use three criteria to determine if I am willing to accept a referral for an IME. First, the subject matter has to be within my area of expertise. For example, I have little training in child-custody issues and I therefore do not accept referrals for that purpose. Second, there should be no potential conflict of interest. For example, if the person who is to be examined by me in an IME has previously or concurrently been served on a routine clinical basis through my department or even another service in the hospital that employs me, I do not want to be in a position of wearing two different professional hats simultaneously. Incidentally, I only do neuropsychological evaluations through the hospital that employs me, and I have no financial incentive to do more IMEs because my salary is the same, regardless of whether I see a clinical patient who is on Medicare or a person in the context of an IME where the reimbursement is at a relatively higher rate. My third criterion to evaluate the appropriateness of an IME referral is that I need to have a clear understanding with the referring party that all relevant records will be made available to me and that I will be expected to provide an unbiased and objective work product, be it a verbal or a written report. Specifically, I make it clear that it is my expertise that can be hired but not my opinion.

Some of the referrals I receive from attorneys, insurance case managers, or IME coordinators involve strictly file reviews. With these, I always make it clear what the limits of such reviews are, consistent with the professional guidelines for psychologists (standard 9.01.b; American Psychological Association, 2002). For example, I typically indicate that I do not feel comfortable making a definitive diagnosis without directly interviewing or otherwise examining the person in question. Several years ago, I reviewed a case file in which a person had demonstrated some isolated but atypical and inconsistent test results after an apparently mild TBI. Most striking were extremely poor results on the Tactual Performance Test, in a manner that did not seem to correspond to any other test results of sensory–motor, perceptual, or problem-solving skills. Rather than concluding that this was simply an aberrant finding or that it might have been the result of insufficient effort, I suggested an interview with this woman to help clarify this and some other unusual aspects of her presentation. It was at that time that I learned that she had previously been the victim of a sexual assault. Apparently, the Tactual Performance Test (blindfold and all) had been administered by a male psychometrist, as one of the first tests in the battery. It was not difficult to imagine how this might have confounded the findings, but, unfortunately, the assault history had not been included in the original report. This is an example of how exclusive reliance on medical records may not be sufficient to form a diagnostic opinion.

IMEs typically involve more of a direct interview with, and examination of, the individual who is claiming acquired neurobehavioral impairment. I typically review available academic, medical, and other relevant records before the interview, so that I have at least some understanding of the background and history of the case. For example, if I know that the person has taken a specific test twice already within the last year with different providers, with unremarkable results on both occasions, I may not necessarily be inclined to repeat that same test again. When possible and allowed, I also interview a spouse or other family member for collateral information.

Occasionally, I receive requests to have a third person present during the evaluation, usually the plaintiff attorney or his or her designee. My standard policy in this regard is that I allow the presence of such a third party during the interview but not during the formal psychometric assessment. Typically, I refer to guidelines from national professional organizations in this regard (American Academy of Clinical Neuropsychology, 2001; Axelrod et al., 2000) as well as to empirical research that has documented the threats to the validity of test results under such circumstances

(Constantinou, Ashendorf, & McCaffrey; 2005; Lynch, 2005). Although this matter is governed by specific laws in some jurisdictions, judges in the state of Michigan (which is where I practice) have considerable leeway in their determination of whether to grant attorneys' requests for third-party observers or to agree with my objections to such. If it is decided that the evaluation may not proceed without a third party present during the psychometric assessment, I typically withdraw from the case.

Once I am able to proceed with the actual IME, I first explain the contingencies to the individual. For example, I indicate who had referred him or her to me and what a neuropsychological evaluation involves. I emphasize that I have no financial stake in the outcome of the legal dispute in question and that my opinion will be objective. I make it clear that we will not have a treating doctor–patient relationship, that the usual limits of confidentiality do not apply, and that I will not be able to provide the examinee with direct feedback about the test results or any treatment recommendations. I also underscore that it is very important for the examinee to consistently do his or her best and to be truthful at all times. I then document the examinee's level of understanding of all of this and at least his or her verbal agreement for the assessment to proceed (some examinees refuse, at the advice of council, to sign any consent forms).

CASE STUDY

Background

Mr. Smith was a 25-year-old, single, right-handed, Caucasian man with 13 completed years of education who was referred to me by an attorney representing a defendant who was being sued by Mr. Smith for alleged sequelae of an accident in which Mr. Smith had been involved as a helmeted bicycle driver, about 20 months prior to my evaluation. Mr. Smith had taken several semesters off from college following the accident, and he had completed some outpatient physical and speech therapy during that time but had not undergone a prior neuropsychological evaluation. The issue in this case was whether he had sustained a "serious neurological injury" and specifically whether that was associated with any permanent cognitive impairment.

Review of acute-care medical records did not suggest any clear loss of consciousness, and head CT scan on the day of injury was unremarkable. Review of collegiate academic records revealed that Mr. Smith's last complete semester GPA (grade point average) just prior to the accident was 1.14 (cumulative: 0.95) and that this actually improved to 2.66 (cumulative: 1.38) when he resumed his studies, about 1 year after the accident. During the interview, Mr. Smith described a fairly benign premorbid history, with no endorsement of any prior neurological, psychiatric, or substance abuse problems. He reported less than 1 hour of posttraumatic amnesia; yet, he complained of persistent difficulties with the learning and retention of new information, some neck and back pain, and frustration with his residual symptoms—all of which he attributed to the accident in question. At the same time, he reported that he was independent with all activities of daily living, including part-time labor as well as riding his bicycle in traffic.

Mr. Smith was then given a battery of neuropsychological tests. Table 1.1 presents the most significant ones of these, defined as those that were specifically referenced in my original report and/or the review by a psychologist retained by the plaintiff. My interpretation of Mr. Smith's obtained scores was as follows:

> I have concerns about the validity of these test results, for a variety of reasons. First of all, Mr. Smith clearly violates criteria for sufficient effort on a forced-choice measure (WMT [Word Memory Test]). On other tasks, assessing skills as diverse as fine motor coordination (Grooved Pegboard) and sustained attention (CPT-II [Continuous Performance Test—Second Edition]), his level of performance is so poor (more than 2 standard deviations below the mean) that it is out of proportion with the mild severity of his head injury. On other tasks, there are atypical responses. For example, on the WCST [Wisconsin Card Sorting Test], Mr. Smith made a high number of nonperseverative errors, sometimes even giving an "Other" response when the stimulus card matched one of the key cards in all three possible attributes. This is extremely unusual. For these reasons, I do not believe that these test results reflect consistent effort, and I doubt strongly that they represent a valid picture of this man's true cognitive abilities.

Note that I did not belabor the individual tests too much, to minimize the potential risk of "coaching" prior to later evaluations with this particular person or other individuals. This is a risk that needs to be considered in the context of IME's (Youngjohn, 1995). In the final "Impression and Recommendations" section of my report, I subsequently wrote:

> I can find no evidence for cognitive deficits that can unequivocally be attributed to head trauma with this man. In fact, I strongly suspect that the current test findings are confounded by inconsistent effort and possible symptom magnification. At the same time, he is telling me that he is having no difficulties in his current job, that he was obtaining B's and C's in his most recent semester at college, and that he is not depressed, so I really have no additional recommendations for his care.

This report was subsequently sent to the attorney who had retained me, who then had a legal obligation to share it with plaintiff's counsel. About 4 weeks

TABLE 1.1. Neuropsychological Test Scores

Test name	Test result
Conners' CPT-II omissions[a]	T 100
Conners' CPT-II commissions[a]	$T = 66$
Conners' CPT-II reaction time[a]	$T = 44$
Conners' CPT-II variability[a]	$T = 89$
CVLT-2 trial A1[b]	$z = -1.5$
CVLT-2 trial A5[b]	$z = -1.5$
CVLT-2 Short Delay Free Recall[b]	$z = -1.5$
CVLT-2 Long Delay Free Recall[b]	$z = -2.5$
CVLT-2 Recognition Hits[b]	$z = 0.5$
CVLT-2 Recognition False Positives[a]	$z = 4$
Grooved Pegboard, right hand[b]	$T = 28$
Grooved Pegboard, left hand[b]	$T = 20$
Trail Making Test, A[b]	$T = 38$
Trail Making Test, B[b]	$T = 37$
WAIS-III Verbal Comprehension[b]	SS = 105
WAIS-III Perceptual Organization[b]	SS = 118
WAIS-III Working Memory[b]	SS = 104
WAIS-III Processing Speed[b]	SS = 84
WCST Perseverative Errors[b]	$T = 41$
WCST Nonperseverative Errors[b]	$T = 36$
WMT Immediate Recall[b]	% correct = 72.50
WMT Delayed Recall[b]	% correct = 87.50
WMT Consistency[b]	% correct = 70.00

Note. CPT-II = Continuous Performance Test—Second Edition; CVLT-2, California Verbal Learning Test–2; WAIS-III, Wechsler Adult Intelligence Scale–III; WCST, Wisconsin Card Sorting Test; WMT, Green's Word Memory Test; T, standardized score with mean = 50 and standard deviation = 10; z, standardized score with mean = 0 and standard deviation = 1; SS, standardized score with mean = 100 and standard deviation = 15.
[a]Higher scores reflect worse performance.
[b]Higher scores reflect better performance.

later, I received a written request from "consulting psychologist" Dr. Jones for a copy of the report of my neuropsychological evaluation of Mr. Smith, along with the raw test data. Apparently, Dr. Jones had been asked by Mr. Smith's attending physician to perform a neuropsychological evaluation but then found out that one had recently been completed by me. Dr. Jones sent with his request a release of information that was signed by Mr. Smith. However, because Mr. Smith was not the client in this medical–legal context, I felt that it was my responsibility to contact the attorney who had retained me in the first place. This attorney then gave me permission to forward my report and test data to Dr. Jones, which is what I subsequently did.

About 3 weeks later, Dr. Jones prepared a letter to Mr. Smith's attending physician, documenting that he had obtained the results from my evaluation. This letter was forwarded to me by the defense attorney about 2 weeks after that. In it, Dr. Jones stated the following:

Predictably, **Dr. Donders questioned Mr. Smith's level of effort and motivation** in taking the tests, and determined that the test scores did not reflect his true cognitive status (1). It is my professional opinion that the test scores do reflect ongoing cognitive problems, very consistent with those reported by Mr. Smith and his father. Thus, I will offer my own interpretation of the test scores from Dr. Donders's evaluation for you and make some recommendations for treatment planning.

Dr. Donders stated that Mr. Smith's test scores were not likely valid due to some of the scores being quite low. The low scores on the evaluation were in areas of processing speed, attention and concentration, and verbal memory. As you know, these are **typically the areas that receive low neuropsychological test scores for individuals who have mild traumatic brain injuries (2).**

Mr. Smith seemed to perform somewhat better on attention span measures on the WAIS-III [Wechsler Adult Intelligence Scale–III] than on other areas of the neuropsychological testing. He had a very low attention span score on the CPT, a more sensitive indicator of the patient's ability to maintain attention on a task over time. Mr. Smith had mildly impaired scores on the Trail Making Test, something that would not likely be seen in an individual of his age and health were there not some other interfering cognitive problems. **He seems to have slowed speed of processing (3).**

The test scores with most significance and relevance for Mr. Smith's efforts to return to college are the results of the California Verbal Learning Test–2. He was only able to recall 4 of the 16 words on the first trial, and by the fifth trial had only been able to learn 9 of the 16 words. His short-term delayed recall was only 6 words, though cuing did help him retain all of the 9 words that he had originally learned from the 16-word list. **His delayed recall of the list was only 5 words. Recognition memory suggests that there had been passive storage of information and also provided a nice indicator of good level of effort and valid test results (4).**

On the basis of his interpretation of my test results, Dr. Jones also offered a number of recommendations for the care of Mr. Smith. These included the following:

Mr. Smith might **benefit from a psychostimulant medication** because of his attention span difficulties (5). Because he takes evening classes, the dosing and timing of stimulant medication must be carefully considered. In the academic environment, it is advisable for Mr. Smith to take a somewhat reduced number of courses because of the limitations in his memory. He should be instructed on how to use an audio tape recorder in class to assist with note taking. He should probably be **treated as a learning disabled student in the community college environment (6).** This will allow him access to help with note taking, extra time for taking tests, and the ability to take tests in a distraction-free environment.

Analysis

(1) Dr. Jones used the term *predictably* to refer to my interpretation of Mr. Smith's effort and motivation. I could not determine the grounds for this assertion although it is possible that Dr. Jones had seen previous reports that were authored by me and that included comments on the validity of test taking by the examinee. It is important to appreciate that I routinely administer symptom validity tests to all my patients, regardless of whether they are children or adults, and regardless of whether they are referred on a routine clinical basis or for an IME. However, I elected not to react to Dr. Jones's somewhat dismissive tone and simply focused instead on the facts of the case.

(2) The assertion that processing speed and other cognitive functions are typically "low" for persons with "mild traumatic brain injuries" is not consistent with the literature on this subject. It is true that Mr. Smith's lowest factor index score on the WAIS-III was Processing Speed. However, that index is typically depressed only by moderate to severe TBI (i.e., with prolonged coma and/or acute intracranial lesions on neuroimaging). Patients with mild TBI tend to obtain levels of performance on this index that are not different from demographically matched controls, as long those patients are not seeking financial compensation and have no forced-choice indicators of possible poor effort (Donders, Tulsky, & Zhu, 2001).

(3) The blanket statement that Mr. Smith had "slowed speed of processing" ignores the fact that his reaction time on Conners's CPT-II was well within normal limits—if anything, about a half a standard deviation better than average. Dr. Jones did not discuss the discrepancy between that index of speed of processing and other ones in the battery. It is well known that inconsistencies in test results occur more frequently in persons who may not give consistent effort (Larrabee, 2005; Slick, Sherman, & Iverson, 1999).

(4) Dr. Jones refers exclusively to the California Verbal Learning Test—2 (CVLT-2) in his discussion of memory impairment. Although it is true that Mr. Smith obtained 16/16 correct on the forced-choice recognition trial of the CVLT-2, this does not negate the fact that he violated relevant validity criteria on Green's WMT, which has been validated more extensively for the assessment of effort and motivation during neuropsychological evaluations. Furthermore, Dr. Jones does not appear to appreciate that a level of impairment of 2.5 standard deviations below the mean on the long delay free recall trial of the CVLT-2 is considerably worse than one would expect on the basis of a fairly mild head injury (with minimal loss of consciousness or posttraumatic amnesia, and a negative head CT scan). In addition, Dr. Jones does not comment on the fact that Mr. Smith had no less than 13 false positives on the Yes/No recognition memory trial of the CVLT-2, which is an even more extreme level of impairment (4 standard

deviations from the normative mean). Such a level of impairment would be unusual, even in persons with moderate–severe TBI (Donders & Nienhuis, 2007).

(5) *Psychostimulant medication* can be a reasonable consideration when a person truly has difficulties with attention. However, Dr. Jones appeared to make this recommendation exclusively on the basis of Mr. Smith's psychometric test scores. Even if Mr. Smith had not violated validity criteria on the WMT, it should still have been apparent that performance on the CPT that was literally worse than 99% of Mr. Smith's peers was hard to reconcile with the facts that at the time of the neuropsychological evaluation, this man was competitively employed.

(6) Finally, a diagnosis of being "learning disabled" requires (at least in the state of Michigan) a significant discrepancy between overall intelligence and academic achievement. No achievement tests were administered during the neuropsychological evaluation, primarily because Mr. Smith's GPA was actually better during the first semester when he returned to college after the accident than it had been before that same accident. Dr. Jones did not appear to appreciate this.

Initial Resolution

Shortly after receiving and forwarding to me Dr. Jones's letter to Mr. Smith's attending physician, the attorney who had retained me initiated a telephone conference with me, during which I reviewed verbally my above-described reactions to Dr. Jones's interpretations of my test findings. I was then asked to summarize the most convincing points in a letter that could be submitted into evidence during a scheduled deposition of Dr. Jones because the attorney was concerned that too much detail about psychometric issues would be potentially confusing or boring to the jury. I was specifically asked to support any of my positions with literature references. In response to this request, I prepared the following rebuttal to Dr. Jones's narrative review:

> I have reviewed the letter by Dr. Jones that you sent me. Dr. Jones apparently disagrees with my assessment findings. To tell you the truth, I find his rationale somewhat difficult to follow, for the following reasons.
>
> A. Dr. Jones does not seem to appreciate that this man violated empirically established and cross-validated measures of effort and motivation. The best example is Mr. Smith's failure to meet such criteria on the WMT, a forced-choice measure of response validity during neuropsychological evaluations. His scores are worse than those of adults with severe brain injury, and even grade-school children would have done better (Green & Flaro, 2003). The validity of the WMT in the assessment of patients with traumatic brain injury has been well es-

tablished in the professional literature (Green, Rohling, Lees-Haley, & Allen, 2001; Hartman, 2002).

B. As I explained in my original report, the level of impairment that Mr. Smith displayed on some of the other tests was way out of proportion with the apparently very mild severity of the head injury in question. It has been well established that significant cognitive dysfunction for more than a year after this kind of mild head injury is rare and typically related to factors other than cerebral compromise (Alexander, 1995; Binder & Rohling, 1996; Dikmen, Machamer, Winn, & Temkin, 1995). Yet, here is a man who scored worse than 99% of his peers on a measure of sustained attention (CPT), at a time point that was almost 2 years postinjury. Keep in mind that he reported that, in real life, he had no problems with riding a bicycle in traffic or performing his job duties—all things for which he would need to be able to concentrate.

In the end, Dr. Jones's documentation does not include anything that leads me to change my previously offered impressions and recommendations.

Follow-Up

About 2 months after I had written this rebuttal to the attorney who had retained me, I received a letter from that same attorney, asking for additional responses to comments that Dr. Jones had made during a deposition that had taken place in the meantime. The attorney indicated that he was surprised that Dr. Jones stated that he had never heard of the WMT, and he asked me to provide information about this test and its general acceptance in the professional community. Around the same time, I received a separate notice of the taking of my trial deposition within the next month. The following is a reproduction of the relevant portion of Dr. Jones's discovery deposition.

Q. I understand that you, at least at the time you dictated your September 13, 2004, report, didn't agree with everything that Dr. Donders said, at least with regard to some of his conclusions?

A. That's correct.

Q. But with respect to the raw data itself, did you have any concerns or disagreements with regard to the tests that were administered, the manner in which they were administered, or the manner in which they were scored?

A. I don't know the manner in which they were administered or scored, because I only have the scores themselves. I do know Dr. Donders has an assistant to do the testing but I am assuming that's all in a very appropriate order and done well, and I would not normally question that. There's a test that he used that he relies heavily upon that I've never heard of, and I don't know of any other neuropsychologist who's heard of it either, because I've been asking. It's called the Word Memory Test. He puts a great deal of weight on that, and it's Green's WMT. And I can't find anyone who knows anything about that test.

Q. That is a test that Dr. Donders relied upon, essentially, because it raised concerns in his mind concerning the validity of the test taking?

A. Yes.

Q. The effort and motivation by Mr. Smith, correct?

A. Correct.

Q. And that's not a test you've administered yourself, correct?

A. No.

Q. And who did you check with?

A. Dr. [name redacted], Dr. [name redacted].

Q. Can you think of any other neuropsychologists or any other health care providers you spoke to questioning the WMT?

A. No. Just those two.

Q. What it means—OK—Have you done . . . ?

A. I looked it up in a book of neuropsychology tests and couldn't find it.

Q. So, I guess, aside from the fact that you couldn't find it, you don't have any opinions concerning the validity or the usefulness of the WMT since you're not familiar with it?

A. No.

I subsequently called the attorney and expressed my surprise at Dr. Jones's ignorance about the WMT. I explained that in 2003, the National Academy of Neuropsychology had awarded its Nelson Butters award to Rohling, Green, Allen, and Iverson (2002) as the most highly rated peer-reviewed article that had been published in the *Archives of Clinical Neuropsychology*, the official journal of that organization. I emphasized that this was a paper that relied heavily on the WMT as a measure of effort and motivation to determine the validity of effort during neuropsychological evaluations.

I also faxed to the attorney a list of papers of which I was aware that had been published in peer-reviewed professional journals at least a year before Dr. Jones wrote his September 2004 letter, and at least 2 years before his deposition, all of which included the WMT. In addition to the articles that I had already cited in my above-mentioned rebuttal, these included several papers that specifically addressed the use of the WMT in persons with TBI in the context of financial compensation seeking, such as the works of Green, Iverson, and Allen (1999), Green, Lees-Haley, and Allen (2002), and Iverson, Green, and Gervais (1999). Mr. Smith's personal injury lawsuit was subsequently settled out of court within a week after I had provided the attorney with this additional information, and my scheduled trial deposition was canceled at that time.

CONCLUSIONS

This case presentation is intended to make a couple of points. The first principle is that it is important in the context of an IME to have all the relevant records, and to use tests that have established standardization, reliability and validity. In other words, the method of application should be a sound, scientifically defensible approach (Greiffenstein & Cohen, 2005; Larrabee, 2005). Had I not been able to compare premorbid and postmorbid academic records, I would not have been able to highlight the fact that the plaintiff's GPA was actually higher afterwards. Had I not used an empirically validated test of effort like the WMT, and appropriately normed instruments like the WCST and CPT-II, I would have had more difficulty rebuking Dr. Jones's critique of my original report.

A second and related objective is to demonstrate the need to be able to support one's opinions with specific empirical references. Sound neuropsychological IME practice includes not only a standardized approach but especially also the use of tests that have been accepted in the scientific community, and a working knowledge of the related literature. Because I could cite research in a peer-reviewed journal concerning the most common findings with the WAIS-III in the evaluation of patients with various degrees of severity of TBI, I was in a better position to respond to Dr. Jones's original commentary about reduced speed of information processing than if I had used an obscure or homemade test for which there was no research background.

Third, it is advisable to present information in a way that can be understood by persons who do not have advanced graduate course work in psychometrics or related field. Although it may be theoretically interesting to other psychologists to argue the fine points of whether standard score A is statistically significantly different from standard score B, attorneys, judges, and jury members will benefit more from a clear explanation of what the data really mean with respect to daily functioning, and the degree to which they "make sense" from a brain–behavior relationship point of view. For this reason, I contrasted Mr. Smith's performance on one of the tests with that of school-age children, and his result on another one in the context of doing worse than 99% of his own peers. In this context, I also referred specifically to the fact that (1) this plaintiff had actually been doing better in college after his accident than before, and (2) he maintained employment and was riding a bicycle in traffic despite his subjective complaints and despite his severely impaired test scores.

I never tried to ascertain what the terms of the settlement in this case were. I wanted to keep my involvement strictly professional, without a significant degree of ownership. Any attempt at ascertaining "how much did he get in the end?" would carry the risk of wanting to "win" more in a subsequent case, or in a possible future interaction with the same plaintiff psychologist. As others have suggested (Sweet & Moulthrop, 1999; Van Gorp & McMullen, 1997), it is crucial to be aware of one's own biases in IMEs. It is important to try to avoid becoming an advocate for one side rather than an expert, or to try to please the referring attorney too much instead of sticking to the facts of the case. This is also why I never agree to any arrangement where my fee is related in any way to the "success" of the party that retains me in the case in question. Without even considering the potential ethical concerns that this might raise (Binder & Thompson, 1995; Grote, 2005), it would simply introduce at least the potential perception of bias and carry with it an inherent risk of perceivêd lack of objectivity.

Finally, I felt throughout this process that it was important to remain professional and neutral in my formal documentation about the case in question. Even if the plaintiff's behavior is unusual or even if the plaintiff's expert takes a dismissive tone in his report, it is advisable to just stick to the facts of the case and not get into a "micturation match." When I initially read Dr. Jones's letter, critiquing my report, I had an initial reaction along the lines of "How can he not see what is so obvious in these data?" However, in the end, I decided that getting involved in a personalized reciprocal diatribe would not likely help the jury determine the facts of the case. I figured that the neuropsychological data would pretty much speak for themselves, even if the other psychologist did not see what I saw.

REFERENCES

Alexander, M. P. (1995). Mild traumatic brain injury: Pathophysiology, natural history, and clinical management. *Neurology, 45*, 1253–1260.

American Academy of Clinical Neuropsychology. (2001). Policy statement on the presence of third party observers in neuropsychological assessments. *The Clinical Neuropsychologist, 15*, 433–439.

American Psychological Association (2002). Ethical principles of psychologists and code of conduct. *American Psychologist, 57,* 1060–1073.

Axelrod, B., Barth, J., Faust, D., Fisher, J., Heilbronner, R., Larrabee, G., et al. (2000). Presence of third party observers during neuropsychological testing: Official statement of the National Academy or Neuropsychology. *Archives of Clinical Neuropsychology, 15,* 379–380.

Binder, L. M., & Rohling, M. L. (1996). Money matters: A meta-analytic review of the effects of financial incentives on recovery after closed head injury. *American Journal of Psychiatry, 153,* 7–10.

Binder, L. M., & Thompson, L. L. (1995). The ethics code and neuropsychological assessment practices. *Archives of Clinical Neuropsychology, 10,* 27–46.

Constantinou, M., Ashendorf, L., & McCaffrey, R. J. (2005). Effects of a third party observer during neuropsychological assessment: When the observer is a video camera. *Journal of Forensic Neuropsychology, 4,* 39–47.

Dikmen, S. S., Machamer, J. E., Winn, H. R., & Temkin, N. R. (1995). Neuropsychological outcome at 1–year post head injury. *Neuropsychology, 9,* 80–90.

Donders, J., & Nienhuis, J. B. (2007). Utility of CVLT-II recall discriminability indices in the evaluation of traumatic brain injury. *Journal of the International Neuropsychological Society, 13,* 354–358.

Donders, J., Tulsky, D. S., & Zhu, J. (2001). Criterion validity of new WAIS-III subtest scores after traumatic brain injury. *Journal of the International Neuropsychological Society, 7,* 892–898.

Green, P., & Flaro, L. (2003). Word Memory Test performance in children. *Child Neuropsychology, 9,* 189–207.

Green, P., Iverson, G. L., & Allen, L. M. (1999). Detecting malingering in head injury litigation with the Word Memory Test. *Brain Injury, 13,* 813–819.

Green, P., Lees-Haley, P. R., & Allen, L. M. (2002). The Word Memory Test and the validity of neuropsychological test scores. *Journal of Forensic Neuropsychology, 1,* 97–124.

Green, P., Rohling, M. L., Lees-Haley, P. R., & Allen, L. M. (2001). Effort has a greater effect on test scores than severe brain injury in compensation claimants. *Brain Injury, 15,* 1045–1060.

Greiffenstein, M. F., & Cohen, L. (2005). Neuropsychology and the law: Principles of productive attorney-neuropsychologist relations. In G. J. Larrabee (Ed.), *Forensic neuropsychology: A scientific approach* (pp. 29–91). New York: Oxford University Press.

Grote, C. (2005). Ethical practice of forensic neuropsychology. In G. J. Larrabee (Ed.), *Forensic neuropsychology: A scientific approach* (pp. 91–114). New York: Oxford University Press.

Hartman, D. E. (2002). The unexamined lie is a lie worth fibbing: Neuropsychological malingering and the Word Memory Test. *Archives of Clinical Neuropsychology, 17,* 709–714.

Iverson, G. L. (2005). Outcome from mild traumatic brain injury. *Current Opinions in Psychiatry, 18,* 301–317.

Iverson, G. L., Green, P., & Gervais, R. (1999). Using the Word Memory Test to detect biased responding in head injury litigation. *Journal of Cognitive Rehabilitation, 17,* 4–8.

Larrabee, G. J. (2005). A scientific approach to forensic neuropsychology. In G. J. Larrabee (Ed.), *Forensic neuropsychology: A scientific approach* (pp. 3–28). New York: Oxford University Press.

Lynch, J. K. (2005). Effect of a third party observer on neuropsychological test performance following closed head injury. *Journal of Forensic Neuropsychology, 4,* 17–25.

Rohling, M. L., Green, P., Allen, L. M., & Iverson, G. L. (2002). Depressive symptoms and neurocognitive test scores in patients passing symptom validity tests. *Archives of Clinical Neuropsychology, 17,* 205–222.

Schretlen, D. J., & Shapiro, A. M. (2003). A quantitative review of the effects of traumatic brain injury on cognitive functioning. *International Review of Psychiatry, 15,* 341–349.

Slick, D. J., Sherman, E. M. S., & Iverson, G. L. (1999). Diagnostic criteria for malingered neurocognitive dysfunction: Proposed standards for clinical practice and research. *The Clinical Neuropsychologist, 13,* 545–561.

Sweet, J. J., & Moulthrop, M. A. (1999). Self-examination questions as a means of identifying bias in adversarial assessments. *Journal of Forensic Neuropsychology, 1,* 73–88.

Van Gorp, W. G., & McMullen, W. J. (1997). Potential sources of bias in forensic neuropsychological evaluations. *The Clinical Neuropsychologist, 11,* 180–187.

Youngjohn, J. R. (1995). Confirmed attorney coaching prior to neuropsychological evaluation. *Assessment, 2,* 279–283.

2

Multiple Chemical Sensitivity

A Sensitive Matter in
Neuropsychological Assessment

Michael McCrea

MULTIPLE CHEMICAL SENSITIVITY

Multiple chemical sensitivity (MCS) is a term used to describe a disorder characterized by a vast array of somatic, cognitive, and affective symptoms, the cause of which is attributed to exposure to extremely low levels of a variety of chemicals. Objective physical findings and consistent laboratory abnormalities are typically not uncovered in MCS cases (LaBarge & McCaffrey, 2000).

Clinical manifestations of MCS are more relevant to psychophysiological than pathophysiological factors (Lee, Pai, Chen, & Guo, 2003). In most cases, symptoms can be explained by well-defined psychiatric and medical conditions other than MCS (Bornschein, Hausteniner, Zilker, & Forstl, 2002). Patients with MCS have a higher rate of psychiatric disorders (Fiedler & Kipen, 1997), with anxiety and depression often significant contributors to the physical and cognitive symptoms and complaints of patients with MCS (Caccappolo-van Vliet, Kelly-McNeil, Natelson, Kipen, & Fiedler, 2002).

Psychiatric comorbidity is especially high in patients presenting to specialized centers for environmental medicine. Somatoform disorders (35%)

are the leading diagnostic category, and there is reason to believe that certain kinds of "environmental" factors contribute to form a special subgroup of somatoform disorders. Personality traits predisposing to somatization and beliefs about environmental sensitivities have also been reported among patients with MCS (Staudenmayer & Kramer, 1999).

Most patients with MCS remain committed to the belief that they have MCS, even in the face of improvement in their condition or consistently contrary opinions and findings (Black, Okiishi, & Schlosser, 2001). Therefore, patients with MCS are often resistant to recommendations for psychological or psychiatric intervention to address their symptoms, with the goal of returning to a more gainful and productive life.

The overall neuropsychological profile of patients with MCS does not reflect cognitive impairment (Fiedler, Kipen, DeLuca, Kelly-McNeil, & Natelson, 1994). Indeed, neuropsychological testing is within normal limits in most cases of MCS, with no evidence of cerebral dysfunction (Caccappolo-van Vliet et al., 2002; Osterberg, Orbaek, & Karlson, 2002) but prominent signs of depression, anxiety, and somatization disorders (Caccappolo-van Vliet et al., 2002). Performance on neuropsychological testing typically does not confirm the most frequently reported subjective complaints of patients with MCS, suggesting that patients with symptoms of MCS do not have compromised central nervous system dysfunction (Bolla, 1996a, 1996b; Simon, Daniell, Stockbridge, Claypoole, & Rosenstock, 1993).

MURIATIC ACID EXPOSURE

Muriatic acid (hydrochloric acid) is typically diluted in bleaching agents (less than 10%). Concentrated solutions (36%) are involved in dye and chemical synthesis, metal refining, and the plumbing industry. Toxicity arises from its corrosive activity on skin and mucous membranes. There are no neurological or neurocognitive sequelae associated with muriatic acid exposure, especially when not directly ingested in large liquid quantity. Acute confusion, delirium, and coma can result in severe cases, but there is no evidence of long-term chronic effects beyond the acute exposure. With respect to pathophysiology, determinants of toxicity after exposure to acids include type of substance ingested, volume ingested, contact time, volume of liquid and material in the stomach, and toxicity of the pyloric sphincter.

Obviously, these factors primarily refer to instances of exposure by ingestion. Phases of potential injury include (1) acute inflammatory phase (first 4–7 days) when vascular thrombosis and cellular necrosis reach a maximum in 24–48 hours and the columnar epithelium, submucosa, and muscularis are destroyed; necrotic mucosa appears by the third or fourth day, and an ulcer forms; (2) latent granulation phase; and (3) chronic cicatrization phase, 2–4 weeks after injury, in which excessive scar tissue forms around the mucosa and the muscularis and produces contractures.

CASE STUDY

Background

In this chapter, I review a case from my practice that involved a claim of MCS referred for independent neuropsychological examination due to complaints of a multitude of physical, cognitive, emotional, and functional deficits secondary to muriatic acid exposure.

Nature of the Evaluation

Mrs. Smith is a 55-year-old, right-handed, Caucasian female referred for neuropsychological examination to assess for any neurocognitive or psychological residuals associated with a reported muriatic acid exposure incident while working as a custodian at a local health club 4 years earlier. The referral was from an attorney representing the insurance company defending against a claim by Mrs. Smith of disability associated with the exposure incident. My consultation in this case consisted of clinical interview with Mrs. Smith, formal neuropsychological testing, and a review of available records. Mrs. Smith was made fully aware of the nature of this independent neuropsychological examination, and she granted written consent to proceed with the examination. She also authorized me to contact her significant other to provide collateral information, which I did, but I did not receive any response back from him. Mrs. Smith acknowledged that there was pending litigation related to her reported exposure incident, with a lawsuit filed against her former employer and her workers' compensation carrier at the time of the incident.

Chemical Exposure Incident

Mrs. Smith reportedly experienced a chemical exposure while performing routine maintenance on the swimming pool at the health club where she was working at the time. Her duties there included changing various chlorine and other chemical lines to the pool. On the day of the reported exposure, she entered the pool area and noticed a "peculiar odor." When she opened the door to the hallway leading to the mechanical room near the pool, she apparently recognized immediately that there had been a muriatic acid leak. She then reportedly went downstairs to the mechanical room, opened the door, and saw a thick, yellow haze in the room, which disallowed her from seeing the equipment in the room. She was accompanied by another employee at the time. Following the exposure, she reportedly returned to the pool area and called her supervisor, who contacted the local fire department. Officials determined that no evacuation was necessary, but people were restricted from entering the pool area. Mrs. Smith was unable to estimate how long she was in the room with the exposure, and was unsure whether her coworker or other people were able to estimate the duration of any exposure. She is also unaware as to whether or not her coworker experienced any residual problems associated with the exposure.

Available records indicated an estimated 1- to 2-minute exposure to muriatic acid by proximity to fumes and probable inhalation without skin contact, followed by acute symptoms of burning in the throat, lungs, stomach, eyes, and exposed skin. Mrs. Smith was evaluated at a local hospital emergency department for chief complaints of burning in her throat and epigastric chest area on the day of the exposure incident. She was diagnosed with acute nasopharyngeal/bronchial inflammation secondary to muriatic acid exposure and released the same day with no work-related restrictions.

Medical Follow-Up

Mrs. Smith initially followed up with her primary care physician, and she has since been evaluated and treated by numerous physicians and health care providers over the past 4 years, including a second primary care physician, occupational and environmental medicine specialists, otolaryngolosts, pulmonologists, and psychologists. Most treating providers attributed Mrs. Smith's initial acute symptoms, but not her chronic symptoms or ongoing subjective complaints, to the exposure and they projected a favorable prognosis for complete recovery without any permanent partial or total disability. Several treating or evaluating physicians documented suspicion of a functional or psychological basis for her ongoing symptoms and associated disabilities, including numerous references to a probable conversion or somatoform disorder diagnosis, along with recommendations for mental health treatment.

At the time of my evaluation, Mrs. Smith was under the primary care of a physician in a distant metropolitan area. He diagnosed Mrs. Smith with chemical sensitivity and multiple related problems and provided a lengthy list of 22 recommendations for additional diagnostic workup and treatment. Mrs. Smith was followed by this physician on several more occasions, which culminated in the impression that she "has not progressed well and is unable to return to work in any capacity at this time. I would encourage her to apply for disability at this point as she continues to remain totally disabled, and it is beginning to look as if it may be permanent."

At the recommendation of this physician, Mrs. Smith then traveled out of state to a clinic that specializes in the diagnosis of MCS, where she was evaluated by a physician and psychologist (Dr. Jones). Mrs. Smith reported that she paid for the out-of-state medical and neuropsychological evaluation by charging several thousand dollars to her credit card the day of the evaluation. The workup resulted in several diagnoses from the physician and psychologist, including toxic encephalopathy, toxic effects of muriatic acid, immune deregulation, chemical sensitivity, chronic fatigue, fibromyalgia, autonomic nervous system dysfunction, and cognitive impairment as a result of her exposure to the chemical fumes from the mixture of muriatic acid, chloride, and concrete in the workplace. The physician considered Mrs. Smith to be completely disabled by her sensitivities and unable to engage in any type of sustained work or work-like activities at that time or in the foreseeable future. According to Mrs. Smith, these providers recommended "lifetime treatment" with vaccines and other forms of intervention to be administered at their clinic.

Records from the out-of-state clinic also referenced results from a SPECT (single-photon emission computed tomography) study as "consistent with neurotoxic exposure." The radiologist's impression was as follows: "The temporal lobes were moderately asymmetric with more activity on the right than the left," and "the mismatch between the early and late phases, salt-and-pepper pattern, and temporal asymmetry are part of a pattern that has been seen in patients with neurotoxic exposure. The degree of involvement is mild." The attending physician concluded that the objective medical data revealed findings consistent with central nervous system dysfunction, and the SPECT brain scan "confirmed the presence of neurotoxicity." The neuropsychological test results are discussed below in greater detail.

Current Chief Complaints

Mrs. Smith presented for my examination with a multitude of systemic, neurological, and cognitive complaints, which she attributes to the chemical exposure incident. She reported that her symptoms had progressively worsened since the exposure, and that her condition was "getting worse instead of better, the sensitivity is getting more and more acute." She felt that her condition was worsening each day and having a more debilitating effect on her daily functioning, to the point whereby she essentially led an "almost completely avoidant lifestyle" at this time.

With regard to her cognitive complaints, Mrs. Smith noted that "I feel like I've become a blundering idiot" since her reported exposure. She described a pattern of significant problems with memory, including difficulty recalling, retaining, and retrieving new information. She also described a pervasive pattern of remote retrograde memory loss, including an inability to remember significant family events far predating the exposure incident. For example, she reportedly had no recall of her children's (then ages 33 and 35) childhood or high school graduation. Mrs. Smith noted that "I've lost a lot of the stuff I used to have [meaning memories], and it's literally wiped out by the exposure, and it doesn't come back." She also indicated that she had difficulties with concentration and distractibility, as well as dysfluency, word-finding difficulties, and a proneness toward word misusage and mispronunciation. She also felt that her vocabulary is "greatly, tremendously" diminished.

Mrs. Smith reported that her symptoms have had a significant effect on her daily functioning. From a social standpoint, she reported, "I can't be among people because I'll get sick from what they're wearing." She was also limited in her ability to participate in household chores or use household products for cleaning, lawn care, and gardening. Mrs. Smith reported that she returned to work approximately 3 days after the exposure incident but could not tolerate being anywhere near the room of the exposure or pool due to smells of chlorine and muriatic acid, all of which apparently exacerbated her symptoms. She then reportedly worked full time for 2–3 years but reportedly was "getting sicker and sicker," with a substantial amount of missed work time due to her symptoms. She eventually discontinued work altogether, and feels that she is unable to return to her former job or any other form of gainful employment. Documentation indicated that Mrs. Smith had applied for social security disability benefits based on the allegation of chemical sensitivities, and she also had an application for a hearing on a workers' compensation claim with an alleged 100% permanent partial disability due to the muriatic acid exposure.

Data from Previous Evaluations

Neuropsychological Evaluation

As part of the out-of-state evaluation at the chemical sensitivity specialty clinic, Mrs. Smith underwent neuropsychological testing by a psychologist, Dr. Jones, "to evaluate neurocognitive and personality/behavioral concomitants of toxic exposure." A battery of cognitive tests and self-report measures were administered as part of the evaluation. Dr. Jones provided a lengthy report and copy of his curriculum vitae, but there was no table of cognitive test scores included. Mrs. Smith's presenting complaints were surveyed on a series of self-report measures, including the Physical Symptom Checklist, Psychological Symptom Checklist, and Neurocognitive Symptom Checklist. A multitude of physical, psychological, and neurocognitive symptoms were endorsed by Mrs. Smith. In addition to her subjective complaints, Dr. Jones documented impairments in general intellectual functioning, severely impaired executive functions, impaired memory abilities, mild to moderate impairment of sensory and motor functions, and mild to moderately severe impairment on the Halstead–Reitan Neuropsychological Battery. Dr. Jones indicated that Mrs. Smith's personality profile was "generally healthy and free of psychopathology, with no suggestion on personality measures of a conversion disorder." Dr. Jones's impression was that there was "no evidence of malingering" during the evaluation, but no response bias measures or other objective measures of effort were referenced.

Dr. Jones's diagnostic impression included "toxic encephalopathy, mild, chronic with reversibility uncertain without continued avoidance of toxic/neurotoxic substances and full participation in her treatment program as prescribed by her treating physician. Considering the duration of time between workplace exposure and evaluation, it is possible that some deficits may be permanent in nature." Dr. Jones also made the diagnosis of cognitive disorder not otherwise specified (NOS) and rated Mrs. Smith's global assessment of functioning as 55–60 (current). Dr. Jones added that "it is more likely than not, considering Mrs. Smith's history and the temporal relationship between the exposure and symptoms, that the observed neurocognitive deficits are a result of toxic/neurotoxic exposure in the workplace either directly or indirectly." He added that "it is important to note that Mrs. Smith was evaluated in an environment relatively free of toxins and incitants and under conditions of reduced stress, with rest periods permitted, as necessary, to elicit her best performance. Had she been evaluated in the ordinary office setting with exposure to contaminants, or under more stressful or demanding conditions, it is likely that greater compromise of functioning would have been observed."

Dr. Jones recommended continued avoidance of toxic/neurotoxic substances and full participation in her treatment program as prescribed by the referring physician to prevent any further compromise of physical, psychological, or neurocognitive functioning. Formal cognitive rehabilitation was recommended, along with stress management, relaxation training, and neuropsychological reevaluation in 18–24 months to assess the effects of treatment and avoidance and to determine whether Mrs. Smith's condition has improved, regressed, or remained static. Dr. Jones indicated that Mrs. Smith was seriously limited or unable to meet competitive standards because she was neuropsychologically and physically impaired, noting that "Mrs. Smith is permanently unable to work in any capacity in any ordinary workplace setting." A 7% to whole-body level of permanent disability was assigned by Dr. Jones.

Psychological Evaluation

Results from an evaluation by a different psychologist, Dr. Pong, were consistent with a probable conversion or somatoform disorder, as well as possible symptom exaggeration, as the basis for Mrs. Smith's ongoing symptoms and claimed level of disability. Mrs. Smith's Minnesota Multiphasic Personality Inventory–2 (MMPI-2) profile was of marginal validity but felt to be consistent with the clinical diagnosis of conversion disorder or somatization disorder. A dependent personality style was also suggested. Mrs. Smith denied experiencing any symptoms associated with posttraumatic stress disorder connected with the exposure.

A brief cognitive battery was administered by Dr. Pong, which included the following results from the Repeatable Battery of Neuropsychological Status (RBANS): immediate memory = 61, visuospatial/construction = 87, language = 99, attention =100, delayed memory = 94. A measure of response bias was also positive for signs of symptom exaggeration or malingering with a recorded score of 0 out of 15 on the Rey 15-Item Memory Test. Mrs. Smith's performance on the Trail Making Test A was also relatively poorer than her score on B. Dr. Pong concluded that Mrs. Smith's chemical exposure at work did not cause her presenting condition. She concluded that Mrs. Smith was capable of working with no psychological or other limitations.

Current Examination Results and Impression

Results from my neuropsychological examination of Mrs. Smith 4 years after the exposure can be found in Table 2.1. My summary of these findings was documented as follows:

> Results from the current neuropsychological evaluation do not indicate any signs of developmentally based or newly acquired neurocognitive dysfunction. Mrs. Smith demonstrated abilities within normal limits for her age and consistent with her estimated baseline level of functioning with respect to general intellectual abilities, anterograde memory functioning, working memory, attention and concentration, language, visuospatial/constructional abilities, and verbal fluency. The lone abnormal finding on the current examination was on a single measure of higher-order executive functioning, the results of which are more indicative of variable effort or motivation than focal impairment. Other measures of executive functioning are fully within or above normal limits. Response bias testing suggested a pattern of poor or incomplete effort by Mrs. Smith, without necessarily confirming purposeful malingering of cognitive impairment. There are no signs of impairment in any stage of auditory or visual memory, including encoding, recall, retrieval, and recognition memory after an extended delay. There was limited variability on select measures of visual scanning speed, but other measures of cognitive processing speed were fully normal. Fine motor speed and dexterity were within normal limits bilaterally, and

TABLE 2.1. Neuropsychological Test Data

Test name	Test score	Normal mean
Gross cognitive functioning		
Folstein MMSE	30	28 (2.5)
Estimate of premorbid abilities		
WRAT-3 Reading Subset	90	100 (15)
WRAT-3 Spelling Subset	98	100 (15)
WRAT-3 Arithmetic Subset	92	100 (15)
General intellectual abilities		
WAIS-III Full Scale IQ	103	100 (15)
WAIS-III Verbal Scale IQ	92	100 (15)
WAIS-III Performance Scale IQ	119	100 (15)
WAIS-III Verbal Comprehension Index	91	100 (15)
WAIS-III Perceptual Organization Index	121	100 (15)
WAIS-III Working Memory Index	106	100 (15)
WAIS-III Processing Speed Index	96	100 (15)
WAIS-III Subtests: Vocabulary	8	10 (3)
WAIS-III Subtests: Similarities	10	10 (3)
WAIS-III Subtests: Arithmetic	9	10 (3)
WAIS-III Subtests: Digit Span	10	10 (3)
WAIS-III Subtests: Information	7	10 (3)
WAIS-III Subtests: Letter–Number Sequencing	14	10 (3)
WAIS-III Subtests: Picture Completion	16	10 (3)
WAIS-III Subtests: Digit Symbol–Coding	11	10 (3)
WAIS-III Subtests: Block Design	11	10 (3)
WAIS-III Subtests: Matrix Reasoning	13	10 (3)
WAIS-III Subtests: Symbol Search	8	10 (3)
Attentional functions		
WAIS-III Working Memory Index	106	100 (15)
WAIS-III Digit Span	10	10 (3)
WAIS-III Arithmetic	9	10 (3)
WAIS-III Letter Number Sequencing	14	10 (3)
WAIS-III Processing Speed Index	96	100 (15)
WAIS-III Symbol Search	8	10 (3)
WAIS-III Digit Symbol–Coding	11	10 (3)
WMS-III Working Memory Index	111	100 (15)
WMS-III Spatial Span Scaled Score	11	10 (3)
WMS-III Letter Number Sequencing	13	10 (3)
WMS-III Digit Span	8	10 (3)
Brief Test of Attention (BTA) Part A	9	
Brief Test of Attention (BTA) Part B	8	
Brief Test of Attention (BTA) Total Score	17	17.3 (2.6)
Trail Making Test A	61"	35 (12)
Trail Making Test B	105"	95 (36)

(*continued*)

TABLE 2.1. (*continued*)

Test name	Test score	Normal mean
Memory		
WMS-III Immediate Memory Index	102	100 (15)
WMS-III General Memory Index	107	100 (15)
WMS-III Auditory Immediate Index	99	100 (15)
WMS-III Auditory Delayed Index	105	100 (15)
WMS-III Auditory Recognition Delayed Index	105	100 (15)
WMS-III Logical Memory I Recall	10	10 (3)
WMS-III Logical Memory II Recall	12	10 (3)
WMS-III Logical Memory Percent Retention—Scaled Score	14	10 (3)
WMS-III Verbal Paired Associates I Recall	10	10 (3)
WMS-III Verbal Paired Associates II Recall	10	10 (3)
WMS-III Word List I Recall Total Score	12	10 (3)
WMS-III Word List II Recall Total Score	12	10 (3)
WMS-III Word List II Percent Retention—Scaled Score	11	10 (3)
WMS-III Word List II Recognition Total Score	8	10 (3)
WMS-III Visual Immediate Index	103	100 (15)
WMS-III Visual Delayed Index	106	100 (15)
WMS-III Faces I Recognition	11	10 (3)
WMS-III Faces II Recognition	11	10 (3)
WMS-III Faces II Percent Retention—Scaled Score	10	10 (3)
WMS-III Family Pictures I Recall	10	10 (3)
WMS-III Family Pictures II Recall	11	10 (3)
WMS-III Family Pictures II Percent Retention—Scaled Score	12	10 (3)
Language		
Boston Naming Test	55	55 (3)
Visual–spatial/constructional skills		
Rey Complex Figure	35.5	34 (2)
Facial Recognition Test	48	45 (5)
Judgment of Line Orientation Test	17	22 (5)
Prefrontal executive functions		
Controlled Oral Word Association Test (COWAT)	43	40 (10)
Wisconsin Card Sorting Test (WCST) Total Trials	128	
WCST Total Correct	47	
WCST Total Errors	81	1%ile
WCST Categories Completed	1	5.6 (1.1)
WCST Percent Perseverative Errors	14%	11.3 (6.9)
WCST Percent Nonperseverative Error	49%	< 55%ile
WCST Trials to Complete First Category	16	11–16%ile
WCST Failure to Maintain Set	0	> 16%ile

(*continued*)

TABLE 2.1. (*continued*)

Test name	Test score	Normal mean
Motor functions		
Finger Tapping—Dominant	47	43 (6)
Finger Tapping—Nondominant	44	40 (6)
Grooved Pegboard—Dominant	67	68 (9)
Grooved Pegboard—Nondominant	84	75 (10)
Depression screening		
Beck Depression Inventory (BDI)	3	< 10
Motivational scales		
Rey 15-Item Memory Test	9/15	
Rey 15-Item Memory Test—15 minute delay	8/15	
Word Memory Test	"Poor or incomplete effort"	

there were no focal sensorimotor abnormalities on gross examination. Psychological test results from the current examination suggest a pattern of chronic psychological maladjustment and are most consistent with a severe somatoform disorder as the basis for Mrs. Smith's persistent somatic complaints and associated disability. She otherwise denied currently experiencing symptoms of depression, anxiety, psychosis, or posttraumatic stress disorder associated with the exposure incident.

Critical Analysis of Examination Findings

Contrary to the earlier interpretation by Dr. Jones, results from my neuropsychological examination did not indicate *any* evidence of a decline in Mrs. Smith's general intellectual abilities, memory functioning, or other areas of cognitive functioning as a result of the reported chemical exposure. With respect to the measurement of general intellectual abilities, Mrs. Smith demonstrated global intellectual functioning consistent with her predicted baseline level of intellectual functioning in the average range of normal adults. Her performance on similar measures of verbal and nonverbal intellectual abilities, however, showed a reverse pattern relative to the results reported by Dr. Jones, which is more consistent with a pattern of variable effort across subtests than an altered pattern of impairment attributable to encephalopathy or other form of cerebral dysfunction. In addition, Mrs. Smith's poorest performance on both neuropsychological examinations was on measures most heavily dependent on education and less sensitive to the acquired effects of central nervous system disease.

Mrs. Smith also demonstrated substantial, measurable improvement on measures of auditory and visual immediate and delayed memory relative to results previously reported by Dr. Jones. The level of improvement in anterograde memory performance on the current exam is well beyond that attributable to normal variability or practice effects due to serial test exposure. Overall, Mrs. Smith demonstrated memory abilities fully within the normal range for her age and there is no evidence from the current examination to suggest an amnestic disorder that would have a negative impact on her daily functioning as suggested by Dr. Jones. Mrs. Smith's self-report of remote retrograde amnesia resulting from the chemical exposure is neurologically implausible. Similarly, severely diminished vocabulary as reported by Mrs. Smith is an extremely improbable deficit even in the context of severe neurological disorder. Mrs. Smith's self-reported course of worsening symptom acuity over the past 2 years is also questionable in the absence of a progressive neurological disease.

There was no clinically or statistically significant discrepancy between intellectual and memory functioning on my exam. There is, however, a significant discrepancy between Mrs. Smith's self reported assessment of her cognitive functioning (i.e., perceived decline in cognitive functioning attributed to muriatic exposure) and her normal performance on formal neuropsychological testing. Mrs. Smith performed well on a lengthy battery of neuropsychological tests in an "ordinary office," despite Dr. Jones's prediction that this type of environmental exposure would result in "greater compromise of functioning."

Dr. Jones also opined, "It is more likely than not, considering Mrs. Smith's history and the temporal relationship between the exposure and symptoms, that the observed neurocognitive deficits are a result of toxic/neurotoxic exposure. . . . " This is a common error observed in medical or neuropsychological evaluations where litigation is in process. The fact that a temporal relationship exists (event A followed by symptom B) does not equate to causation in the absence of other evidence to support such a claim. Also, because Mrs. Smith presented with a multitude of subjective complaints 4 years later does not in any way confirm that the chemical exposure is the cause of her symptoms and claimed level of disability.

My examination and that of Dr. Pong suggested that suboptimal effort and low motivation negatively affected the patient's performance on formal neurocognitive testing. While Dr. Jones indicated that there were no signs of malingering or symptom exaggeration on the previous exam, no formal response measures were administered. Mrs. Smith showed a profile of poor or incomplete effort (Word Memory Test) on my examination, and failed outright a more naive measure of effort administered by Dr. Pong. These findings must be considered in the context of medical legal evaluation where potential for secondary gain is clearly present.

CONCLUSIONS

Overall, there was no evidence of neurocognitive impairment on my examination to support the diagnoses of "toxic encephalopathy" or cognitive disorder NOS cited by Dr. Jones. There was also no evidence of cerebral dysfunction manifested on neuropsychological testing as purported by earlier evaluators on the basis of SPECT imaging results. Furthermore, the validity, sensitivity, and specificity of SPECT in MCS has not been established in the scientific literature. In contrast, objective personality assessment suggested a pattern of significant, chronic psychological maladjustment contributing to Mrs. Smith's presenting symptoms, contrary to Dr. Jones's previous depiction of Mrs. Smith as "generally healthy and free of psychopathology." Evidence from the current examination of a severe somatoform disorder supports the earlier impressions of multiple evaluating and treating experts over the past several years based on the nature and course of Mrs. Smith's symptoms and results from an exhaustive medical workup. This case is considered generally more consistent with a primary somatoform disorder than malingering or a factitious disorder, despite signs of suboptimal effort, ongoing litigation, and a clear potential for secondary gain. This is because Mrs. Smith otherwise denied currently experiencing symptoms of depression, anxiety, posttraumatic stress, or other distress associated with the reported chemical exposure that would cause significant disability on the basis of a primary psychiatric condition.

RESPONSE TO SPECIFIC INTERROGATIVES

In response to the referring attorney's specific interrogatives, the following responses were offered:

1. *What is your diagnosis of Mrs. Smith's present medical/psychological condition?* Severe somatoform disorder: Differential includes DSM-IV diagnoses of undifferentiated somatoform disorder, converion disorder, and hypochondriasis. There is no diagnosis of cognitive dysfunction or disorder.

2. *Did the exposure to muriatic acid directly cause Mrs. Smith's present medical/psychiatric condition?* No.

3. *If not directly, is it probable that the muriatic acid exposure caused her present condition by precipitation, aggravation, or acceleration of a preexisting condition beyond normal progression?* There is no evidence of any neurocognitive impairments in this case, either directly or indirectly resulting from the muriatic acid exposure, or due to the exacerbation of a preexisting condition. Mrs. Smith's primary psychiatric disorder is influenced by a combination of premorbid factors, personality structure, and

environmental stressors. Individuals with severe somatoform disorders, as in this case, typically have a preexisting propensity toward a maladaptive somatic response following any stressor perceived to possibly cause a change in physical, systemic, neurological, or cognitive functioning, regardless of the actual potential threat of the stressor. This patient's somatoform disorder has more to do with a predisposed pattern of maladaptive reaction to stress (not limited to the exposure) than to the chemical exposure incident itself.

4. *Was any exposure to muriatic acid or any other substance or materials in Mrs. Smith's workplace either the sole cause of her present condition or at least a material contributory causative factor in the condition's onset or progression?* Determining the early effects of the exposure on Mrs. Smith's acute symptoms is deferred to other medical specialists. Exposure to the muriatic acid is not considered the sole cause or material contributory causative factor for Mrs. Smith's presenting symptoms or reported disabilities at this time. Please see response to item 3 above.

5. *If it is your opinion that Mrs. Smith's present medical/psychological condition is unrelated to her exposure to muriatic acid, to what do you attribute the development of his condition?* Please see response to item 3 above.

6. *Has Mrs. Smith reached a healing plateau with respect to the muriatic acid exposure? If so, when was the healing plateau reached? If not, when do you anticipate an end of healing to be reached? If she has not reached a healing plateau, please offer your recommendations for further treatment, specifying type, frequency and duration of same.* There is no evidence of neurocognitive impairment resulting from the muriatic acid exposure, and no future decline in neurocognitive functioning is predicted now more than 4 years out from the exposure. Mrs. Smith's primary psychiatric disorder is considered reversible with psychological treatment, most effectively a combination of cognitive-behavioral therapy, patient education, and exposure-based techniques within the recommended standard of care for somatoform disorders of this type. Intensive weekly therapy is indicated based on the severity of her psychological dysfunction. I cannot predict the projected duration of treatment at this time.

7. *Without regard to the causative factor for Mrs. Smith's current medical/psychological condition, is she capable of working? If so, does she require any work restrictions? Would these work restrictions be necessary solely as a result of the muriatic acid exposure?* From a neuropsychological standpoint, this patient is capable of working in her former or other similar capacity without any need for work restrictions or specialty accommodations. There is also no need for work restrictions on the basis of Mrs. Smith's psychiatric disorder. Psychological intervention geared at reversing her pattern of severe somatization should also include an aggressive plan

for Mrs. Smith to return to gainful employment and resume other activities currently integral to her environmental avoidance behavior.

8. *If Mrs. Smith has reached a healing plateau with respect to the muriatic acid exposure, has she sustained and permanent partial disability? If so, what percentage and to which body part(s), pursuant to state workers' compensation guidelines?* There is no rating of permanent partial disability on the bases of any neurocognitive impairment in this case. Mrs. Smith's psychiatric disorder is considered treatable and reversible and not representing any degree of permanent partial disability.

REFERENCES

Black, D. W., Okiishi, C., & Schlosser, S. (2001). The Iowa follow up of chemically sensitive persons. *Annals of the New York Academy of Sciences, 933*, 48–56.

Bolla, K. I. (1996a). Neurobehavioral performance in MCS. *Regulatory Toxicology and Pharmacology, 24*, S52–S54.

Bolla, K. I. (1996b). Neuropsychological evaluation for detecting alterations in the central nervous system after chemical exposure. *Regulatory Toxicology and Pharmacology, 24*, S48–S51.

Bornschein, S., Hausteiner, C., Zilker, T., & Forstl, H. (2002). Psychiatric and somatic disorders and MCS in 264 environmental patients. *Psychological Medicine, 32*, 1387–1394.

Caccappolo-van Vliet E., Kelly-McNeil, K., Natelson, B., Kipen, H., & Fiedler, N. (2002). Anxiety sensitivity and depression in MCS and asthma. *Journal of Occupational and Environmental Medicine, 44*, 890–901.

Fiedler, N., & Kipen, H. (1997). Chemical Sensitivity: The Scientific Literature. *Environmental Health Perspectives, 105*, 409–415.

Fiedler, N., Kipen, H. M., DeLuca, J., Kelly-McNeil, K., & Natelson, B. (1996). A controlled comparison of MCS and chronic fatigue syndrome. *Psychosomatic Medicine, 58*, 38–49.

LaBarge, X. S., & McCaffrey, R. J. (2000). MCS: A review of the theoretical and research literature. *Neuropsychology Review, 10*, 183–211.

Lee, Y. L., Pai, M. C., Chen, J. H., & Guo, Y. L. (2003). Central neurological abnormalities and MCS caused by chronic toluene exposure. *Occupational Medicine, 53*, 479–482.

Osterberg, K., Orbaek, P., & Karlson, B. (2002). Neuropsychological test performance of Swedish patients with MCS–An exploratory study. *Applied Neuropsychology, 9*, 139–147.

Simon, G. E., Daniell, W., Stockbridge, H., Claypoole, K., & Rosenstock, L. (1993). Immunologic, psychological, and neuropsychological factors in MCS: A controlled study. *Annals of Internal Medicine, 119*, 97–103.

Staudenmayer, H., & Kramer, R. E. (1999). Psychogenic chemical sensitivity: Psychogenic pseudoseizures elicited by provocation challenges with fragrances. *Journal of Psychosomatic Research, 47*, 185–190.

3

Cents and Scentability

A Disability Claim Due to Multiple Chemical Sensitivity

Howard Oakes

As a neuropsychological consultant to a private disability company, a major activity is the review of medical records to assist with determining whether an individual meets the contractual requirements to be eligible for disability coverage. Specifically, this involves formulation of an opinion relating to the existence of functional impairments and associated work-related restrictions (things one should not do) and/or limitations (things one is unable to do). This work has afforded me the opportunity to review hundreds of neuropsychological reports as well as the raw test data from these assessments. While the vast majority of reports provide clear and objective results that address the question of cognitive and/or psychological impairment, one is too frequently confronted by the evaluation that reaches conclusions not supported by the data (either for or against impairment) and is based on a test battery that fails to meet any reasonable standard of practice within the field of neuropsychology.

Personal experience has revealed a number of repeating themes that have emerged over time with respect to these substandard evaluations and reports. First, problems associated with evaluations often stem from the reliance on the patient/claimant as the sole source of information relating to his or her reported difficulties. As a consultant often has the totality of an individual's medical records available before reading the neuropsychological evaluation, the presence of marked distortions of an individual's history, prior medical and psychiatric evaluations, and current functioning, as well as the omission of the fact that the individual is claiming disability at the time of the evaluation, is fairly frequent. It is important to note that the disability reviewer may have access to more medical information than the claimant's treatment providers. For many of these reports, it is clear from the outset that the clinical information available may skew the interpretation of the data generated either due to the absence of detailed clinical history or from not having available prior medical and/or psychiatric findings. Although much of this difficulty may result from the nature of a busy clinical practice, other issues lie solely with the individual completing the evaluation. This includes the failure to evaluate effort, an overemphasis on single poor scores with disregard for the totality of the test data, misinterpretation and misrepresentation of findings, and conclusive statements that have no basis in science or the facts at hand. The lack of clearly defined standards for neuropsychological evaluations makes this process an individual judgment call. The recent American Academy of Clinical Neuropsychology (2007) practice guidelines are certainly a positive first step in providing more definitive criteria for evaluation-related standards of practice.

The following report exemplifies many of the issues stated previously. Before proceeding with a discussion of the case, I provide a brief overview of the reported condition (multiple chemical sensitivity) as well as a clarification of the role of the disability reviewer.

MULTIPLE CHEMICAL SENSITIVITY

While first defined as a syndrome in the 1990s, multiple chemical sensitivity (MCS) has a long history as an unverifiable and general label for a constellation of somatic complaints. First described by Randolph in 1952, MCS has had many names, including environmental illness, total allergy syndrome, and chemical AIDS. More recently, the more common label used in the field is *idiopathic environmental intolerance* (i.e., Bailer, Witthoft, Paul, Bayeri, & Rist, 2005).

The core features of MCS include a subjective odor-mediated hypersensitivity toward common chemical agents in the environment such as car exhaust, perfumes, pesticides, drying paint, new carpeting, air pollution, cigarette smoke, and hairspray (Black et al., 2000). Individuals are reported to experience a potential range of symptoms across multiple systems, including difficulties with breathing, cognitive impairment, headaches, dizziness, fatigue, and generalized pain, as well as anxiety and depression.

Although multiple potential explanations have been proposed (i.e., biopsychosocial, classical conditioning, and physiological vulnerability), the etiology of MCS has remained elusive. In large part, the hypothesis that MCS reflects a genuine pathophysiological entity has been rejected (American Academy of Allergy and Immunology, 1986; American College of Occupational and Environmental Medicine, 1999; American College of Physicians, 1989). A number of studies have also failed to support the presence of cognitive deficits in this condition (Bolla, 2000; Labarge & McCaffrey, 2000). However, psychiatric illness has been identified as common in patients with MCS (Fiedler, Kipen, DeLuca, Kelly-McNeil, & Natelson, 1996). Psychiatric factors have also been put forth as a potential etiology for MCS (Staudenmayer, 2001).

In light of the available literature, it would be reasonable to approach an MCS disability claim with a fair degree of skepticism from a neuropsychological perspective. As the determination of an individual's medical status is outside the scope of a neuropsychologist's expertise, the focus of a review often includes identification of psychiatric factors that may offer a more parsimonious explanation of presenting complaints as well as an examination of the data related to neurocognitive functioning.

ELEMENTS OF A NEUROPSYCHOLOGICAL DISABILITY REVIEW

As part of the disability review process it is important to be cognizant of the nature of the particular disability policy and the claimant's contractual obligations. The policy effective in this case was an "own occupation" policy. Thus, the question of impairment was couched in relation to the individual's capacity to perform the "substantial duties" of his or her occupation. As there are a wide range of potential related activities inherent to any occupation, specific information is often requested in relation to the duties the individual had been engaged in prior to filing a claim.

As part of the disability review process, a claimant is typically asked to provide the names and contact information associated with current health care providers. At times, individuals fail to include providers that may have relevant information, either by accidental omission or, at times, via intentional efforts to engage in impression management. The entire medical record may then be requested and included within the file. Disability claim files also often include a statement from the claimant about his or her impressions of the condition, resulting impairment, current activities, and job duties. Copies of correspondence, policy information, and information from collateral sources (i.e., field visit reports, prior independent medical–legal evaluation reports, and surveillance) may also be found in the file.

An additional important element in relation to a disability claim is a certification by a licensed health care provider (generally labeled as the *attending
physician,* irrespective of his or her actual specialty) as to the presence of occupational impairment due to an illness or injury. A form for this purpose is
commonly obtained. It should be noted that psychologists are often referred
to as attending physicians when they are certifying to impairment.

CASE STUDY

Background

Dr. Jones is a 33-year-old female psychologist with a claim of disability secondary to MCS, beginning in September 2004. In this case, the presence of
impairment was being reported by an attending physician with a reported
specialty in MCS. "Multiple chemical sensitivity" was provided as the primary and sole diagnosis. It was reported that the claimant is impaired from
performing her occupation due to sensitivity to environmental stimuli including molds, mycotoxins, dust, mites, danders, trees, grasses, weeds,
chemicals, metals, certain nutrients, and many foods. Intradermal skin testing was reported to have also indicated sensitivity to a variety of chemicals
including solvents, chlorine, natural gas, ethanol, formaldehyde, unleaded
gas/diesel, and fireplace smoke. The individual was specifically reported as
unable to perform her occupation based on cognitive impairment and the
report that follows provided the basis for this conclusion. In terms of her
occupation, the individual provided solely therapy services and was not involved in testing, teaching, research, or other related additional activities
common to psychologists. The presence of any psychiatric difficulties was
specifically denied by her attending physician and no impairment on this
basis was being claimed.

From a medical perspective, a need to avoid exposure to environments
in which she would be exposed to dust, perfumes, or any "environmental
toxins" was also reported. Interestingly, the claimant was not reported to
have current medical impairment but rather was solely at risk for physical
symptoms should she be exposed to a plethora of potentially "toxic" environmental stimuli. Thus, from a medical perspective the issue was of a risk
of disability versus current impairment. The issue of risk can be a significant disability-related issue because of the limitations in quantifying risk.
However, a thorough discussion of risk of disability is beyond the scope of
this chapter. In addition, this issue was to be addressed by a physician reviewing the claim and the neuropsychologist reviewer specifically focused
on whether the presence of cognitive impairment was supported.

The claimant was referred to Dr. Brown, a neuropsychologist, for evaluation of cognitive functioning. His report was cited by the attending phy-

sician as clear evidence of the presence of cognitive impairment. Having been involved in similar claims previously, the neuropsychologist reviewer was aware that Dr. Brown often completed evaluations at the request of Dr. Blue (the attending physician) and had on each prior occasion indicated the presence of marked cognitive dysfunction.

The following section is dedicated to the claimant's neuropsychological evaluation. In order to provide an active sense of the claim review process in association with this case, a verbatim text (altered to ensure anonymity) is provided in numbered paragraphs. Subsequently, observations regarding Dr. Brown's report are offered.

Neuropsychological Evaluation

Background Information

(1) Dr. Brown reported the following background information: Dr. Jones reported unremarkable early developmental years. She stated that she underwent a tonsillectomy at age 9. She reported good health during her undergraduate training, in graduate school, and generally in adulthood until her present illness. However, she stated that she developed nasal stuffiness approximately 10 years ago. She said that she also experienced burping since her pregnancy 10 years ago.

Dr. Jones reported that she was born and raised in the East. She stated that she lived and worked in New England for approximately 3 years and completed her graduate school training. She stated that she relocated in 1991. She reported generally good psychological health throughout the lifespan. She described herself as a child as friendly and well liked by most peers and adults. She said that she was competitive and achieved many of her goals. She reported some anxiety due to neighborhood bullies and due to the bullying of an older sister. She said that she was well behaved and idealistic, attempting to live high Christian values, and sensitive to the feelings of others.

Academically, Dr. Jones reported that she was a B+ and A student throughout high school and perhaps even better in elementary and middle school. She stated that she initially had some difficulty when she started college because she discovered she had to memorize, not "study," for tests. She said that subsequently she earned straight A's for the remainder of undergraduate and graduate school.

In terms of family health history, Dr. Jones reported that her mother, age 82, is generally in good health but has some environmental sensitivities. She stated that her father, age 79, is generally in good health but has some cardiac issues. She said that her two sisters are generally healthy but the older sister also has environmental sensitivities.

Dr. Jones stated that she has been married on three occasions. She said that her second husband is the father of her daughter, age 11. She reported that she has been divorced from her third husband since 2001 and that her illness probably contributed to the demise of the marriage. She reported good relationships with family members and described her mother as the more supportive parent. She stated that her illness has had a negative impact on interpersonal relationships, as others find it difficult to understand. Dr. Jones reported undergoing counseling associated with a divorce and custody dispute with her second husband approximately 6 years ago. She stated that therapy lasted for approximately 1 year.

Occupationally, Dr. Jones stated that she worked for 1 year as a secretary at a community health center before attending graduate school. She said she subsequently worked as a counselor in a group home for troubled adolescents, in an inpatient psychiatric unit providing group therapy, and as a psychotherapist since completing her PhD. She stated that most recently she worked at the university medical center in the adolescent program (partial hospital and intensive outpatient programs). She said that she had also been in private practice for approximately 2 years prior to accepting the hospital position.

Dr. Jones denied any drug or alcohol abuse, past or present. However, she said that she experimented briefly with a few illicit drugs when she was in her mid-20s. She stated that she has never smoked cigarettes. She denied any history of head injury or loss of consciousness. She said that she is not taking any prescription medications at the present time.

Description of Illness

(2) Dr. Jones stated that, in retrospect, she believes she has had symptoms of allergies throughout her lifespan, and she now realizes that her allergic responses are neurological as well as sinus related. She believes that during her college years she was somewhat compromised by these allergies but unaware of them. She was teased about being "spacey" as she often became absorbed in her thoughts, having to reread assigned materials due to poor concentration, as well as losing track of time, being easily distracted, sleeping excessively, etc. She has recently observed these types of symptoms, which come and go associated with the skin testing to various substances.

(3) Dr. Jones believes that the beginning of her toxic overload occurred approximately 15 years ago when she lived near orchard country and developed a seasonal cough and a new form of digestive difficulty. She learned to work around these symptoms and when standard medical evaluations, testing, and treatment were ineffective, she ignored her symptoms. She avoided some foods but nothing affected her cough until she was evalu-

ated and treated by Dr. Blue in October 2004. Her cough had been an ongoing daily problem by then, which she failed to notice at times; however, others seemed to notice it.

(4) Dr. Jones had moved into a new home in the early 1990s and was reexposed to many chemicals associated with new construction. She and her husband finished the basement of the home in the mid to late 1990s and she alleges that she was exposed to additional construction chemicals. Her employer installed new carpets in the building and painted her office and other rooms, which exposed her to additional chemicals.

(5) Dr. Jones believes that during this long period of exposure to numerous chemicals, her system became gradually worn down. She began to experience fatigue. She sought out assessments and information for attention-deficit disorder as others suggested this might be a problem for her. Ritalin and later Adderall were prescribed but did not help. She noticed that most medications prescribed for her were too strong if taken in full doses. She used smaller amounts when possible.

(6) She had a leg biopsy in the mid-1990s that required a 2-week recovery period due to exposure to anesthesia. She experienced many physical complaints that she described as nagging, including digestive problems, concentration problems, excessive sleepiness after meals, poor sleep quality, fatigue, etc. She found it necessary to make lists and to keep reminders to stay on schedule. Her motivation and sex drive decreased. She became stressed due to her cognitive difficulties.

(7) Dr. Jones noticed that she could feel other people's electromagnetic fields in January 2002. Prior to that time, she had experienced several occasions of electricity coursing through her body during the night. Her home, at the time, was located near large power lines and the transformer was in her yard. She became intolerant of her home and other people, including her husband. She subsequently divorced and experienced concomitant depression and alienation. She could not find any appropriate health care provider to help her.

(8) She terminated her job of 5 years in July 2003 and took a position as a therapist in the adolescent program. The offices had new carpet, flooring, furniture, computers, etc. She used an air purifier in her office.

(9) She sought treatment with Dr. Blue. She wanted to recheck mercury levels and find help for electromagnetic sensitivity, as being around electrical equipment such as computers produced a variety of symptoms. For example, she noticed that any watch she wore stopped working and she had occasional difficulty with electrical devices malfunctioning around her such as light fixtures and hair dryers.

(10) After she sought care, Dr. Jones noticed that she had "unmasked" and her degree of sensitivity increased. She also noticed that when she returned to work in November 2004, she had more difficulty concentrating

than ever before. She smelled chemicals and was informed that new flooring had been laid in the adjacent office; new carpeting had been laid on the floor above her office as well. Additional construction was scheduled to continue throughout the building. She became ill that night after work with nausea, headache, a chemical taste in her mouth, fatigue, and feeling "sick all over." She was off work within a week and she did not return to her position because of the continuous "outgasing" of noxious chemicals. She returned to Dr. Blue for further treatment and she learned through testing that her sensitivities had worsened since her trip home. She has been attempting to detoxify her system since that time. Dr. Blue referred Dr. Jones for neuropsychological evaluation.

(11) Dr. Jones reported that she experienced anxiety and depression from her many stressors, including environmental toxins. She said that she experiences more anger, irritability, and other negative characteristics when exposed to environmental incitants, which then have a negative impact on her work, particularly because of her neurocognitive deficits. She stated that when she is not experiencing significant stressors, her mood appears to be normal.

Testing

The following tests were and administered to Dr. Jones: Wechsler Adult Intelligence Scale—Revised (WAIS-R), Wechsler Adult Intelligence Scale—III (WAIS-III: 2 subtests), Wechsler Memory Scale—III (WMS-3), Benton Visual Retention Test, Grooved Pegboard Test, Wide Range Achievement Test—Revised (WRAT-R), Test of Memory Malingering, Halstead–Reitan Neuropsychological Battery (including Reitan–Indiana Aphasia Screening Test, Reitan–Klove Sensory–Perceptual Examination, Halstead Category Test, Tactual Performance Test (TPT), Speech Sounds Perception Test, Seashore Rhythm Test, Hand Dynamometer Test, Finger Tapping Test, Trail Making Test A/B), and Beck Depression Inventory.

TEST OF MOTIVATION AND EFFORT

(12) Dr. Jones earned perfect scores on Trials 1 and 2 and the Retention Trial of the Test of Memory Malingering (TOMM). Scores suggested that she had put forth her best effort on the neuropsychological tests administered.

INTELLECTUAL FUNCTIONING

(13) Dr. Jones's age-corrected subtest scores on the WAIS-R ranged from the population mean (50th percentile) to the very superior range (99th per-

centile). She scored in a very superior range (99th percentile) on the Verbal measures in general learning ability; range and richness of ideas, words, and expression; and utilization of words. She also scored in a very superior range (98th percentile) in commonsense reasoning, social judgment, and the ability to recognize antecedent–consequent relationships to make good decisions. She scored in a superior range (95th percentile) in long-term memory and retention of general fund of information from education and experience.

The remaining three Verbal subtest scores fell in the high-average ranges. She scored at the 84th percentile in short-term, rote, and immediate auditory memory, attention, concentration, and auditory sequencing. She scored at the 75th percentile in numerical reasoning and problem-solving ability as well as in abstract reasoning requiring the capacity for associative thinking and ability to separate essential from nonessential details. Her Verbal IQ (VIQ) score of 130 fell in a very superior range at the 98th percentile.

Four of five WAIS-R Performance subtest scores fell in the average range. She scored at the population mean (50th percentile) in visual–motor–spatial integration and analyzing and synthesizing ability and in the ability to synthesize concrete parts into meaningful wholes and grasp patterns. She scored at the 63rd percentile in visual sequencing and planning ability as well in the ability to attend to and observe inconsistencies and incongruities in the environment and attend to details, in general. She scored in a high-average range (75th percentile) in perceptual–motor learning, speed of mental operation, and psychomotor speed. Her Performance IQ (PIQ) core of 117 fell in a high-average range at the 87th percentile. Her Full Scale IQ score of 127 fell in a superior range at the 96th percentile ranking. The 13-point difference between VIQ and PIQ scores in favor of the Verbal measures is significant but not necessarily abnormal. The difference in scores may represent better verbal comprehension abilities in contrast to perceptual organization skills as suggested by her scores on the primary factors of the WAIS-R. She scored at the 95th percentile on measures of Verbal Comprehension and at the 71st percentile on measures of Perceptual Organization. She scored at approximately the 86th percentile, overall, on measures of Freedom from Distractibility.

MEMORY

(14) Dr. Jones's scores on WMS-III fell generally in the average ranges with better recall of visual than verbal information. Her Auditory Immediate Memory Quotient score fell at the 34th percentile; her Visual Immediate Memory Quotient score fell at the 73rd percentile.

She scored at the 47th percentile in the ability to recall the same verbal information after a delay of 30 minutes. Her Visual Delayed Memory score improved to the high-average range (84th percentile). She scored in an average range (63rd percentile) on high-level, attention and concentration tasks.

Scores on the Benton Visual Retention Test, a task measuring visuospatial memory and visuomotor response, fell within normal limits. This particular measure is included in the World Health Organization core battery of tests with known sensitivity for neurotoxic effects (no reference provided by Dr. Brown).

Dr. Jones demonstrated significant incidental verbal learning deficits. She was able to recall only two of four words after a 30-second distractor and after delays of 5 and 15 minutes. She scored in a perfectly normal range on one measure of incidental memory from the TPT—that is, recall of the shapes of the blocks after three trials (TPT Memory: 10). However, she scored in the severely impaired range in her ability to recall the correct location (TPT Localization 2). The localization score in considered one of the most sensitive to dysfunction on the Halstead–Reitan Neuropsychological Battery.

GENERAL NEUROPSYCHOLOGICAL BATTERY

(15) Dr. Jones earned a General Neuropsychological Deficit Scale score of 17 on the Halstead–Reitan Neuropsychological Battery, falling within normal limits (normal range 0–25). Her Impairment Index of 0.3 (30% of Halstead's test in an impaired range) was low normal. She scored in a severely impaired range on one of the five most sensitive indicators of dysfunction on the battery, in a low-normal range on two of the indicators, and in a perfectly normal range on two of the indicators.

She scored in a low-normal range on a measure of executive functions, including new learning and problem solving, abstract reasoning, concept formation, mental efficiency, and judgment with a Category Test Error score of 31. Her score fell at the 34th percentile ranking compared with her age, sex, and educational peers. She also scored in a low-normal range on a complex psychomotor problem-solving task (TPT) requiring the executive functions, noted above, in addition to the ability to sustain adequate strength and speed of movement in the upper extremities and tactile perception. Her score fell at the 39th percentile compared with that of her peers.

She scored in a perfectly normal range on two measures of attention and concentration for verbal and nonverbal auditory stimuli. She scored in a mild to moderately impaired range on a simple measure of visual tracking and scanning (Trail Making Test A: 4th percentile compared with her peer group) and in a perfectly normal range on a more complex measure requiring mental flexibility (Trail Making Test B: 70th percentile compared with her peers).

No dysphasic symptoms were noted on the Reitan–Indiana Aphasia Screening test. She committed no errors upon bilateral, simultaneous stimulation in the auditory, visual, or tactile modalities. She scored within normal limits on measures of sensory–tactile functioning with the exception of Tactile Form Recognition, which was low normal.

She scored in a mildly impaired range on a measure of motor speed with the index finger with the dominant right hand; she scored in a low-normal range with the nondominant left hand. She scored at the 39th percentile with the dominant right hand on a measure of grip strength and at the 70th percentile with the nondominant left hand, compared with her peers. However, she demonstrated greater impairment with the dominant right hand on a measure of manual speed and dexterity (10th percentile), in contrast to the nondominant left hand (55th percentile). These scores indicated greater dysfunction in the right hemisphere but the difference in right and left hemisphere scores is not significant.

ACADEMIC ABILITIES

(16) Dr. Jones's Reading and Spelling scores had post-high school grade equivalents, falling at the 73rd and 91st percentile rankings, respectively. Her Arithmetic score had a high school grade equivalent, falling at the 55th percentile ranking. These scores are generally consistent with prior levels of educational achievements. Inattention appears to have contributed to this relatively lower score on Arithmetic. For example, she added figures, although subtraction was indicated.

PERSONALITY AND BEHAVIOR

(17) Dr. Jones did not endorse the presence of significant depressive symptoms on a self-report inventory of depression. She reported mild difficulties with low energy and physical malfunctioning consistent with her medical condition. She also reported feelings of social isolation and withdrawal due to others not understanding her condition. At the present time, she may require more help, sympathy, and understanding from others. She probably enjoys working alone rather than in groups, as she appears temperamentally independent, self-sufficient, and resourceful.

Summary and Conclusions

(18) Dr. Jones is a 33-year-old clinical psychologist with disabilities who sought evaluation and treatment with Dr. Blue, an environmental medicine specialist, due to declining health and neurocognitive functioning after being exposed to a variety of chemicals for many years. Her health

particularly declined following a variety of toxic exposures in the workplace. She reported exposure primarily to construction chemicals and vehicle exhaust as well as to lawn chemicals. She also reported sensitivities to many substances in the environment resulting in a variety of symptoms, including neurocognitive dysfunction. Dr. Blue referred her to this office for neuropsychological evaluation.

(19) Neurocognitive test results indicated general neurocognitive functioning within normal limits as demonstrated by a General Neuropsychological Deficit Scale score of 17 on the Halstead–Reitan Neuropsychological Battery (normal range 0–25). However, she demonstrated severe impairment on one (TPT Localization) of the five most sensitive indicators of dysfunction on the battery. She scored in a low-normal range on two of the indicators, and in a perfectly normal range on two of the indicators. She scored in low-normal range on a measure of executive functioning and psychomotor problem solving. Although her scores were not as impaired as many of the patients evaluated in this office associated with environmental illness/toxic exposure, she showed the usual pattern of impairment observed in chemically sensitive individuals including greater impairment of higher-order functions, relative to other abilities.

(20) Dr. Jones's Full Scale IQ score of 127 fell in a superior range at the 96th percentile; her VIQ score of 130 fell in a very superior range at the 98th percentile. Her PIQ score of 117 fell in a high-average range at the 87th percentile. The 13-point difference between Verbal and Performance measures in favor of the Verbal measures may represent better developed verbal comprehension abilities. However, the impaired PIQ score may also represent the negative impact of toxic exposure on perceptual organization abilities.

(21) Scores on a formal measure of memory fell generally in the average ranges. She also scored within normal limits on the Benton Visual Retention Test with known sensitivity for neurotoxic effects. However, scores have been observed to fall within normal limits when the individual is removed from the primary incitant(s). She demonstrated severe impairment on two measures of incidental memory; one measure from the TPT and one on a measure of incidental verbal memory. Incidental memory is more like the memory requirements of everyday life when one is not specifically instructed to store information for later recall. Academic abilities fell generally within an expected range considering prior educational achievements. Some inattention was observed on the Arithmetic subtest.

(22) Her personality and behavior indicated some disturbance of emotional equilibrium associated with toxic exposure and chronic physical illness with moderate levels of tension, depression, anger, and fatigue indicated at the present time and diminished level of vigor and activity. Her profiles are typical of other patients who have been evaluated in this office

associated with toxic/neurotoxic exposure showing a pattern of cognitive impairment and emotional difficulties to a lesser degree. It is important to note that Dr. Jones was evaluated in an environment relatively free of toxins and incitants and under conditions of reduced stress, with rest periods permitted, as necessary, to elicit her best performance. Had she been evaluated in her workplace or under conditions of greater demands and stress, it is likely that greater compromise of functioning would have been observed. Despite the fact that this examiner's office is much safer, environmentally, than the vast majority of general offices, Dr. Jones reported a significant number of symptoms during and after the evaluation. Test results are considered a valid indication of her current level of neurocognitive and personality/behavioral functioning under environmentally safe, nonstressful conditions. Her reported degree of sensitivity appears consistent with skin-testing results and probably argues most strongly against return to work in any ordinary workplace setting. Continued avoidance of toxic/neurotoxic substances and full participation in her treatment program as prescribed by Dr. Blue is recommended. It is quite likely that physical, psychological, and neurocognitive functioning would worsen if she continues to be "reexposed." It has been observed in some patients that continued exposure has resulted in permanent neurocognitive and/or personality dysfunction.

Analysis

The following is a review of the background, testing, and conclusions referenced to the appropriate sections of Dr. Brown's report above.

(1) Review of her past history did not indicate the presence of any significant medical conditions that would need to be considered as likely etiologies in relation to her cognitive complaints. It is interesting to note Dr. Jones's report of similar symptoms in family members. Also, no strong family history of either psychiatric or medical difficulties was reported.

The description of her early interpersonal relationships is notable for her perception of being idealistic, moral, and sensitive to others. Her mental health history is most consistent with a likely adjustment disorder in the context of her divorce and the subsequent child custody issues with no clear periods of reported major depressive episodes. Her history of multiple failed marriages is unclear as a potential indicator of issues with close relationships. Her occupational history is generally consistent with an ability to sustain effective work performance and no difficulties with interpersonal conflict were noted. No past disability claims were noted.

Her educational history is not consistent with an individual likely to have experienced a learning or attention-deficit disorder that might result in abnormal cognitive test findings. There were no reported standardized test scores (SAT, GRE) that may have been of assistance in estimating her premorbid functioning. As no medications are presently prescribed, one also does not have to be concerned with potential cognitive side-effect profiles. Overall, the background information suggests a fairly benign history and no clear differential diagnosis emerges from this information.

(2) It should be noted that while the claimant was asserting the presence of cognitive impairment secondary to her MCS dating back to college, the prior section of the report had noted that she was a straight A student through undergraduate and graduate school. Dr. Brown implies that her cognitive functioning was compromised and gives the sense of an individual struggling to maintain her performance since her early 20s despite no prior periods of occupational impairment.

(3) The insertion of pseudoscientific terminology such as "toxic overload" and "outgasing" and how this is described in a manner that suggests a clear etiology and disease process is concerning. As the reported condition is a syndrome and not a disease, there is a degree of embellishment in this description that raises concern. In addition, on the one hand there is a description of an individual struggling, but on the other hand the symptoms are reported as capable of being ignored and possibly such that she might not actually notice them (i.e., her cough).

(4) Again, the claimant's assertion regarding exposure is now reported as fact—she "was exposed." While this section of the report is clearly an opportunity to present the history from the perspective of the claimant, there is a sense of a translation of the claimant's self-report as a factual recollection of events rather than her own perspective of events.

(5) The claimant is a trained mental health provider with no history of learning and/or attention problems through school, yet the first hypothesis when she reportedly began to feel fatigued was attention-deficit disorder. No information was provided in relation to what, if any, type of evaluation may have been completed. Had neuropsychological testing been completed at the time, this may have served as a valuable source of data by which to make comparisons. As most are aware, a prescription for a stimulant medication does not indicate the presence of attention-deficit/hyperactivity disorder (ADHD), nor does her reported nonresponse indicate the absence of this condition. One might question whether the claimant was actually experiencing symptoms of emotional distress at this time. As noted previously, this was about the time of her marital difficulties and pending divorce.

(6) The range of reported symptoms covers a broad spectrum for which diagnostic workup would require an extensive array of diagnostic testing to rule out other potentially causative factors. No mention of any diagnostic testing done during this time period was made. There is also

question as to whether her symptoms, if accurate, are best accounted for by a single process or may reflect multiple processes.

(7) At the time of this evaluation, her reported symptoms have now moved into a range that might be considered somewhat bizarre. The report does not include much detail in relation to what she experienced when feeling other people's "electromagnetic" fields. Similarly, the experience of electricity "coursing through her body" does not sound like restless leg syndrome or other forms of movement-related sleep disorders. The insertion of the statement that her home was near power lines provides a specious link that is not otherwise supported in this report or in her other medical records.

(8) The history also suggests that despite a growing constellation of symptoms causing her emotional, cognitive, and physical distress, the claimant opted to change jobs to one with increased responsibility and demands.

(9) The claimant sought a workup with Dr. Blue who practices several states away. Of note in this section is the introduction of increasingly bizarre symptoms such as her causing the malfunctioning of both electrical and battery-operated devices.

(10) The narrative cites physiological processes that are not supported by the empirical literature. The claimant's reported symptoms are stated as facts rather than statements of opinion. It is also interesting to note the psychological process of being informed of likely worsening of symptoms should she return to the "toxic" environment of her workplace and her rather rapid decline in functioning when this occurred. Dr. Blue also offers a range of medically unsubstantiated treatment services that the claimant had not yet attempted.

(11) While the presence of significant anxiety and/or depressive symptoms is denied, there appears to be at least some acknowledgement of psychological factors in relation to her reported physical symptoms. This description is strongly consistent with a somatoform disorder. However, the presence of a disability claim may also be a factor in the perpetuation of her reported difficulties.

(12) While there were no indications of poor effort on the TOMM, the absence of evidence on a single validity measure of course does not indicate maximal effort throughout the examination. It is notable that psychological testing that included validity scales was not included in this evaluation. Moreover, the lack of a standardized psychological assessment inventory in light of the clinical history is a striking omission.

(13) It is not clear what Dr. Brown's rationale was for using the WAIS-R instead of the WAIS-III, especially when the WMS-III is also used in the same test battery. This would have provided the opportunity to make more direct comparisons between her IQ and memory abilities. Review of the

WAIS-R raw data was notable for generous scoring on verbal measures with a number of responses credited as a 2 rather than 1. Dr. Brown discusses the WAIS-R findings in terms of index scores and recalculation of these scores indicated trivial errors (Verbal Comprehension Index = 129—97th percentile, Perceptual Organization 111—77th percentile, and Freedom From Distractibility 115—84th percentile). It is also notable that the age-corrected scores were reported for the Verbal but not Performance subtests from the WAIS-R. Had these scores been reported, four of five subtests would have fallen in the high-average versus average ranges.

(14) Memory scores were somewhat lower than expected but solidly in the average range. Dr. Brown cited impairment on an incidental verbal learning task but no data for such a test was included nor does the list of tests include a measure similar to what was described in his report. The TPT Localization score was not accurate and was more reasonably scored as 5: this changes the interpretation to a T-score of 44, which while below average (using Heaton terminology), falls at the 27th percentile (Heaton, Miller, Taylor, & Grant, 2004).

(15) The Halstead Impairment Index (HII) was reported as low normal. However, as calculated by Dr. Brown, her score of .3 falls as at the 50th percentile and is normal. With correction of the erroneously scored TPT Localization score, the HII is .15 (Finger Tapping below cutoff) and perfectly normal. There was a fairly consistent pattern of reporting scores in normal ranges below their actual levels. For example, on the Category Test, her T-score was 46 and in the normal, not "low-normal" range. Similarly, her TPT—Time was a T-score of 47 and in the normal, not "low-normal" range. There was a significant discrepancy between her Trail Making Test A/B performance, with times that were almost identical. Tactile Form Recognition scores included a T-score of 57 (right) and 60 (left), neither of which could be construed as low-normal performances. Finger Tapping scores bilaterally were at T-scores above 50, again inconsistent with "mildly impaired" and "low normal." The Grooved Pegboard scores were accurately reported but the conclusion of "greater dysfunction" in the right hemisphere is spurious. Dr. Brown infers in his statement the presence of left-hemisphere dysfunction as well but that it was not as bad as her right-hemisphere dysfunction. Neither of these conclusions is reasonably supported by the data.

(16) Overall, her WRAT-3 scores are somewhat lower than expected based on her IQ (primarily her Reading score). Again, the generous scoring of the WAIS-R may have artificially accounted for this difference. Nonetheless, her scores were generally within expectancy.

(17) The psychological testing completed was limited to the Beck Depression Inventory–II. Her score was in the range of minimal symptoms and is less than what would be expected based on the clinical history dis-

cussed earlier. The failure to incorporate a standardized psychological inventory (e.g., Minnesota Multiphasic Personality Inventory–2 [MMPI-2]) with validity scales as well as a more comprehensive assessment of her psychological/emotional functioning was striking in light of her overall presentation.

(18) It is notable that again that the claimant's self-report is treated as fact by Dr. Brown and that attribution of her difficulties has been clearly established.

(19) The mislabeling of Dr. Jones's performance now conveys a level of impairment not supported by the actual data. The data are more reasonably interpreted as a normal profile with no clear areas of cognitive weakness or deficit. The failure to consider the presence of normal variation in scores within a battery is also notable (Palmer, Boone, Lesser, & Wohl, 1998; Schretlen, Munro, Anthony, & Pearlson, 2003). Dr. Brown also indicates a normative database for individuals with MCS that is idiosyncratic to his practice and not consistent with the peer-reviewed literature.

(20) The previously reported nonsignificant VIQ–PIQ split is now interpreted as both clinically meaningful and evidence of toxic exposure.

(21) Note that data contrary to his hypothesis are readily dismissed. Again, the measure of "incidental memory" was not included in the data provided and the TPT was within normal limits.

(22) Despite the absence of psychological test data to support his conclusions, Dr. Brown opines that the claimant suffers from emotional difficulties but argues that these difficulties are normal for her condition. His hypothesis of greater dysfunction in another setting is not supported by any findings in his evaluation and implies a risk of further impairment than was present at the time of his assessment. Dr. Brown's recommendation to avoid "ordinary" work settings is based on a medical rather than neuropsychological risk and is clearly outside the bounds of the competency of a psychologist. The citing of dire consequences of a return to work and a strong recommendation against resuming her prior activities runs contrary to the majority of opinion as to how best address MCS from a behavioral standpoint.

CONCLUSIONS

Based on a detailed review of this report as well as review of the additional materials available in her claim file, the presence of cognitive impairment to a degree to preclude the claimant from performing her occupation was not reasonably supported. A careful review of the data (as well as rescoring of some data) indicated a normal profile with no clear areas of cognitive impairment. The evaluation also did not reasonably support the presence of a psychiatric condition causing functional impairment, though in fairness, the evaluation was markedly limited in this area and failed to include appropriate assessment in this domain. A recent study by Binder, Storzbach, and Salinsky (2006) illustrates the value of the MMPI-2 in this population. The insistence of Dr. Blue that no impairment was present on this basis also argues further against a psychiatric condition causing occupational impairment. A concurrent medical review of the file by a board-certified internal medicine physician did not support the presence of impairment on a medical basis.

As impairment was not reasonably supported by the information available and several issues were raised in reviewing the neuropsychological report, both Dr. Blue and Dr. Brown were contacted via phone to obtain further clarification.

Dr. Blue reported that she was doing well from a medical perspective and he anticipated a return to work in the next month. He noted that he was concerned about her experiencing a "relapse" if she were exposed to environmental "toxins." He was not able to identify any specific concerns but noted that this was based on her report of what substances may cause her to experience an adverse reaction. He noted that he did not have an opinion in relation to her exposure to "electromagnetic fields" from other people but expressed concern about potential adverse effects if she used a phone or computer. When issues were raised in relation to the neuropsychological evaluation and the lack of evidence to support cognitive impairment, he indicated that he relied solely on the conclusions of Dr. Brown and deferred to him for any additional comment.

Discussion with Dr. Brown was generally antagonistic when the issues of scoring and labels of performance were addressed. While conceding that the labels he employed may have been misleading, he emphasized that this was missing the forest for the trees. Dr. Brown emphasized that he had a vast experience of testing such individuals and that these results were consistent with those he finds in patients with MCS. When asked about the missing incidental memory testing data, he reviewed his file and did not find any such measure. He responded that he generally includes such a measure in his MCS test battery and it may or may not have been given. He also noted that he often "writes over" an old report when generating a new one and that these data may have been from a prior evaluation rather than the current one.

The presence of any psychiatric symptoms was minimized and attributed solely to adjustment issues to her serious medical condition. Dr. Brown had no response to the question of why he used the Beck Depression Inventory–II versus a more comprehensive measure of emotional functioning, vaguely citing time issues. In the end, he reluctantly conceded that her neuropsychological scores were consistent with no present impairment but emphasized that these findings were in a "safe" environment free of the common toxins in the "real" world. He added that Dr. Jones would likely evidence marked decline in her cognitive functioning upon exposure to less "safe" environments. When asked about the "safe" environment he provides, he noted that his office was very clean and free of dust and that environmentally "friendly" chemicals were used to clean the office. He also noted that he uses an air purifier. He was not willing to discuss that the claimant had to travel to his office and ate lunch in an "unsafe" environment on the day of testing without any apparent ill effects and that the use of a tape recorder, stopwatch, and at least one computer-based test also did not have an ill effect (nor did any of these instruments malfunction in her presence). In terms of risk of further symptoms, he agreed that this issue was more appropriately in the purview of Dr. Blue (though he insisted that this was the likely case).

In conclusion, the foregoing case is a clear example of the benefit of the use of a neuropsychological disability reviewer when cognitive impairment is alleged to be a cause of occupational impairment. A review of the report by an individual without a detailed knowledge and understanding of neuropsychological assessment may have erroneously relied on the conclusions of Dr. Brown without questioning the data used to reach his conclusions. Furthermore, the raw test data were indispensable in detecting scoring errors and the misreporting of performance.

REFERENCES

American Academy of Allergy and Immunology. (1986). Position Statement: Clinical ecology. *Journal of Allergy and Clinical Immunology, 78*, 269–271.

American Academy of Clinical Neuropsychology. (2007). Practice guidelines for neuropsychological assessment and consultation. *The Clinical Neuropsychologist, 21*, 209–231.

American College of Occupational and Environmental Medicine. (1999). Multiple chemical sensitivities: Idiopathic environmental intolerance. *Journal of Occupational Medicine, 41*(11), 940–942.

American College of Physicians. (1989). Clinical ecology. *Annals of Internal Medicine, 111*, 168–178.

Bailer, J., Witthoft, M., Paul, C., Bayeri, C., & Rist, F. (2005). Evidence for overlap between idiopathic environmental intolerance and Somatoform Disorders. *Psychosomatic Medicine, 67*, 921–929.

Binder, L. M., Storzbach, D., & Salinsky, M. C. (2006). MMPI-2 profiles of persons with multiple chemical sensitivity. *The Clinical Neuropsychologist, 20*, 848–857.

Bolla, K. I. (2000). Use of neuropsychological testing in idiopathic environmental testing. *Occupational Medicine State of the Art Reviews, 15*, 617–624.

Black, D. W., Doebbeling, B. N., Voelker, M. D., Clarke, W. R., Woolson, R. F., Barrett, D. H., et al. (2000). Multiple chemical sensitivity syndrome. Symptom prevalence and risk factors in a military population. *Archives of Internal Medicine, 160*, 1169–1176.

Fiedler, N., Kipen, H. M., DeLuca, J., Kelly-McNeil, K., & Natelson, B. (1996). A controlled comparison of multiple chemical sensitivity and chronic fatigue syndrome. *Psychosomatic Medicine, 58*, 38–49.

Heaton, R. K., Miller, S. W., Taylor, M. J., & Grant, I. (2004). *Revised comprehensive norms for an expanded Halstead–Reitan Battery: Demographically adjusted neuropsychological norms for African American and Caucasian adults.* Lutz, FL: Psychological Assessment Resources.

Labarge, A. S., & McCaffrey, R. J. (2000). Multiple chemical sensitivity: A review of the theoretical and research literature. *Neuropsychology Review, 10,* 183–211.

Palmer, B. W., Boone, K. B., Lesser, I. M., & Wohl, M. A. (1998). Base rates of "impaired" neuropsychological test performance among healthy older adults. *Archives of Clinical Neuropsychology, 13,* 503–511.

Randolph, T. G. (1952). Sensitivity to petroleum including its derivatives and antecedents. *Journal of Laboratory and Clinical Medicine, 40,* 931–932.

Schretlen, D. J., Munro, C. A., Anthony, J. C., & Pearlson, G. D. (2003). Examining the range of normal intraindividual variability in neuropsychological test performance. *Journal of the International Neuropsychological Society, 9,* 864–870.

Staudenmayer, H. (2001). Idiopathic environmental intolerances (IEI): Myth and reality. *Toxicology Letters, 120,* 333–342.

4

Noncredible Competence

How to Handle "Newbies," "Wannabes," and Forensic "Experts" Who Know Better or Should Know Better

Joel E. Morgan

Most practicing neuropsychologists are probably familiar with the terms *noncredible performance* and *suboptimal effort* in discussions concerning poor effort by examinees, but how about *noncredible competence?* Forensic neuropsychology is a specialty requiring a specific knowledge base beyond that required in a general clinical practice. Clinical neuropsychologists involved in the forensic setting are sometimes confronted with reports from the "other side," which may display the grossest errors in terms of methodology, practice, interpretation, and/or report writing. In reading one of these reports for the first time, a competent neuropsychologist may think, "What is this?" or "How can this be?" Sometimes, such "experts" are really practitioners who are new to the field of forensic neuropsychological assessment. Some others may be experienced clinically but have an apparent lack of sufficient knowledge of the specific issues concerning competent forensic clinical neuropsychological practice. Sometimes, such "experts" are actually experienced, highly competent, and quite knowledgeable people who, unfortunately, alter or bend their views in accordance with the demand characteristics relative to the side that retained them (i.e.,

53

plaintiff vs. defense [civil cases] or prosecution vs. defense [criminal cases]). These practitioners might be referred to as newbies, wannabes, or those who probably should (or do) know better, respectively. Newbies and wannabes often coexist and are not mutually exclusive. In all cases, however, the work produced by these practitioners is substandard and often unethical.

Having practiced forensic clinical neuropsychology for over 20 years in both the civil and criminal arena, I have encountered many examples of substandard work. It has become my practice to carefully review both the reports and the raw neuropsychological/psychological test data provided by the other side's expert in all cases. When reviewing such neuropsychological information I pay particular attention to the methodology, raw and normed scores, and the classification range of the scores. In all cases, I review the medical record carefully to determine as much as possible if the examinee's performance makes sense in light of the medical information. For instance, it makes little sense when an examinee reportedly has severe cognitive deficits subsequent to what is normally considered to be an extremely mild or minor injury. In this instance, the medical history does not support the test findings. Yet, as common and apparent as this scenario may be to the experienced reader, it is actually a scenario that is frequently encountered in forensic neuropsychological work. Neuropsychological reports by newbie or wannabe practitioners not uncommonly attribute poor/impaired test scores to severe dysfunction and underlying brain damage subsequent to the most trivial injuries. Often, well-trained clinicians, including those who actually know better, avoid giving symptom validity tests altogether—for example, Test of Memory Malingering (TOMM; Tombaugh, 1996) or other tests of validity or response style, such as Minnesota Multiphasic Personality Inventory/Minnesota Multiphasic Personality Inventory–2 (MMPI/MMPI-2; Butcher, Dahlstrom, Graham, Tellegen, & Kaemmer, 1989). Why, you may ask? It could be to give the appearance that his or her exam is valid and in the hope that the expert retained by the other side (you!) doesn't know any better. The reader is therefore cautioned to pay particular attention to the medical record and juxtapose the record against the obtained test scores, behavior, and overall performance of the examinee. In all circumstances, whether in a purely clinical or a forensic context, the medical history and the neuropsychological/psychological test data must stick together in a sensible way; the obtained performance must make neuropsychological sense. The competent and ethical forensic practitioner will know the scientific literature of the field, with regard to both the explosion of research in the area of effort and the neuropsychology of the disorder/illness/injury at hand.

Similarly, one must pay special attention to the effects of serial testing, when test scores obtained in one examination are compared to the test scores in another examination. It is not uncommon in forensic practice for a neuropsychologist providing the second exam to obtain scores from an examinee that are markedly lower than those obtained on the first exam in the context of a disorder or injury that clearly improves over time rather than gets worse (a head injury, stroke, etc.). Worse performances in serial testings, in the absence of a progressive central nervous system (CNS) disorder, should raise a red flag, particularly in a forensic/secondary gain context.

These and many other types of errors are commonly found in expert reports in clinical neuropsychological practice. When doing forensic work, the competent and ethical clinical neuropsychologist should carefully review the other side's expert neuropsychology report. The following two case examples illustrate these and other common errors produced by individuals who may be said to demonstrate "noncredible competency." Sometimes, these experts may also demonstrate "suboptimal ethics," but this is another matter for a different chapter.

CASE STUDY 1: PLAINTIFF EXPERT— NEWBIE–WANNABE

Background Information

This case concerns a 53-year-old Caucasian female who was allegedly sexually assaulted while performing her duties as a custodial worker in a university classroom building. The records indicated that the alleged assault took place while she was cleaning classrooms at 10:00 P.M. and consisted of the assailant "cutting her clothes with a knife, pulling her blue jeans down, and having intercourse with her" (from the plaintiff expert's report). The plaintiff alleged that "he put the steel handle of the knife in my private parts. He pulled my hair. He made me do it with my mouth. . . . " The victim further stated that the assailant banged her head on the floor until she "passed out." The patient (victim) told the doctors at the emergency room that she estimated the length of loss of consciousness as lasting "a few seconds." Reportedly, after the assault, the victim then went to the bathroom where she cleaned herself and then attempted to go back to work. Shortly thereafter, she reportedly became emotionally distressed and reported the incident to authorities, after having cleaned a few classrooms.

I reviewed the report of the plaintiff expert neuropsychologist prepared as part of a civil suit emanating from this alleged incident. The victim retained counsel to sue the university for failure to provide a safe atmosphere for its employees. Plaintiff counsel hired a local "neuropsychologist" who ostensibly conducted a neuropsychological evaluation of the victim/plaintiff. I requested the raw psychological/neuropsychological test data of victim/plaintiff and reviewed them, as well as the written report of the plaintiff expert neuropsychologist and his or her curriculum vitae (CV).

Two volumes of medical records accompanied the neuropsychology examination report. Ten days later, I received another neuropsychological report by the same expert, which was actually a rewrite of the first report. In the first report, there was no mention of the tests administered, no mention of observations of the patient, and, oddly, no date on the report. In the second report, these discrepancies were rectified. Clearly, writing two reports of the same examination, let alone submitting them to counsel for review, is certainly not standard practice.

Quickly skimming through the report, I found the diagnostic conclusion section. The diagnoses opined by the plaintiff's expert included "dementia due to head trauma, major depressive disorder, and posttraumatic stress disorder."

In reviewing the medical record, there was little doubt from the start that "dementia due to head trauma" was completely inaccurate. How was it possible that someone hitting his or her head on the floor, even several times, without a substantial loss of consciousness or positive neurological exam, could lead to dementia? The medical record recorded a normal neurological exam in the emergency room (ER); the patient was "awake, alert, and fully oriented. . . . " A computed tomography (CT) of the patient's head at the time was completely normal with "no observable abnormalities . . . normal adult brain scan consistent with age. . . . " A review of the neuropsychological raw test data indicated that the victim/plaintiff essentially "bottomed out" on all cognitive tests.

Intellectual Functions

In terms of general intelligence as assessed with the Wechsler Adult Intelligent Scale—Revised (WAIS-R), the victim/plaintiff had a Full Scale IQ of 57 with a Verbal IQ of 57 and a Performance IQ of 57. These results are clearly in the mentally retarded range, yet the victim/plaintiff had no history of mental retardation. In fact, she was a high school graduate. Scaled scores for Information and Digit Span were 1; she earned scaled scores of 2 on Arithmetic and Comprehension; a 3 on Similarities and a 5 on Vocabulary. She earned scaled scores of 1 on all Performance subtests except Picture Completion where she earned a 2. In order to convey an idea of the examinee's effort, she had a raw score of 2 on Digit Span, having correctly recalled only one trial of three digits forward and two in reverse! The plaintiff expert never questioned this (i.e., administered the Reliable Digit Span [RDS]; Greiffenstein, Baker, & Gola, 1994).

Amazingly, no symptom validity tests (SVTs) were administered, despite the fact that the patient was examined many years *after* a number of

SVTs were commercially available with a growing scientific literature! Because there was no assessment of effort, plaintiff's expert never discussed the plausibility of such IQ scores vis-à-vis the medical history; the scores were taken at face value.

Memory and Other Cognitive Functions

The California Verbal Learning Test (CVLT) was administered. The patient scored in the moderately or severely impaired range on each score. On the recognition trial, she had 7 hits but 15 false positives, which reflects insufficient effort (Millis, Putnam, Adams, & Ricker, 1995).

In addition to the absurdly low score on the WAIS-R scales and CVLT, all other neuropsychological tests administered by plaintiff's expert were grossly impaired. Trail Making B, for example, required greater than 300 seconds and was not completed. On the Aphasia Screening Test of the Halstead–Reitan Neuropsychological Battery, the claimant got only three items correct. On the Wechsler Memory Scale—Revised, Logical Memory subtest, she scored below the first percentile for both immediate and delayed recall.

In the plaintiff expert's report, no discussion whatsoever was made of the particularly abysmal test results obtained in that examination. The neuropsychologist opined that there had been a severe injury to the claimant/plaintiff's brain during the alleged assault resulting in "severe dementia. . . . " Plaintiff's neuropsychologist considered the test results valid and considered the banging of the plaintiff/victim's head on the floor by the assailant to cause sufficient injury resulting in such severe neuropsychological impairment.

Excerpts from My Defense Report[1]

Sadly, Dr. X so misinterpreted the data of the neuropsychological exam as to reach absurd proportions. It makes no sense whatsoever to conclude that the examinee's performance in plaintiff expert's exam genuinely reflects her actual ability—particularly in light of (1) the medical history simply cannot support conclusions of dementia and (2) no tests of effort or symptom validity/malingering were given. From that perspective, it follows naturally that one would question the validity of these test results. Although I have not had an opportunity to examine the plaintiff, the only possible explanation for her test performance is poor effort. The scenario reported by the plaintiff during the alleged assault would have resulted in little more than a headache with

---

[1] I did not evaluate the patient/plaintiff but wrote the report based solely on the record review.

no effect at all on cognition. Yet, her scores on neuropsychological tests are more consistent with widespread damage to the brain, massive hemorrhage, extended coma, hemiparesis, and the like. None of that occurred. The scores reported by Dr. X, then, are not to be believed; they are invalid.

This case may seem to be a "no-brainer" to the well-trained neuropsychologist. However, I considered this an instructive example of some of the work that is being done by newbies and wannabes. It is quite apparent that plaintiff expert neuropsychologist had virtually no understanding of the nature of traumatic brain injury, concussions, their natural history and course, and the effect on cognitive functioning. Nor did the expert have adequate knowledge of issues concerning effort, despite the fact that during this period there were many SVTs available assessing effort. The fact that none of them was administered or that the expert did not consider the pattern and severity of scores on traditional neuropsychological measures is almost absurd especially in a forensic, civil litigation context.

It is unlikely that the reader will encounter very many of such gross examples of incompetence in their practice of forensic neuropsychology. However, it would be surprising if during one's career one did not find at least one or two cases of such noncredible competence. It is also interesting to note that in this particular case, the plaintiff expert's CV indicated that his or her training in neuropsychology consisted of a postgraduate year with the developmentally disabled. This case might represent newbie/wannabe status all rolled into one!

CASE STUDY 2: MAKING MOUNTAINS OUT OF MOLEHILLS
Background Information

In case 1, the work may be considered to be an example of a "newbie/wannabe," representing someone with a paucity of adequate training in clinical neuropsychology and frankly performing work that is worse than bad. Case 2 may be considered an example of the work of a pure "wannabe." This is someone who has *some* experience in neuropsychology but little experience in the forensic arena or little experience in a highly challenging, extremely competitive, and complex forensic arena (i.e., where one's work is liable to be scrutinized and criticized). Common among such practitioners is the tendency to magnify the importance of rather irrelevant "blips" in the neuropsychological exam, a common procedure when major indices and measures are within normal limits. Such efforts are designed to give the impression of "significant problems" when little or none exist.

Such practitioners have requisite training and experience in neuropsy-chology and are sufficiently savvy at impression management to give the appearance of a credible exam, at least superficially.

Case 2 involves a 52-year-old, right-handed, Caucasian male who was referred for an independent medical–legal evaluation (IME) after he had been seen in a civil litigation context by plaintiff's expert neuropsy-chologist. The plaintiff in this case was suing a major pharmaceutical com-pany alleging that over-the-counter medications that he had consumed had caused a hemorrhagic stroke. This case was part of the well-known phenylpropanolamine (PPA) litigation wherein many over-the-counter med-ications contained phenylpropanolamine, a substance thought to lower the threshold of cerebral hemorrhages. It was alleged that this plaintiff had suf-fered a hemorrhagic stroke of the left cerebral hemisphere. He was admit-ted to an ER on the evening in question and was worked up by a team con-sisting of internists, neurologists, and cardiologists. He had a CT scan of the head, which showed a small intracerebral hemorrhage in the area of the left temporal–parietal junction. There was some evidence of extremely mild atrophy, which was considered to be compatible with the patient's age. The overall radiological impression was that of a resolving bleed of a minor ex-tent. The radiologist believed that the man had a small aneurysm that rup-tured; that is, "a small amount of hemorrhage in the temporal–parietal junction likely represents rupture of a sacular micro aneurysm of a branch of the left MCA [middle cerebral artery], now obliterated by the bleed. . . . "

Neurological examination revealed the patient to have normal neuro-logical functions. Physical examination revealed normal sensory and motor functions, normal speech, and normal cranial nerve functions. Normal mental status was also noted in the progress notes. Thus, at the time of the alleged stroke, the claimant's symptoms consisted only of mild word-find-ing difficulties and reported right-sided weakness, which was not corrobo-rated, on neurological exam. No cognitive problems were noted. The re-cord indicated that one neurologist who saw the patient in the ER found a completely normal neurological exam while a resident found extremely mild right-sided, "if equivocal," weakness.

The claimant reported that he had contacted an attorney after he saw a TV commercial for a law firm advertising their services to individuals tak-ing over-the-counter cold pills, alleged to cause "strokes and cerebral hem-orrhages. . . . " When I saw this man during the IME, he stated that he "thought" he took "those pills on the TV. . . . " With that medical history in mind, the plaintiff attorney hired an expert neuropsychologist who com-pleted an exam, which was rather comprehensive in nature.

A review of the raw data eventually received from the plaintiff expert provided a basis for concern about the conclusions in the report. The plaintiff neuropsychologist expert had a consistent habit of classifying scores into a lower classification range than they should be. For instance, in reading the report, she consistently called the 16th percentile "mildly impaired." She called the 17th percentile "borderline impaired," and the 11th percentile was simply "impaired." This is clearly wrong. The 16th and 17th percentiles fall into the low average range and so does the 11th percentile. This "dumbing down of the range" is not uncommon in some neuropsychological expert reports and is intended to mislead the reader, particularly the unsophisticated and unschooled reader. In this particular case, it is very possible that the plaintiff neuropsychologist knew very well the correct category that such scores fall into. Yet, these types of interpretations were incorrectly made throughout the report.

Intellectual Functions

When examined by the plaintiff neuropsychologist, the plaintiff had scaled scores within the average or high average range on all the Wechsler Adult Intelligence Scale–III (WAIS-III) subtests and an IQ score that fell within the average range. However, a comparative analysis of the raw data from the plaintiff expert's examination and the raw data from my subsequent exam revealed marked, inexplicable discrepancies. For instance, in my exam, the plaintiff earned a scaled score of 8 on the WAIS-III Arithmetic; however, when previously examined by the plaintiff expert he had a scaled score of 12 on the same test. In other words, in 6 months his arithmetic ability dropped by more than 1 standard deviation! He also showed qualitatively odd responses on the Arithmetic subtest. For instance, on two occasions in my exam, he answered very simple subtraction questions incorrectly, being off by one digit. I confronted him both times and he quickly changed his answer to the correct one. This must be considered extremely unusual behavior, to say the least.

Sometimes, the intrasubtest scatter on various tests is also instructive. For instance, plaintiff could not answer the Similarities item "how are a table and a chair alike," stating that he did not know. Yet on the same test, he correctly answered items that were considerably more difficult such as "democracy and monarchy." This type of variability occurred throughout the raw test data, yet the plaintiff neuropsychologist expert made no mention of it. The selective highlighting of data supportive of the claims and ignoring contradictory data is common in forensic venues.

Comparing the two examinations, the plaintiff also showed unusual behavior on the WAIS-III Block Design where he became frustrated quite early in my exam ostensibly unable to complete the design. But, in the first assessment with the plaintiff neuropsychologist, he had no trouble accurately completing the design. Scaled scores on Block Design fell from a 10 on the first exam to a 6 in mine. He was unable to complete several designs on which he earned bonus points the first time around!

Sometimes experts in forensic settings use vague statements to describe behaviors or test results, or to make allusions to putative underlying neurological abnormality. For instance, in the plaintiff expert's report, she spoke of "weaknesses in word retrieval and/or expressive language were noted as implied by his relatively low scores in other language subtests." What plaintiff's expert was referring to was the plaintiff's performance on the Vocabulary and Similarities subtests of the WAIS-III, both of which were performed at the 37th percentile (scaled score = 9). Where was such "weaknesses in word retrieval or expressive language" one wonders, especially when scores are average. Sometimes, forensic experts use such vague language in order to seemingly bolster the impression that abnormalities are present or to promote the perception of abnormalities in the unschooled reader. It is a wise practice for forensic neuropsychological experts to carefully review the raw data in conjunction with medical history and the other side's expert's report.

Other Cognitive Functions

Plaintiff performed poorly on the Wide Range Achievement Test—Third Edition (WRAT-3) Reading subtest, where he apparently could not pronounce words such as "contagious, bibliography, benign, or discretionary," as well as some others. His reading score was at the 6th percentile. Yet, importantly on the plaintiff expert's exam, the plaintiff had no difficulty reading many of these words and his Reading score fell at the 25th percentile.

On the Arithmetic subtest of the WRAT-3 in my examination, the plaintiff's overall score fell at the 12th percentile. To the question "7 times 6" he answered 13, as if the question required addition rather than multiplication. In the first examination with plaintiff's expert, he correctly answered the question as "42." Other errors were made in the present examination that were not made in the first exam. For instance, on WRAT-3 Spelling the first time, plaintiff spelled the word *table* correctly," but in the present exam with me, he spelled the same word as *tabel*.

Analysis of Findings

I found an abundance of other misleading statements in this report, and again a careful examination of raw data, the norms for the raw data, and an analysis of where these scores fall is crucial. For instance, in the plaintiff expert's report, the claimant was ultimately found to have "auditory selective attention impairment." Yet, on what is arguably the most complex and difficult of auditory selective attention tests, the Paced Auditory Serial Addition Test (PASAT), the claimant scored within normal limits. In fact, he had an atypical profile where he performed more poorly on the easier trials and better on the more difficult trials. Yet, the plaintiff neuropsychologist expert failed to interpret or even mention this.

Probably, the most blatant and dramatic discrepancy between the two examinations occurred on one of the figures of the Beery–Buktenica Developmental Test of Visual–Motor Integration (VMI). Although the plaintiff's expert gave this test, which is normed for children, to an adult, I decided to use it in my examination in order to precisely compare test results. On one of the figures, the Necker cube, plaintiff drew a perfect Necker cube in the first examination. In my exam, he pretended to be completely unable to draw the figure only drawing one line and saying, "Doc, I don't know how to do it. . . . "

This claimant's apparent feigning of impaired drawing ability was dramatically presented during my deposition testimony. When I was asked questions about this section of my report, I first held up an enlarged example of the plaintiff's successful rendition of the Necker cube in the first exam. Then, I showed an enlarged copy of a one-vertical-line rendition of the same figure produced by the examinee in my exam, stating what the examinee said to me, "Doc, I don't know how to do it. . . . " The examining plaintiff attorney asked how I interpreted his client's behavior. I said that there was only one possibility—and one did not need a PhD in psychology to figure that out. A long moment of silence followed. At that point, the plaintiff attorney asked for a break, a recess shortly ensued, and 3 days later the case settled.

These behaviors, observations, and test results and comparisons of serial testing point out the inconsistency of an apparent and unsophisticated malingerer. Inexperienced forensic examiners will either not appreciate unsophisticated malingerers or will ignore their blatant feigning. An unsophisticated malingerer is defined as someone possessing no scientific or medical knowledge of mental disorders or neurological/cognitive disorders but only that which they suppose them to be. Typically, their clinical presentation is immediately observed to be grossly absurd to the experienced clinician; it makes no sense based on what is well known about mental disorders. Although this individual scored within normal limits on symptom validity tests administered in both examinations, (including the TOMM in the first exam and the TOMM, Victoria Symptom Validity Test, and the Portland Digit Recognition Test in my exam), he nonetheless went on to manifest completely noncredible test results. That fact became completely transparent when comparing the results of one examination to those from a previous exam.

It should be abundantly clear to the reader how crucial it is to compare test results in forensic settings, where serial assessment has taken place over time. As the reader likely knows, a static neurological injury, disorder, or illness generally gets better over time. This of course is certainly not true in progressive disorders such as dementia, multiple sclerosis, Parkinson's disease, and many others. But generally, in dealing with cerebral hemorrhage, stroke, traumatic brain injuries, and many other forms of neurological abnormality, especially in cases that come to be seen in forensic venues, the "disorder" in question is typically not progressive. It should be remembered that the brain, like any other organ in the body, typically heals; neuropsychological performance in such cases should also improve. Thus, in a putative cerebral hemorrhage in the acute state, there may in fact be neurocognitive deficits, but these should logically get better over time, not worse.

Again, it should be understood that the expert in such forensic venues should constantly be asking the question, "What would possibly contribute to reduced performance in the second examination relative to the first?" This has been termed *late symptom development* (M. F. Greiffenstein, personal communication, June 2004). If medical history supports a chronic progressive condition such as a demyelinating disorder, or there has been a recent neurological insult between the exams, or there is a chronic progressive psychiatric illness such as schizophrenia, then one may legitimately expect or at least not be surprised if neurocognitive performance declines over time. In cases in which there is no progressive illness, where there has been a static insult, one would expect improvement or no change at the least. But, of course, science is sometimes put on hold in forensic settings.

The wording of a neuropsychological report must also be considered by practicing forensic neuropsychologists. Some experts purposefully report things in a rather vague or misleading way; some use unusual descriptive language, expressing a cognitive function in ways seldom used by the majority of practicing neuropsychologists. Sometimes attributions of a disorder are declared that have absolutely no basis in neuroanatomy and/or that represent an invalid interpretation of data. In this case, the plaintiff expert diagnosed "dyscalculia"—even though the patient scored normally on WAIS and WRAT-3 Arithmetic subtests. Upon what basis the diagnosis was made was never made clear—other than the patient's self-report! Similarly, even though the plaintiff scored within normal limits on almost all tests of perception and construction, the plaintiff expert diagnosed "constructional dyspraxia"—despite the purported brain insult being in the left hemisphere, or "impaired manual motor praxis" in the absence of any frontal lobe injury! The reader may wonder, "On what basis do such neuropsychologists make these claims in the absence of scientific evidence?" I have been wondering that, as well, for over 20 years. I suppose they simply hope that the "other side" won't pick it up, a sneak-it-through mentality.

In an apparent attempt to portray the examinee as being more impaired than he or she might be, some experts classify performances into an incorrect classification range, placing low average scores (15th percentile, say) into the impaired range or calling them "mildly impaired." This is impression management. The reader is therefore cautioned to carefully review the raw data, the normative data set used, as well as the classification range that such scores would normally fall into. This case example illustrates how an expert in a forensic setting who probably knows better misleads the reader in many of these ways.

SUMMARY AND CONCLUSIONS

This chapter addresses common errors often seen in neuropsychological experts' reports, by individuals who are either ill-prepared to do forensic work or who are actually well trained and well prepared to do the work but for other reasons have not taken the high road in presenting or interpreting their data. Readers of this chapter should be aware that such tactics exist even in an era where more specific guidelines for education and training (Hannay at al., 1998) and practice (American Academy of Clinical Neuropsychology, 2007) have been articulated in our profession. Although the cases highlighted in this chapter represent criticisms of "plaintiff" work in civil litigation, it should be stressed that such tactics are freely used by both defense and plaintiff experts.

It is incumbent upon all neuropsychologists, whether they practice exclusively in a clinical setting or do primarily forensic work, that they provide the most competent services to the public that they possibly can. Forensic neuropsychologists' work comes under considerably greater scrutiny than the work of those who practice exclusively in clinical venues. Such scrutiny is often done by neuropsychologists retained by the other side in criminal or civil forensic settings. Thus, it is crucial that reports be accurate, that the medical history be consistent with the test findings, that interpretations be made that represent standard and typical interpretations in the field, that they have a scientific basis, and that all efforts be made to "dot all the i's and cross all the t's" in reports. Examining sources of bias via a logical and consistent approach (Sweet & Moulthrop, 1999) is strongly recommended. Always report the facts, remain objective, and be honest in your testimony. Do not allow yourself to become a member of a legal "team," but retain your professional independence. Remember that the final outcome of the legal case usually does not hinge on your opinions. Nor is it your duty or responsibility to "win the case" for the side that has retained you.

REFERENCES

American Academy of Clinical Neuropsychology. (2007). Practice guidelines for neuropsychological assessment and consultation. *The Clinical Neuropsychologist, 21,* 209–231.

Butcher, J. N., Dahlstrom, W. G., Graham, J. R., Tellegen, A., & Kaemmer, B. (1989). *MMPI-2 manual for administration and scoring.* Minneapolis: University of Minnesota Press.

Greiffenstein, M. F., Baker, W. J., & Gola, T. (1994). Validation of malingered amnesia measures with a large clinical sample. *Psychological Assessment, 6,* 218–224.

Hannay, H. J., Bieliauskas, L. A., Crosson, B. A., Hammeke, T. A., Hamsher, K. deS., & Koffler, S. P. (1998). Proceedings: The Houston Conference on Specialty Education and Training in Clinical Neuropsychology. *Archives of Clinical Neuropsychology, 13*(2).

Millis, S. R., Putnam, S. H., Adams, K. M., & Ricker, J. H. (1995). The California Verbal Learning Test in the detection of incomplete effort in neuropsychological evaluations. *Psychological Assessment, 7,* 463–471.

Sweet, J., & Moulthrop, M. (1999). Self-examination questions as a means of identifying bias in adversarial cases. *Journal of Forensic Neuropsychology, 1,* 73–88.

Tombaugh, T. N. (1996). *Test of Memory Malingering.* Los Angeles: Western Psychological Services.

5

Maturation into Impairment

The Merit of Delayed Settlement
in Pediatric Forensic Neuropsychology Cases

Ida Sue Baron

Normal human brain development involves an enormously complex geneti-
cally programmed maturational sequence. The developmental course becomes even more intricate following brain injury at an early age, and prognosis is confounded by a need to consider diverse brain reserve, cognitive
reserve, family, socioenvironmental, and medical factors that differentially
influence outcomes. Pediatric neuropsychologists are acutely aware that injured young children may not manifest signs or symptoms of dysfunction
until they "grow into their impairment" (Baron, 2004). That is, one cannot
identify deficit until the child has matured to an age when the expected capacity or skill should be apparent but is not evident or cannot be demonstrated sufficiently well.

In forensic practice, it becomes crucially important for an attorney
to determine when litigation should be concluded on behalf of a brain-
injured infant or preschool child. This chapter presents a case of a
2-year-old child injured in a motor vehicle accident (MVA) but whose
settlement was delayed until a final neuropsychological evaluation was
conducted 10 years later when many neuropsychological functions are

approaching adult competence levels. Yet, significant and persisting late effects of the early injury were objectively documented over the decade since injury. The full extent of any residual dysfunction consequent to early injury cannot be appreciated until such time as a full range of neuropsychological functions can be assessed. A temporal delay was helpful in this case, and would be in many others, because maturation continues through the preschool and early elementary school years into adolescence and young adulthood. As a result, by delaying settlement, the attorney established the basis for a successful and large settlement. This case serves as an excellent example of (1) how long-term effects of early brain injury in general, and traumatic brain injury (TBI) specifically, may be underappreciated until such time as the immature brain develops and the capacities at risk are demanded, and (2) how less than comprehensive neuropsychological evaluations may fail to identify the full extent of injury-related dysfunction and unintentionally create obstacles to diagnosis and treatment for the child and family.

PERSONAL FORENSIC EXPERIENCE

Forensic cases represent a small percentage of my child and adult private practice work. My involvement in a forensic case is typically as a treating professional, when patients I have evaluated on clinical referral enter the forensic arena, often years after the evaluation. Commonly, the etiology is a TBI from an MVA, as in this case report, but requests for evaluation of neuropsychological competence are quite varied. At other times, I have accepted a role as expert witness, as in the case presented here, with the stipulation clearly stated that I will provide an independent and objective opinion, irrespective of whether the interests of the attorney, my client, is benefited. It is commendable when, after hearing results counter to their interests, an attorney replies, "That's OK, I just really needed to know." A third role, as a "secret" consultant, has been an interesting type of forensic work. In this role, I have had the opportunity to objectively review and critically analyze the reports and depositions of colleagues, at the request of both plaintiff and defense attorneys. It has been interesting to educate attorneys about the science and practice of neuropsychology and qualifications for neuropsychologists, and to assist in their preparation for depositions of experts based on the facts of the case and the quality of the opposing neuropsychological testimony. This has afforded me the unanticipated opportunity to learn which colleagues may uphold responsible and objective practice, and it has had an untoward result of learning which colleagues adjust their work product for the attorney's benefit, counter to the profession's ethical and professional standards.

CASE STUDY

Background

F. C. was a 12-year-old right-handed child first referred to me for neuro-psychological evaluation 10 years after injury from an MVA, and after four intervening psychological evaluations by others. F. C. was 18 months old and strapped into a car seat in a stopped car when a truck traveling at high speed struck the car and sent it tumbling into a ravine. It required approximately 1 hour to extract F. C. from inside the crushed and demolished vehicle. Whether F. C. had a brief loss of consciousness was undocumented, but there were multiple external scalp lacerations requiring stitches, a forehead contusion, and limb fracture. F. C. was discharged home after a brief hospitalization in a pediatric intensive care unit without subsequent complications. Computed tomography (CT) of the head and X-ray findings on the day of the accident were interpreted as normal. Whereas settlement with the liable driver's insurance company for injuries incurred by the parents and two older brothers occurred early, settlement was postponed for F. C., due to young age and developmental immaturity. The plaintiff's attorney waited 10 years and now requested that I first review the records for merit and then provide a current, comprehensive neuropsychological evaluation and opinion to enable settlement to be reached and the case concluded.

Early medical records indicated that F. C. was the product of a full-term gestation and uneventful pregnancy, with normal birthweight and no pre-, peri-, or postnatal complications. Developmental motor, language, and social milestones were all achieved at age-appropriate times and development had progressed uneventfully and well. Routine well-baby evaluations by the pediatrician prior to F. C.'s injury consistently documented normal growth and development. F. C.'s language development was developing at least age appropriately and, in some respects, at an advanced rate (e.g., F. C. could sing the alphabet correctly by 16 months of age). However, postaccident records clearly indicated that immediately following the accident, F. C. no longer knew previously well-learned automatic language sequences, could not recall names of close relatives, and would occasionally retrieve the wrong names for pets.

Prior Psychological and Neuropsychological Evaluations

Four psychological and neuropsychological evaluations were conducted at three different centers in the interim 10 years before my evaluation of F. C. When F. C. was 4 years old, the pediatrician noted that despite speech and language therapy and a normal neurological evaluation, F. C. continued to have "difficulty acquiring new information, remembering old information, retrieving names, and reciting numbers from 1 to 10." The pediatrician attributed these deficits to "massive head injury secondary to an MVA," expressed concern about an incipient learning disability consequent to the injury, and referred F. C. for a baseline neurodevelopmental evaluation. This evaluation was conducted 2 years postinjury at Center 1. F. C. obtained an IQ of 115 on a standardized intelligence test. Tests of preacademic skills found F. C. falling at average to superior limits (e.g., vocabulary standardized score = 120), with the exception of especially poor letter and word skills (standardized score = 73). F. C. had only borderline to low average performance on a design copying test (standardized score = 84). The developmental psychologist concluded that F. C. had "cognitive skills in the upper range of normal . . . remarkable difficulty and divergent scores on Letter and Word scores . . . visuomotor abilities in the low average/borderline range discrepant from superior visuospatial abilities . . . intact short term memory but isolated difficulty storing long term memory items, such as names . . . it may well be that F. C. suffered some subtle insult to the memory centers in the accident or a learning disability may have preexisted." After equivocating about apparent dysfunction as directly consequent to the injury by invoking the possibility of a preexisting learning disability and referring to long-term memory without actually assessing it formally, recommendation was made for reevaluation. This second testing was conducted at Center 1, 7 months later but only included a standardized memory battery. F. C. obtained scaled scores consistently within average limits for picture memory, design memory, verbal learning, and story memory, resulting in a summary Memory Index of 98. It was concluded, based on these limited additional data and interview with F. C. and parents, that there was "continued progress . . . difficulties with word retrieval and naming persist . . . better memory for perceptual information . . . no specific interventions are needed beyond . . . " more multimodal presentations of stimuli.

On school entry, F. C. required significant help with prereading skills. Speech and language therapy was provided and continued until second grade. A third evaluation, the first neuropsychological evaluation, was conducted at Center 2 when F. C. was 6 years old. F. C. obtained a Wechsler Intelligence Scale for Children—Third Edition (WISC-III) Verbal IQ of 104, Performance IQ of 117, and Full Scale IQ of 111, and scores of 107 for Verbal Comprehension, 120 for Perceptual Organization, 104 for Freedom from Distractibility, and 96 for Processing Speed. Receptive language (assessed by having F. C. point to the picture of a named word), nonverbal responses to increasingly complex verbal commands, and word-list learning and retrieval were intact. Despite noting parental concerns about backward number writing, impaired naming, poor word retrieval, an inability to recite number sequences or the months of the year, and problems with visual tasks, these abilities were not directly tested, and therefore these persistent deficits were not well documented beyond the notes from the history taking. The report also did not mention the significantly lowered scores obtained on measures of oral arithmetic, abstract verbal reasoning (similarities), coding, and symbol search (visual recognition of symbols). On a task requiring motor performance while blindfolded, F. C. demonstrated average psychomotor problem solving with each upper extremity and average recall of tactual stimuli manipulated earlier while blindfolded but mildly impaired recall of their location. Notably, this evaluation failed to include examination of lateral dominance, dyspraxia, or comparative fine motor or sensory–perceptual function of the two sides of the body.

The report, stating the "General Cognitive Index of 120 fell within high average limits" (although the manual clearly indicates this score falls within superior limits), concluded that these data revealed "average to above average performance in language and most aspects of memory . . . mild weaknesses in gross motor skills and spatial memory . . . good recovery from a closed head injury . . . the two mild weaknesses (gross motor skill and spatial memory) are the only significant possible sequelae found during this evaluation." The motor and other mild weaknesses were attributed to developmental variability, "poor self-esteem," and/or F. C.'s "resistance to taking risks." In view of this "generally good recovery," only mental health intervention and physical/occupational therapy were recommended, with emphasis on spatial orientation. It was concluded, "unlikely that F. C. would experience cognitive decline" and neuropsychological reevaluation was recommended, "only if significant changes in signs or symptoms are noted."

Despite these conclusions of only mild nonverbal weaknesses and an overly optimistic prognosis regarding future function, and without recommendation for pertinent resource help, quite serious academic problems continued and increased for F. C. through the early elementary school years. Also, concerns increased about fearfulness, extreme shyness, and anxiety and by the third grade there was a precipitous decline in school grades. An individualized education plan (IEP) was formulated to strengthen language mechanics, study skills, mathematics, recall of verbal information, word retrieval, processing information, and listening. Speech and language therapy was resumed in fifth grade and a tutor was hired to further assist F. C. in learning how to retain linguistic material.

A fourth evaluation was conducted at Center 3 when F. C. was 10 years old. The WISC-III Verbal IQ of 112, Performance IQ of 111 and Full Scale IQ of 112 were commensurate with prior testing. The scores for Verbal Comprehension (111), Perceptual Organization (113), Freedom from Distractibility (112), and Processing Speed (93) were equivalent to prior results. The design copying score of 84, obtained at 4 years old, was now 118 and within high-average limits. The neuropsychologist wrote, in error, "The standard score is 118 where the mean is 50 and the standard deviation is 10." With regard to nonverbal abstract problem solving, the report erroneously states that "performance was intact with a standard score of 53 where the mean is 100 and standard deviation is 15. That places F. C. at the 62nd percentile." Although it was written that "F. C.'s performance on a task of unimanual and bilateral motor coordination was in the average range, although the nondominant left hand was somewhat faster than the dominant right hand," the significance of inefficient right-upper-extremity motor performance was not discussed in the report, and supportive data from other comparative motor function tests were not obtained. A conclusion of "mild" deficits in verbal auditory concentration was, in fact, based on solidly average digit span performance (scaled score = 12; average range) and average letter fluency ("the ability to generate words for a letter cue was at the low end of intact"). Weaknesses were observed on measures of visuospatial planning and problem solving (mazes = 4) and processing speed (symbol search = 7). The neuropsychologist concluded that F. C. "does not appear to be exhibiting difficulties related to an attention-deficit disorder, with the exception of being somewhat inattentive," that F. C. was "showing signs of significant improvement," given good grades obtained in fourth grade. (*Note:* F. C.'s grades were acknowledged to be the result of the extraordinary and intensive 3 hours/night minimum of parental assistance with homework.) It was further concluded that "both susceptibility to anxiety and attentional difficulties are secondary to frontal lobe damage caused by the motor vehicle accident." The report indicated that "mild deficits in verbal auditory concentration and visual sustained attention are likely to be fairly permanent," and "intensive effort in academic pursuits" was the only recommendation along with a suggestion for individual therapy to relieve anxiety.

Final Evaluation

I first met 12-year-old F. C. for the fifth and final evaluation. It was apparent from records review and prior evaluations that F. C. was a highly intelligent child developing well prior to injury in the MVA but who subsequently began a long struggle with language, and some visual–motor, developmental milestones. Successes appeared due, in large part, to strong parental advocacy and the intensive structure and interventional strategies they and, ultimately, the school provided. F. C.'s high average-to-superior intellectual abilities were well established by the prior psychological evaluations and further general intelligence testing was judged unnecessary for the purposes of this evaluation. Among the substantial weaknesses apparent in the prior reports was the less than a comprehensive assessment, underreporting and failure to integrate data that were supportive of brain dysfunction, interpretive errors leading to inappropriate conclusions, and minimal recommendations. There was a pattern of overreliance on existing medical and neurological records, without attempts to confirm their accuracy. Parental concerns were not fully investigated. Overall, these prior evaluations provided minimal data regarding comparative motor functions, and no examiner included sensory–perceptual tests. Consequently, my intent was to better understand a pattern of impaired academic and interpersonal skills persisting for many years despite inherent competencies and reports of only "mild" impairment. While this evaluation was scheduled before effort testing for children was a common pediatric neuropsychological practice, and before publication of normative data for symptom validity test administration for children (Constantinou & McCaffrey, 2003; Donders, 2005), it should be noted that there was nothing about F. C.'s behavior or responses that provided grounds for suspicion of invalid effort.

My evaluation found clear evidence of significant impairment of several functions not assessed in any of the earlier evaluations. F. C. demonstrated impaired extrapersonal right–left discrimination on lateral dominance examination, unexpected for a 12-year-old but a deficit that is closely linked to left temporoparietal dysfunction. Apraxia testing revealed clear and repeated evidence of ideomotor dyspraxia. Praxis, a nonlinguistic function associated with left cerebral hemisphere functioning, was not assessed earlier despite its correspondence to F. C.'s presumptive dysfunctional brain regions. F. C.'s difficulty self-monitoring verbal output (evidenced by frequent repetitive errors) was demonstrated clearly across tests, including tests of verbal fluency and auditory/verbal list learning. Spelling errors inconsistent for age and intelligence were made. In addition, F. C. had slowed information-processing speed, susceptibility to interference on a measure of divided attention, especially for the longest interference interval, and quite poor working memory.

Of considerable interest, and implicating contralateral (right) cerebral hemisphere brain dysfunction, sensory–perception screening identified left-sided neglect of space, notable on tests of visual search, trail making, clock drawing, paragraph formulation (wide left margin to edge of right margin), and line bisection. Importantly, such errors are unanticipated under conditions of normal brain development, or even in the presence of developmental delay. Strongly lateralized cerebral dysfunction was not evident on tests of double simultaneous tactile, visual, or auditory stimulation or fingerwriting recognition but bilateral errors were made on finger-recognition testing. Had primary motor and sensory measures been included in earlier evaluations, it could be presumed that deficits would have been found at an early age corroborating the existence of significant TBI, and the pattern of impairment would have implicated both right and left cerebral hemisphere dysfunction. Such a profile of bilateral dysfunction (in this case, left impaired to a greater extent than right) is entirely consistent with a history of TBI. Table 5.1 presents selected test results.

I summarized the results as follows (and omit here the detailed recommendations that were attached):

F. C. is a 12-year-old right-handed, Caucasian, sixth-grade student. This evaluation was administered 10 years after F. C. was injured in a motor vehicle accident and following interim cognitive assessments, as documented above. Over time, it was documented that F. C. consistently demonstrated above-average intelligence. Therefore, one important issue that arises in interpreting the current results is whether "average" for F. C. may indicate poorer functioning than might otherwise have been expected had there not been a traumatic brain injury at 2 years of age. With respect to the current data, there are numerous instances of above-average functioning (some scores falling within the superior range), making lower (merely average) scores notable areas of potential weakness.

Importantly, a number of current test results supported the interpretations of earlier results and indicated probable maximal left cerebral hemisphere deficit. Such data were obtained across a range of tests, including those assessing apraxia, verbal fluency, right–left discrimination, number sequencing, spelling, and automatic language sequencing. The presence of perseverative responding is important, due to its strong association with neurological compromise and its unlikely occurrence in the normal population, particularly to the extent demonstrated by F. C.

It could be argued that none of these test results considered individually was strongly indicative of impairment. However, neuropsychological evaluation is an examination of profiles of functioning rather than an attempt to link a single test result to a specific brain region. Given this necessary integration of data, the combined results provide a strong basis for considering the resultant profile as indicative of the residua of long-standing cerebral lesions. A child as bright and as capable as F. C. is not expected to demonstrate the above-noted abnormalities and their presence needs to be taken seriously. Of importance as well, these results are entirely compatible with the profiles demonstrated across the earlier neurodevelopmental, psychological, and neuropsychological evaluations, and are consonant with the behavioral reports over the years.

The implications of these deficits have strong relevance to the academic setting, which depends to a large degree on the higher-order integration of language symbols and intact functioning of the left cerebral hemisphere. F. C.'s struggle over the years attempting to master the academic curricula is completely understandable, given these results. Teachers' observations are consistent with this observed profile and provide further confirmation of the ecological validity of the findings. The literature emphasizes that injury at very young ages can result in persistent deficit over the lifespan, and can sometimes be even more problematic than when injury is acquired at an older age. A manifestation of these early injuries may be delayed until the school years, and thus F. C.'s neuropsychological profile is of particular interest in this regard.

Continued special educational resource help (e.g., tutoring) is expected to be necessary. One has to be especially concerned about F. C.'s ability to master the increasingly complex demands of higher grades. F. C.'s mother has served in a tutoring capacity for some time but this

TABLE 5.1. Selected Sampling of Neuropsychological Data

Test name	Test result
WISC-III Digit Span	SS = 13
WISC-III Symbol Search	SS = 15
WIAT Mathematics Reasoning	SS = 104
D-KEFS Trail Making Test–Visual Scanning	SS = 15
D-KEFS Trail Making Test–Number Sequencing	SS = 9
D-KEFS Trail Making Test–Letter Sequencing	SS = 13
D-KEFS Trail Making Test–Number–Letter	SS = 10
D-KEFS Trail Making Test–Motor Speed	SS = 13
D-KEFS Letter Fluency	SS = 9
D-KEFS Category Fluency	SS = 11
D-KEFS Switching: Total Correct	SS = 11
D-KEFS Switching: Total Switching	SS = 12
D-KEFS Design Fluency: Filled Dots	SS = 12
D-KEFS Design Fluency: Empty Dots	SS = 11
D-KEFS Design Fluency: Switching	SS = 12
TEA-Ch Sky Search Attention Score	SS = 8
TEA-Ch Sky Search Number Correct	SS = 14
TEA-Ch Sky Search Time/Target	SS = 9
TEA-Ch Score	SS = 13
TEA-Ch Creature Counting Total Correct	SS = 13
TEA-Ch Creature Counting Timing Score	SS = 9
TEA-Ch Sky Search Dual Task	SS = 9
TEA-Ch Map Mission	SS = 10
TEA-Ch Score Dual Task	SS = 9
TEA-Ch Walk–Don't Walk	SS = 10
TEA-Ch Opposite Worlds: Same World	SS = 9
TEA-Ch Opposite Worlds: Opposite World	SS = 8
TEA-Ch Code Transmission	SS = 11
WCST-64 Total Number of Errors	T = 61
WCST-64 Perseverative Responses	T = 70
WCST-64 Perseverative Errors	T = 65
WCST-64 Nonperseverative Errors	T = 57
WCST-64 Conceptual Level Responses	T = 62
Selective Reminding Test Long-Term Storage	Raw = 47
WRAML Sentence Repetition	SS = 12
WRAML Story Memory	SS = 9
WMS-R Visual Reproduction, immediate	%ile = 50–84
WMS-R Visual Reproduction, delayed	%ile = 50–84
Beery–Buktenica Visual–Motor Integration	T = 55
Stroop Color–Word Test—Words	T = 54
Stroop Color–Word Test—Colors	T = 44
Stroop Color–Word Test—Color–Word	T = 54
Stroop Color–Word Test—Interference	T = 43
Finger Tapping Test, Dominant Hand mean	Mean = 41.4
Finger Tapping Test, Nondominant Hand mean	Mean = 35.4
Grooved Pegboard, Dominant Hand	Time = 53 seconds
Grooved Pegboard, Nondominant Hand	Time = 64 seconds

(continued)

TABLE 5.1. (*continued*)

Test name	Test result
Auditory Consonant Trigrams Test	15, 10, 12, 3
Auditory Analysis Test	Raw = 30
Boston Naming Test	Raw = 47
Cancellation of Targets Test	3 standard deviations < mean
Children's Depression Inventory	0

Note. Automatic Language Sequences, Line Bisection, Rey–Osterrieth Complex Figure Test, Behavior Rating Inventory of Executive Function, Ramparts Design, Reitan–Klove Sensory–Perceptual Examination, Boston Diagnostic Aphasia Examination Paragraph Formulation, Luria Motor Sequences, Apraxia Screening, Rapid Alternating Movements, and Draw-a-Clock Test were also administered. D-KEFS, Delis–Kaplan Executive Function System; WIAT, Wechsler Individual Achievement Test; TEA-Ch, Test of Everyday Attention for Children; WRAML, Wide Range Assessment of Memory and Learning; WMS-R, Wechsler Memory Scale—Revised; WCST, Wisconsin Card Sorting Test—64; *T*, standardized score with mean = 50 and standard deviation = 10; SS, standardized score with mean = 100 and standard deviation = 15.

is not ideal and will not be equally possible once the academic curricula become more complex. Required resource help will be costly if the school does not provide it sufficiently and the likelihood, given the somewhat subtle nature of F. C.'s problems, is that the school may not provide all the resource help needed. Individualized help will be essential, along with other specific assistance as needed, to meet the demands of each respective class.

Another notable complication is impairment within the attention and executive function domains. F. C. demonstrated slowed information-processing speed, susceptibility to interference, and impairment when required to demonstrate intact divided attention and working memory capacity. These important abilities are recognizable problems in the real world, as already identified by both parent and teacher report of clinically significant problems within these domains.

The current data provided a more comprehensive explanation for the observed auditory/verbal integration and learning and recall problems noted at school and at home than previously documented. F. C.'s teachers should be alerted to detect any difficulty attending to information in the left hemispace that may be further contributory to academic problems. Such deficit strongly implicates right cerebral regions as dysfunctional and may further assist in understanding the reasons for academic weaknesses.

The emotional concomitants of brain injury can be debilitating. Indeed, what begins as secondary concerns to the primary concern of an injury may become more prominent over time and achieve primary-level concern. Already, there is a sense that F. C. may be experiencing a poor self-image and is certainly intelligent enough to recognize the added effort that must be produced to function adaptively. There needs to be careful monitoring of F. C.'s emotional health along with

directed attention to the academic weaknesses. Individualized psycho-
therapeutic assistance may be required as F. C. matures. F. C. has considerable intellectual potential, yet F. C. appears to be a child who has
had the edge taken off the ability to always operate at the expected
high level. This can be an intrusive dynamic. As well, others may not
appreciate the true extent of the problems especially since subtle difficulty can be masked in interpersonal interactions and the perceptions
of intact capacity by others may be quite inaccurate.

CONCLUSIONS

Maturation is a prepotent force in pediatric neuropsychology. The developmental trajectory therefore becomes a major consideration in any pediatric
neuropsychological evaluation, and it is equally pertinent when there is litigation about injury to a young child. Chronological age and developmental
stage at the time of any insult are important factors determinant of outcome, along with nature and extent of the insult. However, there are other
influences on the developing child, such as genetic, personality, socioenvironmental, and family factors. The pediatric neuropsychologist must consider a full range of influences and review the behavioral profile dispassion-
ately in order to reach conclusions regarding the late effects consequent to
an insult.

Neurological insult at a very young age presents special limitations regarding the ability to comprehend the full extent of both transient and permanent impairments consequent to injury. Although total brain volume
reaches 90% of its adult size by 6 years (Giedd et al., 2004), there are brain
regions that continue to mature into adolescence and early adulthood. The
phylogenetically most recent prefrontal cortex, which is part of a distrib-
uted neural network influencing a range of executive functions, is late developing (Giedd, 2003; Giedd et al., 1999). This region mediates several
abilities that proved especially problematic for F. C., such as working memory and divided attention. Posterior temporal cortices, primarily in the left
hemisphere, which mediate language function, also have a more protracted
course of maturation than other cortical regions (Sowell et al., 2003).
These were also implicated in F. C.'s clinical course and were especially
prominent immediately postinjury and emerged in a more subtle yet persistent presentation as F. C. aged. Whereas the effects of early damage to these
late-maturing regions may not be recognized until later in the brain development time course, early disruption of function, as occurred in this case,
may be a marker of the potential for profound difficulty. Deficits that were
immediately apparent in this case, including loss of ability to name, retrieve
words, and produce learned automatic language sequences, persisted throughout F. C.'s development and were still evident qualitatively on the final eval-

uation, albeit sometimes in the context of merely average functioning for this highly intelligent child.

Despite several prior evaluations, the import of the effects of injury were not entirely clarified until the final evaluation. The earlier psychological evaluations each contained evidence of persisting deficits, but there were omissions in data acquisition or interpretive weaknesses that made those results inconclusive. Notably, examiners at Centers 1, 2, and 3 failed to sufficiently assess several of the parent-reported concerns, omitted sensory–perceptual tests, and assessed motor function inadequately. These weaknesses negatively affected the formulation of each of their conclusions and recommendations. My finding of consistent evidence of left-hemispace neglect underscored the severity of injury in a child whose medical history remained unremarkable after injury and its protracted effect. Independent neurological evaluation by the plaintiff attorney's expert witness corroborated the presence of left neglect. This impairment is not found in the course of normal development and therefore it highlighted the significance of the injury and strengthened the attorney's arguments on behalf of F. C. Finding left neglect also emphasized the likelihood of bilateral brain dysfunction, damage more broadly represented and not confined only to the left cerebral hemisphere. Sufficient data were available from the earlier evaluations to support this hypothesis but the interpretation had not been communicated. Furthermore, a profile of bilateral damage is entirely compatible with residual impairment secondary to the presumptive forces associated with F. C.'s TBI.

With a comprehensive neuropsychological evaluation, including measures comparing the efficiency of the two sides of the body, difficulties were detected that were presumed certainly present at younger ages. Earlier confirmation of these deficits could have led to better appreciation for the range of impairment F. C. was experiencing in each subsequent academic year and for a more appropriate set of recommendations than were offered in the early evaluations. For example, just knowing that stimuli (e.g., letters) on the left side of a paper might be neglected may have aided F. C. in accommodating to the deficit and enabled teachers to provide more appropriate strategies and interventions earlier.

Young age complicates appreciation for the full range of impairment consequent to a brain injury. While F. C. experienced immediate repercussions, notable in auditory/verbal processing and expression, the full extent of this damage could not be known until such time as F. C. matured and had to integrate information mediated by these damaged brain regions. Only then were the debilitating problems revealed for this highly intelligent child. Above-average to superior intelligence provided a basis for performance expectations that were not met in repeated evaluations, but these pockets of strength likely also lulled teachers into expecting even more adaptive function than F. C. could provide.

Forensic neuropsychological evaluation of a very young child carries with it responsibility for acknowledging that there is no predictable direct correlation between injury and outcome, although some very good guesses may be made. That F. C.'s attorney delayed settlement until such time as F. C. had matured to an age of nearly adult brain development when persistent neuropsychological deficits could be clearly identified proved to be a wise decision. Whereas early settlement could have been made based on one or more of the sequential evaluations conducted at different institutions with individuals of different degrees of neuropsychological proficiency, that series of evaluations failed to adequately document the progressive course of emerging neuropsychological deficit as F. C. matured. Those reports only provided minimal or suggestive evidence and fluctuated between interpretations of impairment, stability, and inaccurate reporting of functional improvement. By attributing some poor performances to variables other than brain injury, such as anxiety and mood disorders, they did a disservice to F. C. in not addressing these as reactive to the underlying neurological compromise.

In conclusion, the attorney's patience and request for comprehensive evaluation truly paid off. The defense attorney did not request that I appear for a deposition. Settlement was reached for the maximum amount possible under the truck driver's insurance plan. This case highlights the substantial conceptual and material value in deferring settlement until such time as a child has matured into deficits—that is, until such time as functions not yet emergent at the time of injury are indeed developed and able to be quantified, observed, and documented.

REFERENCES

Baron, I. S. (2004). *Neuropsychological evaluation of the child*. New York: Oxford University Press.

Constantinou, M., & McCaffrey, R. J. (2003). Using the TOMM for evaluating children's effort to perform optimally on neuropsychological measures. *Child Neuropsychology, 9*, 81–90.

Donders, J. (2005). Performance on the Test of Memory Malingering in a mixed pediatric sample. *Child Neuropsychology, 11*, 221–227.

Giedd, J. N. (2003). The anatomy of mentalization: a view from developmental neuroimaging. *Bulletin of the Menninger Clinic, 67*, 132–142.

Giedd, J. N., Blumenthal, J., Jeffries, N. O., Castellanos, F. X., Liu, H., Zijdenbos, A., et al. (1999). Brain development during childhood and adolescence: a longitudinal MRI study. *Nature Neuroscience, 2*, 861–863.

Giedd, J. N., Rosenthal, M. A., Rose, A. B., Blumenthal, J. D., Molloy, E., Dopp, R. R., et al. (2004). Brain development in healthy children and adolescents: magnetic resonance imaging studies. In J. K. M. Keshavan & R. Murray (Eds.), *Neurodevelopment and schizophrenia* (pp. 35–44). Cambridge, UK: Cambridge University Press.

Sowell, E. R., Peterson, B. S., Thompson, P. M., Welcome, S. E., Henkenius, A. L., & Toga, A. W. (2003). Mapping cortical change across the human life span. *Nature Neuroscience, 6*, 309–315.

6
Electrical Brain Injury and a Case of Examiner Shock

Shane S. Bush

PROFESSIONAL HISTORY AND APPROACH

My postdoctoral training and early professional work occurred primarily in physical medicine and rehabilitation programs. Thus, I provided inpatient and outpatient clinical evaluation and treatment services to individuals who had sustained a variety of neurological injuries and illnesses. Many of those patients also sustained injuries to other areas or systems of the body or were experiencing additional health problems. A primary purpose of neuropsychological services was to assist the patient, the patient's family, and the treatment team to better understand the patient's neurocognitive, emotional, and behavioral functioning, with the overarching goal of facilitating treatment, recovery, and reintegration into a meaningful and productive life.

Because many of my patients were involved in litigation, I gradually experienced increasing involvement in forensic matters. Initially, most of my professional contact with the legal system was through plaintiff attorneys; they contacted me for copies of my records and requested treatment summaries for the patients I treated. I also began to be retained by plaintiff attorneys specifically to serve as an expert in personal injury litigation. However, I noticed a gradual increase in defense[1] work. I believe that the increased defense referrals occurred because I had based my conclusions on an understanding of the science underlying recovery from traumatic brain injury (TBI), including the impact of effort and honesty on examinee presentation, which was inconsistent with the needs of many plaintiff attorneys. Also, it was my impression that some referring physicians who had diagnosed patients with a disabling accident-related condition were not particularly pleased to have their diagnoses contradicted by a neuropsychologist who assessed symptom validity quantitatively; such physicians seemed to stop referring patients for clinical evaluations. Of course, plaintiff attorneys and physicians interested in what I consider to be objective neuropsychological test results continue to contact me for services. Outside medical–legal contexts, I continue to receive referrals from a variety of sources to examine and treat children and adults with a variety of presenting problems.

When reviewing the work of colleagues, I attempt to determine the bases on which their conclusions are drawn. I check the sources of information on which they relied, including medical and other records, interviews of collateral sources, behavioral observations, and standardized symptom inventories and tests. I also determine whether the conclusions and opinions are empirically based, taking into account what is known about (1) the neuropathology of the injury, (2) typical neuropsychological deficits associated with the injury, (3) dose–response impairment and recovery patterns, (4) base rates of neuropsychological symptoms in various populations, and (5) base rates of invalid effort or responding.

Any neuropsychological evaluation performed in a medical–legal context that does not include a multimethod approach to the assessment of symptom validity and rely on empirically based interpretation strategies is considered incomplete, and the neurocognitive and psychological test scores cannot be accepted as reflecting the examinee's full neurocognitive potential or true psychological state. I have been amazed at the lengths to which highly credentialed and experienced colleagues will go to contort their interpretations of invalid effort to fit what can only be described as preestablished positions (e.g., confirmatory bias). For example, such practitioners may use descriptive terms such as *below expectations* or *below recommended cutoffs but not below chance* to describe clear failures on multiple symptom validity tests (SVTs) so that they can then appear to the unsophisticated reader to be justified in interpreting the test data as valid and providing clinical or forensic opinions. The opinions, of course, are ultimately baseless and misleading.

Similarly, such creative practitioners have gone to great lengths to provide neurophysiological or psychological explanations for failure on SVTs,

---

[1]*Defense* is used broadly to include defense attorneys, disability insurance companies, and no-fault insurance companies.

such as explaining that an individual with a mild TBI had such impaired memory or attention that the failed SVT performance reflected true neurocognitive impairment rather than poor effort. It has also been observed that such practitioners may not include the result of SVTs for some examinees while providing it for others; such variable inclusion of SVT results indicates to me a selective omission of unfavorable data.

I suspect that it is because of my commitment to empirically based conclusions and to assessing symptom validity and reporting the findings in a consistent, complete, and accurate manner that my referrals have shifted from being primarily plaintiff oriented to being more defense oriented. However, I am glad to accept referrals from plaintiff and defense attorneys seeking an objective opinion rather than from those who expect me to be an advocate for their client. I anticipate further evolution of my practice over the years, both by design and because of the perceived fit between the needs of potential consumers and the manner in which I practice.

ELECTRICAL BRAIN INJURY

Electrical injury (EI), its mechanisms of damage, and its neuropsychological sequelae have previously been described in detail (e.g., Duff & McCaffrey, 2001; Martin, Salvatore, & Johnstone, 2003; Pliskin et al., 2006). EI may affect a variety of organs and bodily systems, including cardiac, respiratory, and central nervous systems, which may have a direct or an indirect effect on neuropsychological functioning. The possible neurological etiologies of impaired neurocognitive performance include (1) contact from the electrical power source to the head; (2) TBI resulting from falls; (3) anoxia secondary to cardiac or respiratory arrest; and (4) peripheral electrical contact, possibly resulting in neurochemical changes. Of course, a given individual may experience a combination of these brain injuries, and in clinical contexts it is often extremely difficult, if not impossible, to determine which one or more of the injuries resulted in the reported and/or detected neuropsychological deficits.[2]

Electrical brain injury (EBI) has been found to result in a wide variety of reported symptoms and diffuse neurocognitive deficits (Duff & McCaffrey,

---

[2]A note on terms. Because EI may or may not affect central nervous system (CNS) functioning, a more specific term is needed to indicate CNS impairment resulting from exposure to electrical current. Therefore, I propose the term *electrical brain injury* (EBI) to more clearly reflect the origin of neuropsychological problems associated with EI. In addition, because EBI can result from four types of CNS injury that can be extremely difficult to differentiate, EBI should be used to describe any CNS-based neuropsychological impairment following exposure to electrical current, with the specific origin noted if known (i.e., EBI–head contact, EBI–TBI, EBI–anoxia, EBI–peripheral contact, EBI–combined, or EBI–undetermined origin).

2001). However, in a recent, well-designed study involving individuals who experienced peripheral electrical contact injury only, Pliskin and colleagues (2006) found impairment in the domains of attention, processing and psychomotor speed, Full Scale IQ, and motor speed and dexterity. Pliskin and colleagues noted that although the pathophysiology underlying these impairments is unclear, their data suggest that electrochemical alterations in brain systems, in the absence of detectable structural lesions, underlie the neuropsychological impairments. Duff and McCaffrey (2001) also reported that because of the affinity of electrical current for nerve fibers and blood vessels, brain functioning is compromised more than brain structure in persons with EBIs.

As is evident from the foregoing studies, there is considerable overlap between EBI neuropsychological profiles and TBI profiles. In the absence of focal TBI (e.g., subdural hematomas), neuroimaging and electrodiagnostic studies suggest that neurological function rather than structure is affected by EBI. EBI symptoms typically emerge immediately (Cherington, 1995) and follow a dose–response injury pattern (primarily involving amperage of the current and duration of contact) (Lee, 1997), although factors such as resistance of different bodily tissues, type of current (alternating or direct), and course of current through the body can also affect the severity of injury. Deficits evident in the acute period may improve over time (Hopewell, 1983); however, delayed effects and symptom progression have also been reported (Cherington, 1995; Martin et al., 2003). The specific nature of the injury (e.g., EBI–TBI vs. EBI–head contact) may affect course and outcome, and a failure of some studies to control for such differences may account for the variable research findings.

In addition to the direct neurological effects of EBI, neuropsychological functioning and performance may also be affected by the interference-related effects of pain syndromes resulting from peripheral nervous system injuries, headaches, parasthesias, and burn injuries, as well as pain medications. Emotional distress, commonly associated with EI and other types of trauma, was found not to contribute significantly to neuropsychological dysfunction for individuals with EBI–peripheral contact (Pliskin et al., 2006).

CASE STUDY

Background

Mr. A., a 34-year-old, married, white, high school graduate, was working as a chef when he sustained an EI. The injury occurred when he put one hand on a stainless steel oven and the other on a stainless steel preparation table. He recalls putting his hand on the oven and intending to open it. His next memory is of being on the ground, his body convulsing, and someone standing over him. Although he does not know how much time elapsed between his last memory before the injury and his first memory after the injury, he reported that EMS (emergency medical services) workers had already arrived. He estimates that the period for which he is amnestic is approximately 10 minutes. He was later told that a coworker had given him cardiopulmonary resuscitation, although he does not know whether he experienced cardiac arrest.

Mr. A. was taken by ambulance to a local university medical center. He has intermittent memories of that night and the following day, with his recall improving and becoming continuous by the time of discharge home 2 days later. Regarding his physical injury, Mr. A. stated that the entrance point involved one or both hands, with his left upper extremity injured more than his right upper extremity. He does not know the duration of electrical contact; he was informed that a coworker saw him grab the surfaces, stand up straight and shake, and then fall. The exit point appears to have been the bottom of his left foot where a very small wound was noted. He reported that the electrical current was from an alternating current (AC) source, 200 volts. He is unaware of having sustained direct trauma to his head when he fell, although he was unable to take protective actions.

During the first 6 to 8 weeks following his injury, Mr. A. experienced considerable physical pain, including headaches and abdominal pain. He stated that as a result of these symptoms, he could not perform his usual activities at home and could not return to work. He was prescribed pain medications and sleep medication. Following the initial 2 months, he began to try to reintegrate into prior activities and experienced cognitive problems, primarily with concentration, memory, and processing speed. Three months after his injury he was seen for neurological examination by Dr. M. D., which revealed normal cranial nerve functioning and mental status. A magnetic resonance imaging (MRI) of the brain and an electroencephalogram (EEG) were both normal. Nerve conduction studies were abnormal, and an MRI of the cervical spine revealed disc bulges and herniation.

Dr. M. D. noted that in the year following his injury, Mr. A. had made physical and cognitive gains, but he continued to experience multiple symptoms. Physical symptoms included weakness, numbness, spasms, and pain, primarily in his left hand and arm. Headaches and fatigue also persisted. Cognitive symptoms included memory problems, slowed information processing, and trouble concentrating. With the passage of time and the persistence of physical and cognitive symptoms, emotional symptoms emerged, including depressed mood and anxiety. He was anxious when using electrical appliances, changing light bulbs, and plugging cords into electrical outlets. He also reported intrusive thoughts, hyperarousal, and avoidant behaviors related to his injury and electricity, and he reported having trouble sleeping. Despite these symptoms, Mr. A. had stopped taking medications. He had taken a full-time job driving a fork lift in a warehouse, at significantly less pay than he had earned as a chef. He no longer socialized with friends, which he had done frequently before his injury. Despite the symptoms reported by Mr. A., Dr. M. D.'s neurological examination revealed no gross cognitive, sensory, or motor deficits, and no emotional distress was evident. Mr. A. was referred by his neurologist to Dr. Truedough for a neuropsychological evaluation 13 months after his injury. Using board certification, experience in medical–legal practice, and regular attendance at conferences as markers of professional competence, Dr. Truedough would clearly be considered competent for the present case.

Because Mr. A. was reportedly unable to perform his prior occupation following his EI, he was receiving long-term disability benefits. In addition, he was involved in litigation against his former employer. Three months after the completion of Dr. Truedough's neuropsychological evaluation, I was retained by Mr. A.'s disability insurance carrier to make a determination about the nature and extent of his neuropsychological disability and the appropriateness of his current treatment. Because Mr. A. had recently completed a fairly comprehensive neuropsychological test battery similar to one that I would administer, I determined that I would address the referral questions by reviewing medical, neuropsychological, historical, and accident-related records and interviewing Mr. A. Based on those procedures, I would determine if additional testing were necessary.

Neuropsychological Evaluation and Report

Dr. Truedough conducted a fairly thorough evaluation, assessing each neurocognitive domain with multiple well-standardized measures and assessing psychological functioning with the Minnesota Multiphasic Personality Inventory–2 (MMPI-2) (see Appendix 6.1 for a summary of scores[3]). As part of the evaluation, he administered two measures of symptom validity, the Test of Memory Malingering (TOMM; Tombaugh, 1996) and the Word Memory Test (WMT; Green, 2003a). Based on the results of those two measures (scores were not included in the report), Dr. Truedough concluded, "While the patient's performance on two measures of effort was below expectations, it was not significantly below chance. It appeared that the patient's performance on these measures was affected by impaired attention skills. Therefore, the neuropsychological test results are considered valid for interpretation." No other indicators of effort from the neurocognitive tests were reported. With regard to the validity of Mr. A.'s responses to the MMPI-2, Dr. Truedough stated, "Review of standard validity scales

---

[3]It is expected that the reader will understand the symptom validity concerns reflected in the test scores; therefore, detailed description of symptom validity indicators has not been provided.

revealed an honest and valid approach to the MMPI-2." There was no mention of which specific validity scales were reviewed.

Based on his neuropsychological evaluation, Dr. Truedough wrote a *preliminary* report. He stated that the report was considered preliminary because the evaluation was for clinical services and an expedited report was needed to facilitate treatment planning. Dr. Truedough further stated that the report was considered preliminary because he had not reviewed all relevant historical and injury-related materials, had not interviewed collateral sources, and had not fully assessed symptom validity or considered alternative explanations for the findings. Despite these limitations, he concluded that Mr. A. was experiencing severe deficits in most neurocognitive domains, that the deficits were due to damage to frontotemporal systems and subcortical circuitry, and that, as result of his work-related injury, he was totally and permanently disabled. Thus, Dr. Truedough overstepped the parameters of a clinical evaluation by addressing forensic issues (e.g., causality, and disability status), despite acknowledging that he had insufficient information to make such determinations. To his credit, Dr. Truedough did state that on request, the inherent limitations of the preliminary evaluation would be addressed and a "forensic report" would be provided.

Dr. Truedough recommended that Mr. A. receive individual neuropsychological treatment, which Dr. Truedough provided for Mr. A. However, despite the severity of Mr. A.'s impairment, as determined by Dr. Truedough, no recommendations for increased safety, such as supervision or cessation of driving, were made. Because Dr. Truedough assumed the role of a treating doctor in this case, his offer to provide a forensic report invited a dual, conflicting role for himself (Bush, 2005; Bush, Connell, & Denney, 2006; Fisher, Johnson-Greene, & Barth, 2002). Ironically, as seen in the present report and in other cases, Dr. Truedough includes a paragraph in all of his reports that states that he has considered potential sources of bias in his work and has taken steps to minimize the possible impact of such bias, consistent with the recommendations of Sweet and Moulthrop (1999).

Review of Records and Interview

When I reviewed Dr. Truedough's test data, the most striking finding was the overwhelming evidence of Mr. A.'s poor effort on the tests and thus his invalid approach to the evaluation. The results of the SVTs and multiple indicators from the neurocognitive test results indicated that Mr. A. did not approach the evaluation in a valid manner. In addition, his score of 32 on the Fake Bad Scale (FBS; Lees-Haley, English, & Glenn, 1991), which Dr. Truedough apparently failed to consider, was consistent with exaggeration of somatic symptoms (Greiffenstein, Fox, & Lees-Haley, 2007). Although the body of neuropsychological research on EBI is not nearly as extensive as it is for TBI, the only conclusion that could be drawn from the test data was that Mr. A. was exaggerating or fabricating his deficits. Dr. Truedough's interpretation of the test data and his conclusions revealed a remarkable ability and willingness to disregard the science of the profession and to approach the case in a biased manner. More disturbing to me than Mr. A.'s invalid approach to the evaluation was the examiner invalidity.

During my clinical interview of Mr. A., I administered two standardized symptom inventories: the Memory Complaints Inventory (MCI; Green, 2003b) and the Structured Inventory of Malingered Symptomatology (SIMS; Widows & Smith, 2005). With all MCI scores (including a GMP [General Memory Problems] of 20 and a NIP [Numeric Information Problems] of 23) significantly elevated compared to known patient groups, his responses reflected significantly more subjective memory impairment than the following groups of individuals: those who sustained severe TBIs that rendered them comatose with abnormal CT (computed tomography) scans, men with moderate to severe TBIs, men with orthopedic injuries, and men with chronic pain, all of whom passed symptom validity testing. His scores were more consistent with individuals who failed symptom validity testing. His SIMS Total Score of 22 was significantly elevated above the recommended cutoff score for the identification of intentional exaggeration or fabrication of symptoms. Thus, he endorsed a high frequency of symptoms that are highly atypical in patients with genuine psychiatric or cognitive disorders.

Based on the information obtained in the records, including the neuropsychological test data, and from the interview of Mr. A., including the results of standardized symptom inventories, I concluded that there was insufficient evidence to establish the presence of neurologically based cognitive impairment. As a result, there was insufficient evidence to establish the need for neuropsychological treatment (there had been no evidence of emotional distress, so there was no need for psychological treatment). Because Mr. A. approached both Dr. Truedough's neuropsychological evaluation and my interview in an invalid manner, I determined that additional neuropsychological testing was not warranted.

Dr. Truedough's Response

Dr. Truedough was provided a copy of my report by the plaintiff attorney. He wrote:

> Dr. Bush met with Mr. A. on only one occasion. His independent medical–legal evaluation (IME) consisted of an interview, a review of records, and the administration of two measures of "validity of self-reported neuropsychological symptoms." As the patient complains of and dem-

onstrates a variety of cognitive difficulties postinjury, the lack of support for a psychological/neuropsychological diagnosis to which Dr. Bush refers is apparently based on the fact that he does not believe the patient. In actuality, there is no concrete evidence that Mr. A. is exaggerating in any purposeful manner. So, if we put aside the issue of exaggeration, we are left with a series of symptoms and deficits that are very consistent with impaired cerebral functioning.

I have spent much more time with this patient than has Dr. Bush. In the time spent with this patient there has been nothing of a clear and overt nature to suggest that he was exaggerating or fabricating his symptoms. Inconsistency in presentation is not highly atypical or necessarily evidence of exaggeration/malingering. As opposed to Dr. Bush, I have also obtained some information from the patient's wife, which has, in essence, confirmed the patient's subjective complaints and the test results. We know that patients sometimes "overstate" their symptoms not because they are intentionally exaggerating but because that is how the symptoms appear to them. I have discussed Dr. Bush's IME with several other experienced neuropsychologists (of course, with all identifying data regarding the patient and IME examiner removed); to a person, our colleagues did not feel comfortable with the conclusions drawn from the recent neuropsychological IME.

I would like to know how sure Dr. Bush is that this patient is intentionally exaggerating or malingering his symptoms. If his "confidence" in his conclusions is not of a very high level, then we must accept that the patient's (and his wife's) reporting of symptoms might well be valid.

My Response to Dr. Truedough's Letter

In a correspondence to the defense attorney, I wrote:

I recently performed an independent neuropsychological examination of Mr. A. At this time I have been provided with a letter from Mr. A.'s treating neuropsychologist, Dr. Truedough, and have been asked to state whether my opinion has changed based on the information contained in the letter.

First, there exists a considerable body of research on the assessment of symptom validity (for reviews, see Bianchini, Mathias, & Greve, 2001; Iverson, 2003; Larrabee, 2005a; Sweet, 1999). Dr. Truedough's interpretation of Mr. A.'s test results is inconsistent with an actuarial approach to symptom validity assessment, without which the remaining test results cannot be considered valid. Second, research has established that there is a dose–response relationship between brain trauma and neurological symptom outcome; that is, the less severe the injury, the fewer persisting cognitive problems (Dikmen, Machamer, Winn, & Temkin, 1995; McCrea, Kelly, Randolph, Cisler,

& Berger, 2002). The severity of this claimant's reported cognitive symptoms is clearly inconsistent with patterns of brain functioning following electrical injury.

Third, cognitive symptoms are nonspecific; that is, they may be associated with many clinical conditions. Lees-Haley, Fox, and Courtney (2001) found that 51% of their sample of litigating individuals with nonbrain injuries reported feeling dazed immediately after the trauma, and 65% reported feeling confused. In addition, Lees-Haley and Brown (1993) found that 62% of outpatient family practice patients report having headaches and 20% report having memory problems. These symptoms increase in relation to stress, even for individuals without brain trauma (Gouvier, Cubic, Jones, Brantley, & Cutlip, 1992). Following an accident, there can be increased and selective attention paid to bodily sensations (Putnam & Millis, 1994; Watson & Pennebaker, 1989). Failure to appreciate the nonspecific nature of many neurological symptoms can lead to misdiagnosis and iatrogenesis of persisting complaints (Larrabee, 1997, 2005b; Newcombe, Rabbitt, & Briggs, 1994).

Mr. A.'s self-reported cognitive symptoms were inconsistent with my observations of his cognitive functioning during my exam. Despite reporting severe problems with memory, he was able to recall detailed information from his recent and distant past. In addition, no problems with attention and concentration were noted. The inconsistencies between Mr. A.'s reported symptoms and the established dose–response nature of brain injury recovery and between reported symptoms and observations raises significant questions about the validity of Mr. A.'s neurocognitive symptoms. To further evaluate the extent of his cognitive symptoms, I administered two standardized symptom inventories.

On the symptom inventories, Mr. A.'s reported cognitive symptoms are inconsistent with the nature of his injury, are inconsistent with groups of individuals with well-documented brain injuries of various severities, are inconsistent with groups of individuals with orthopedic and pain disorders and psychological disorders, and are thus invalid. Dr. Truedough indicated that, despite Mr. A.'s inconsistencies, there is no concrete evidence that he is exaggerating in any purposeful manner. However, inconsistencies or discrepancies such as those described earlier are the key feature of symptom exaggeration or fabrication. Dr. Truedough stated, "If we put aside the issue of 'exaggeration,' we are left with a series of symptoms. . . . " Given the information presented previously, it is difficult to understand wanting to put aside the issue of exaggeration Furthermore, the issue of time spent with Mr. A. has little bearing; objective consideration of the available information would require little time before a determination could be made that a neurological explanation for Mr. A.'s complaints is not supported.

I did not diagnose malingering; I stated that a neuropsychological disorder was not supported. However, disorders that must be considered include undifferentiated somatoform disorder or malingering; Factitious disorder cannot be considered due to the presence of external incentives. I cannot speak to Mr. A.'s intent; thus, consistent with a reasonable doubt strategy, I am not stating that Mr. A. is intentionally trying to deceive for the purpose of secondary gain. What I can speak to is the lack of an established neurological basis for his symptoms and complaints.

Based on (1) the scientific evidence presented above, (2) multiple discrepancies associated with Mr. A.'s complaints, (3) the results of a standardized symptom questionnaires, (4) the results of Dr. Truedough's neuropsychological evaluation, and (5) my interview and observations of Mr. A., my opinions as stated in the report have not changed. It is difficult to imagine that the information that Dr. Truedough provided to his colleagues was as complete and accurate as that presented here.

Case Resolution

After providing my data-based response to Dr. Truedough's letter, I received no further contact or information regarding this case. I do not know how the disability insurance company used the information that I provided, nor do I know what became of the Mr. A.'s lawsuit against the restaurant. This lack of closure is not all that unusual in these kinds of cases, but it increases my curiosity about whether my opinions had any significant impact on the outcome.

CONCLUSIONS

My involvement with Mr. A.'s case served to reinforce for me three main points. First, reliance on research-based evidence of neuropsychological impairment provides a stronger argument than reliance on subjective interpretations of test data based on clinical judgment. Dr. Truedough seemed to disregard a considerable body of symptom validity assessment research and go to great lengths to contort his opinions to fit the position he intended to represent. Second, despite the importance of basing opinions on research, the research on the neuropsychological effects of some conditions, such as EBI, remains inconclusive. Although we must base our conclusions on the available research, limitations must be considered and incorporated into our opinions.

Third, we must approach medical–legal cases with the understanding that each and every aspect of our work and reasoning will be critically evaluated by our peers (and certainly by a cross-examining attorney), with more or less adherence to objective information and civility. Some neuropsychologists will go to great lengths to undermine the competent, good-faith work of another, including assisting their patients with deception (e.g., encouraging secret taping of examinations) and advising patients to file specious complaints with ethics committees or licensing boards or file lawsuits against the independent examiner. Through such actions, clinicians go beyond appropriate patient advocacy and intentionally sacrifice the interests of justice, affecting not only their reputations but also that of the profession. Ultimately, consumers of neuropsychological services and the public at large are the ones most likely to be harmed by the self-serving pseudo-advocacy perpetuated by some treating neuropsychologists.

REFERENCES

Bianchini, K. J., Mathias, C. W., & Greve, K. W. (2001). Symptom validity testing: A critical review. *The Clinical Neuropsychologist, 15*, 19–45.

Bush, S. S. (2005). Ethical challenges in forensic neuropsychology: Introduction. In S. S. Bush (Ed.), *A casebook of ethical challenges in neuropsychology* (pp. 10–14). New York: Psychology Press.

Bush, S. S., Connell, M. A., & Denney, R. L. (2006). *Ethical practice in forensic psychology: A systematic model for decision making.* Washington, DC: American Psychological Association.

Cherington, M. (1995). Central nervous system complications of lightening and electrical injuries. *Seminars in Neurology, 15*, 233–240.

Dikmen, S. S., Machamer, J. E., Winn, H. R., & Temkin, N. R. (1995). Neuropsychological outcome at 1–year post head injury. *Neuropsychology, 9*, 80–90.

Duff, K., & McCaffrey, R.J. (2001). Electrical injury and lightening injury: A review of their mechanisms and neuropsychological, psychiatric, and neurological sequelae. *Neuropsychology Review, 11*, 101–116.

Fisher, J. M., Johnson-Greene, D., & Barth, J. T. (2002). Examination, diagnosis, and interventions in clinical neuropsychology in general and with special populations: An overview. In S. S. Bush & M. L. Drexler (Eds.), *Ethical issues in clinical neuropsychology* (pp. 3–22). Lisse, The Netherlands: Swets & Zeitlinger.

Gouvier, W. D., Cubic, B., Jones, G., Brantley, P., & Cutlip, Q. (1992). Postconcussion symptoms and daily stress in normal and head-injured college populations. *Archives of Clinical Neuropsychology, 7*, 193–211.

Green, P. (2003a). *Green's Word Memory Test for Windows: User's manual.* Edmonton, Alberta, Canada: Author.

Green, P. (2003b). *Memory Complaints Inventory for Windows* [Computer software]. Edmonton, Alberta, Canada: Author.

Greiffenstein, M. F., Fox, D., & Lees-Haley, P. R. (2007). The MMPI-2 Fake Bad Scale in detection of noncredible brain injury claims. In K.B. Boone (Ed.), *Assessment of feigned cognitive impairment: A neuropsychological perspective* (pp. 210–236). New York: Guilford Press.

Hopewell, C. A. (1983). Serial neuropsychological assessment in a case of reversible electrocution encephalopathy. *Clinical Neuropsychology, 5*, 61–65.

Iverson, G. L. (2003). Detecting malingering in civil forensic evaluations. In A. M. Horton & L. C. Hartlage (Eds.), *Handbook of forensic neuropsychology* (pp. 137–178). New York: Springer.

Larrabee, G. J. (1997). Neuropsychological outcome, postconcussion symptoms, and forensic considerations in mild closed head trauma. *Seminars in Clinical Neuropsychiatry, 2*, 196–206.

Larrabee, G. J. (2005a). Assessment of malingering. In G. J. Larrabee (Ed.), *Forensic neuropsychology: A scientific approach* (pp. 115–158). New York: Oxford University Press.

Larrabee, G. J. (Ed.). (2005b). *Forensic neuropsychology: A scientific approach.* New York: Oxford University Press.

Lee, R. C. (1997). Injury by electrical forces: Pathophysiology, manifestations, and therapy. *Current Problems in Surgery, 34*, 677–764.

Lees-Haley, P. R., & Brown, R. S. (1993). Neuropsychological complaint baserates of 170 personal injury claimants. *Archives of Clinical Neuropsychology, 8*, 203–209.

Lees-Haley, P. R., English, L. T., & Glenn, W. J. (1991). A Fake Bad scale on the MMPI-2 for personal injury claimants. *Psychological Reports, 68*, 208–210.

Lees-Haley, P. R., Fox, D. D., & Courtney, J. C. (2001). A comparison of complaints by mild brain injury claimants and other claimants describing subjective experiences immediately following their injury. *Archives of Clinical Neuropsychology, 16*, 689–695.

Martin, T. A., Salvatore, N. F., & Johnstone, B. (2003). Cognitive decline over time following electrical injury. *Brain Injury, 17*, 817–823.

McCrea, M., Kelly, J. P., Randolph, C., Cisler, R., & Berger, L. (2002). Immediate neurocognitive effects of concussion. *Neurosurgery, 50*, 1032–1042.

Newcombe, F., Rabbitt, P., & Briggs, M. (1994). Minor head injury: Pathophysiological or iatrogenic sequelae? *Journal of Neurology, Neurosurgery, and Psychiatry, 57*, 709–716.

Pliskin, N. H., Ammar, A. N., Fink, J. W., Hill, S. K., Malina, A. C., Ramati, A., et al. (2006). Neuropsychological changes following electrical injury. *Journal of the International Neuropsychological Society, 12*, 17–23.

Putnam, S. H., & Millis, S. R. (1994). Psychological factors in the developmental and maintenance of chronic somatic and functional symptoms following mild traumatic brain injury. *Advances in Medical Psychotherapy, 7*, 1–22.

Sweet, J. J. (1999). Malingering: Differential diagnosis. In J. J. Sweet (Ed.), *Forensic neuropsychology: Fundamentals and practice* (pp. 255–286). Lisse, The Netherlands: Swets & Zeitlinger.

Sweet, J.J., & Moulthrop, M.A. (1999). Self-examination questions as a means of identifying bias in adversarial assessments. *Journal of Forensic Neuropsychology, 1*, 73–88.

Tombaugh, T. N. (1996). *Test of Memory Malingering.* Toronto, Ontario, Canada: Multi-Health Systems.

Watson, D., & Pennebaker, J. W. (1989). Health complaints, stress, and distress: Exploring the central role of negative affectivity. *Psychological Review, 96*, 234–254.

Widows, M. R., & Smith, G. P. (2005). *Structured Inventory of Malingered Symptomatology.* Lutz, FL: Psychological Assessment Resources.

APPENDIX 6.1

Neuropsychological Summary of Scores

WAIS-III	IQ/Index	Verbal	SS	Performance/Visual	SS
FSIQ	83	V	11	PC	5
VIQ	97	S	11	DSy	5
PIQ	68	A	9	BD	4
VCI	105	DSp (5/3)	6	MR	4
POI	67	I	11	PA	6
WMI	80	C	10	SS	1
PSI	66	L-N	5		

NAART	
FSIQ	99

CVLT-II	Raw score	T score
List A		
Trial 1	3	30
Trial 5	5	15
Trials 1–5	22	21
List B	4	40
List A		
Short Delay Free Recall	3	25
Short Delay Cued	3	10
Long Delay Free Recall	2	15
Long Delay Cued	2	15
Semantic cluster	−0.3	40
Serial cluster	1.6	60
% primacy	9%	15
% middle	64%	25
% recency	27%	50
Total learning trials 1–5	0.5	30

(continued)

Appendix 6.1. (*continued*)	Raw score	*T* score
Consistency	65	40
List B versus Trial 1	33.3%	60
SDFR versus Trial 5	−40%	60
LDFR versus SDFR	−33.3%	40
Total repetitions	0	40
Total intrusions	0	40
Y/N recognition	8	10
Response bias ("no")	0.7	70
Forced-choice recognition (% accuracy)	38	Cumulative % with better score = 100

CVMT

Total	34	40
Delayed recognition	1	35 (raw score ≤ 2 = chance level performance)

WCST 128

No. of categories	3	(6–10%ile)
Trials for 1st	12	(>16%ile)
No. of trials correct	68	
No. of errors	60	30
PSV Responses	30	37
PSV Errors	28	35
Non-PSV errors	32	28
% conceptual	49	31
Failure to Maintain Set	1	(>16%ile)
Learning to Learn	−14.52	(2–5%ile)

TMT

A	120	9
B	307	4

GP

Dominant	127	20
Nondominant	116	27

HD

Dominant	26.5	48
Nondominant	21.5	45
CIM	5	3
BNT	39	10
FAS	10	18
SRT	18	27

(*continued*)

Appendix 6.1. (continued)	Raw score	T score
RCFT		
Copy	9 (≤ 1%ile)	
Time to Copy	96 seconds	
	(> 16%ile)	
Immediate Recall	5.5	22
Delayed Recall	4	< 20
Recognition	14	< 20
WRAT-3		
Reading	50	53
Spelling	46	54
Arithmetic	43	53
TOMM		
Trial 1	21	
Trial 2	20	
Retention	18	
WMT		
IR%	42.5	
DR%	37.5	
Consistency%	50.0	
MMPI-2		
?	0	
L	3	46
F	11	75
Fb	5	62
Fp	2	57
K	13	46
S	22	46
VRIN	4	46
TRIN	9	50
FBS	34	99
1	26	92
2	38	88
3	46	106
4	24	66
5	34	55
6	15	67
7	39	95
8	35	84
9	22	65
0	34	58

Note. WAIS-III, Wechsler Adult Intelligence Scale–III; SS, standardized score; FSIQ, Full Scale IQ; VIQ, Verbal IQ; PIQ, Performance IQ; VCI, Verbal Comprehension Index; POI, Perceptual Organization Index; WMI, Working Memory Index; PSI, Processing Speed Index; NAART, North American Adult Reading Test; CVLT-II, California Verbal Learning Test–II; SOFR, short delay free recall; LDFR, long delay free recall; FC, forced choice; CVMT, Continuous Visual Memory Test; WCST-128, Wisconsin Card Sorting Test–128; TMT, Trail Making Test A/B; GP, Grooved Pegboard; HD, Hand Dynamometer; CIM, Complex Ideational Material; BNT, Boston Naming Test; RCFT, Rey Complex Figure Test; WRAT-3, Wide Range Achievement Test—Third Edition; TOMM, Test of Memory Malingering; WMT, Word Memory Test; MMPI-2, Minnesota Multiphasic Personality Inventory–2; VRIN, Variable Response Inconsistency; TRIN, True Response Inconsistency; FBS, Fake Bad Scale.

7

A Second Look at Pain and Concussion

Kevin W. Greve

Traumatic brain injury (TBI) is one of the most common causes of brain damage. According to the National Institutes of Health (NIH), about 5 million Americans alive today have experienced a TBI with an annual incidence of 100 per 100,000 (NIH Consensus Development Panel on Rehabilitation of Persons with Traumatic Brain Injury, 1999). Financially, the direct and the indirect costs of TBI are measured in the tens of billions of dollars (Rose, 2005). The average insurance cost of work-related TBIs is $171,000 (Wrona, 2006) and the relationship between severity of brain injury, early functional outcome, and neurobehavioral indicators often predicts the magnitude of the reward (Novack, Bush, Meythaler, & Canupp, 2001). Most neuropsychologists are familiar with TBI and related issues. However, they are less familiar with the incidence and consequences of chronic pain after TBI, a common problem and an important predictor of functional outcome after TBI (Alexander, 1995). An understanding of pain-related issues following TBI is important to the practicing neuropsychologist.

Pain complaints result in millions of physician office visits per year (Woodwell & Cherry, 2004) and as many as 150 million lost workdays (Guo et al., 1995; Guo, Tanaka, Halperin, & Cameron, 1999). Of all the major musculoskeletal complaints, low back pain is the most common (Picavet & Schouten, 2003), with the 6-month incidence of clinically significant low back pain at approximately 8% of the general adult population

(George, 2002); estimates of lifetime incidence range from 11 to 84% (Walker, 2000). The incidence of neck pain is estimated to be as high as 15% in the adult population (Hardin & Halla, 1995). Approximately half of all motor vehicle accidents (MVAs) result in neck pain symptoms and complaints (Galasko, 1997, as cited in Dvir & Keating, 2001). These MVA-related neck injuries alone result in costs of over $600 million per year in Canada (Navin, Zein, & Felipe, 2000).

A significant portion of the cost of low back pain is accounted for by disability claims (Frymoyer & Cats-Baril, 1991). Compensation status has been linked to outcome in surgery (Vaccaro, Ring, Scuderi, Cohen, & Garfin, 1997) and outpatient rehabilitation (Rainville, Sobel, Hartigan, & Wright, 1997) for back pain. Also, return-to-work rates are lowest for patients with back pain relative to all work-related injuries (Tate, 1992). The high incidence of disability claims for low back pain has had an "explosive socioeconomic impact" (Hazard, Reeves, & Fenwick, 1992, p. 1065), with estimates that it costs the equivalent of 1.7% of the gross national product of some Western countries (van Tulder, Koes, & Bouter, 1995). Much of the cost of neck injuries associated with MVAs may be generated by the incentive inherent in compensation systems. When one Canadian province instituted tort reform (changed to a no-fault system) the incidence of neck pain (whiplash) claims declined by 28% and the length of disability declined by 200 days, despite an increase in the overall number of MVAs during the same period (Cassidy et al., 2000).

In this chapter, I review a case from my own practice that involved a claim of TBI and cervical pain following a work-related MVA. At the time I was retained, the workers' compensation claim had been settled and the claimant was pursuing a third-party suit against the parties associated with the vehicle that struck the claimant. From my understanding of the case, liability had been established and what remained was a question of damages. My services were retained by the attorney representing the defendant's insurance company in the third-party suit. At that time, I was asked to review the available medical records, including a neuropsychological evaluation, and provide a scientifically supported summary of the issues that could be used to assist in settlement negotiations.

In this particular case, my role was as a consultant and I did not anticipate evaluating the claimant or being called to testify. Because of attorney work-product privilege, the presence of a consultant may never be revealed to the opposing side. However, it is good policy to assume that written communications by the neuropsychologist are discoverable and to act accordingly. There are times when changing circumstances of the case will alter the legal strategy such that it is advantageous to reveal the neuropsychologist's communications. It is important to keep in mind that it is the attorney's obligation to represent his or her client zealously and that the necessities of representation may be inconsistent with the professional interests and ethical obligations of the neuropsychologist.

My early discussions with the attorney (my client) led me to believe that my review would likely be made part of the record just as the report of a formal evaluation would be. What follows is based on the text of that review as well as the text of the report of the evaluating neuropsychologist. Identifying information has been altered to protect privacy, but the text of the report is essentially unchanged. The record review and conclusions are mine. The examination results and summary/integration are those of the evaluating neuropsychologist.

CASE STUDY

Background

Records included the traffic collision report, ambulance run report, emergency room report, and records from orthopedic, neurological, and pain management physicians. The most recent record I reviewed was from the pain management doctor dated a year before my involvement with the case With the exception of the traffic collision report and the few pain management records produced after the neuropsychological evaluation, the same records were reviewed by the evaluating neuropsychologist. A summary of the records follows.

Mr. Morgan was injured approximately 2 years earlier when the truck he was driving was struck from behind by a loaded tractor-trailer rig and shoved off the road and into a ditch. When the emergency medical services (EMS) arrived about 30 minute later, Mr. Morgan was still in his vehicle. He complained of pain to the top of his head and soreness to his neck. He was noted to be fully oriented and to have a steady gait. His Glasgow Coma Scale (GCS) was 15/15 at the scene of the accident. He was transported to the emergency room (ER), arriving 1 hour after the accident and was noted to be amnestic for events immediately postaccident. An occipital laceration was repaired and he was diagnosed with a concussion. A computed tomography (CT) scan of the brain at that time was normal.

In a follow-up note 2 days later, it was noted that he had not lost consciousness at the scene. This notation is inconsistent with the patient's statement to his orthopedist that he lost consciousness for 1 minute. When evaluated by a neurologist 2 weeks after the accident, he reported a 5-minute loss of consciousness; he gave the same report to his pain management doctor almost 1 year later. He did not report any loss of consciousness to the neuropsychologist who evaluated him 11 months later. However, the neuropsychologist noted that the patient may have experienced "a very brief period of unawareness."

The orthopedist's primary impression was "cervical sprain/strain," which is generally considered to be a self-terminating condition, often requiring minimal treatment. This is consistent with the orthopedist's report 2 months later, that the symptoms of the sprain/strain had resolved. Nine days after the accident, the orthopedist released Mr. Morgan to full duties without restrictions and he reiterated that impression 6 weeks later. Mr. Morgan's primary complaint to his orthopedist was of pain in his right hand, which he feared might be aggravated by driving. Nonetheless, he did return to work and apparently continued to work.

Mr. Morgan was seen by a neurologist and complained of headaches and blurry vision. The neurologist documented grossly normal cognition with some diminished concentration. He agreed with the ER doctor that Mr. Morgan had suffered a minor head injury. He ordered a magnetic resonance imaging (MRI) and electroencephalogram (EEG), both of which were normal. There are no records for the following 7 months until Mr. Morgan was seen by a pain management doctor upon referral from his attorney. This doctor noted a number of pain-related conditions, including postconcussion headache, persistent neck pain attributed to cervical facet joint pathology, myofascial neck and shoulder pain, and mechanical low back pain with myofascial pain. Remember, the other records indicated the neck pain had resolved within 2 months postinjury.

The pain doctor suggested that Mr. Morgan may have suffered "permanent brain damage" due to what he characterized as a concussion. He also stated that the 5 minutes of unconsciousness reflected a "fairly significant closed head injury." In my experience, such assessments, though not empirically supported, are not uncommon among physicians and other clinicians (e.g., psychologists) and the scientific literature suggests that they can be psychologically damaging (Ferguson, Mittenberg, Barone, & Schneider, 1999; Mittenberg, Canyock, Condit, & Patton, 2001; Mittenberg, DiGiulio, Perrin, & Bass, 1992; Suhr & Gunstad, 2005). Despite this bleak assessment, the pain doctor did not assign any work restrictions, though he did recommend a neuropsychological evaluation, which was completed 11 months postinjury.

Report

Following are the results and conclusions of the neuropsychological evaluation excerpted from the report prepared by the neuropsychologist retained by Mr. Morgan's attorney. Where possible, raw scores have been removed from the text and presented in tables. Raw data were not available and the actual test scores were often not presented. Table 7.1 lists the procedures administered, and Tables 7.2 and 7.3 list the scores for these procedures (when reported).

TABLE 7.1. Procedures Administered

• Aphasia Screening Exam	• Post Mild Traumatic Brain Injury
• Behavioral Dyscontrol Scale	Symptom Checklist
• California Verbal Learning Test–2	• Sensory Perceptual Examination
• Cognitive symptom checklists	• Stroop Test
• Conners' Continuous Performance	• Tactual Performance Test
Test—Second Edition	• Test of Memory Malingering
• Controlled Oral Word Association Test	• Trail Making Test
• Finger Tapping Test	• Wechsler Test of Adult Reading
• Grooved Pegboard Test	• Wechsler Memory Scale–III
• Judgment of Line Orientation Test	• Wechsler Adult Intelligence Scale–III
• Paced Auditory Serial Addition Test	• Wisconsin Card Sorting Test
• Personality Assessment Inventory	

Examination Results

NEUROBEHAVIORAL STATUS

Mr. Morgan was appropriately attired with good personal hygiene and he maintained appropriate eye contact. There was no evidence of psychomotor retardation or excitement. Mr. Morgan was friendly and cooperative in his interactions with the examiner. There was no evidence that depression, anxiety, or pain interfered with his test performance. Affect was euthymic and sensorium was clear. Mr. Morgan had no difficulty understanding instructional sets. He was observed to put forth good effort

TABLE 7.2. Wechsler Adult Intelligence Scale–III and Wechsler Memory Scale–III Results

Wechsler Adult Intelligence Scale–III	Standard score	Percentile
Full Scale IQ	89	23
Verbal IQ	88	21
Performance IQ	91	27
Verbal Comprehension Index	88	21
Perceptual Organization Index	91	27
Processing Speed Index	103	58
Working Memory Index	92	30
Wechsler Memory Scale–III		
Auditory Immediate	94	34
Auditory Delayed	83	13
Auditory Recognition Delayed	Not reported	—
Visual Immediate	109	73
Visual Delayed	106	66
Working Memory Index	96	39

TABLE 7.3. Other Test Results

Test/variable	Score value	Derived score
Controlled Oral Word Association	40	T-score
Finger Tapping Test	WNL	
Grooved Pegboard Test (Nondominant)	41	T-score
Stroop Test		
Word	44	T-score
Color	52	T-score
Paced Auditory Serial Addition Test	30	T-score
California Verbal Learning Test–II		
Trials 1–5 total recall score	75	Percentile
Judgement of Line Orientation	9	Percentile
Trail Making Test A	39	T-score
Trail Making Test B	34	T-score
Wisconsin Card Sorting Test		
Categories Completed	≤ 1	Percentile
% Perseverative Errors	29	T-score
Failure to Maintain Set	≥ 16	Percentile
Tactual Performance Test (TPT)		
Initial dominant hand performance	39	T-score
Nondominant hand performance	34	T-score
Both hands performance	36	T-score
Incidental memory score	38	T-score
Location score	30	T-score

Note. WNL, within normal limits.

throughout the evaluative process. Specific assessment of effort was undertaken via administration of the Test of Memory Malingering (TOMM). Mr. Morgan's performance on the TOMM was well within stringent criteria consistent with our observation of providing good effort. The obtained test results are viewed as a valid sample of his present functioning.

LANGUAGE FUNCTIONS

The evaluation failed to reveal any evidence of aphasic symptomatology. Conversational speech was prosodic, fluent, and of normal rate and tone without evidence of dysarthria or paraphasic errors. Mr. Morgan's performance on a formal test of verbal fluency was below average. There was no evidence of word-finding difficulties in conversational speech and no evidence of receptive language dysfunction.

SENSORY–MOTOR FUNCTIONING

Evaluation failed to reveal any evidence of imperceptions or suppressions affecting tactile, auditory, or visual modalities during unilateral or bilateral stimulation paradigms. Mr. Morgan made a few unsystematic errors on a tactile finger recognition test as well as a test of graphesthsia. He had no difficulty recognizing gross tactile forms in each of his extremities.

Mr. Morgan reports being right-hand dominant. He was observed to ambulate without difficulty or complaint. Mr. Morgan's performance on a test demanding fine motor speed (Finger Tapping Test), was within average limits. On a test demanding fine motor speed and dexterity (Grooved Pegboard Test), he was mildly below average with regard to the nondominant hand.

ATTENTION/MEMORY FUNCTIONING

Mr. Morgan was errorless in his performance on a test of extended information and orientation. On the Stroop Test, he demonstrated adequate processing speed for word and color stimuli; he did not demonstrate a decrement in his performance on a divided attentional task. Mr. Morgan's performance on Wechsler Adult Intelligence Scale–III (WAIS-III) tasks assessing working memory placed his score at the 30th percentile. Mr. Morgan demonstrated difficulty meeting the demands of the Paced Auditory Serial Addition Test (PASAT), a measure of information-processing speed and attentional regulation. Observation of his test performance revealed him to be slow in the initial trial performance with significant decrements as the trials became more rapid and demanding. His total score on the PASAT was suggestive of mild impairment for someone of his age and educational level.

Mr. Morgan was administered the Conners' Continuous Performance Test—Second Edition (CPT-II) to further assess his attentional skills; his performance was suggestive of impairment. The CPT discriminant function indicated that the results better matched a clinical than nonclinical profile at a confidence index of 98.8%. Observation of the test performance revealed that he was generally erratic in his responding, indicative of poor attentional capacity. He was negatively affected by changes in the interstimulus interval. Specifically, his responses became more erratic and inconsistent when the interstimulus interval was slowed from 1 second to 2 and 4 seconds. The finding may reflect difficulties in adapting to changes in task requirements. There was also evidence of difficulty sustaining attention as Mr. Morgan's reaction times became more erratic as the test administration progressed.

Mr. Morgan was administered the Wechsler Memory Scale–III (WMS-III) to assess different components of anterograde memory. His performance on tasks assessing immediate auditory memory placed him at the 34th percentile. Mr. Morgan was more efficient in his performance on tasks assessing immediate visual memory. He demonstrated difficulties retaining auditory information after a delay, but an adequate ability to retain and recall visual information after a delay. Mr. Morgan's performance on WMS-III tasks assessing working memory placed his score at the 39th percentile.

Analysis of separate WMS-III scale performance revealed Mr. Morgan to have an average ability to immediately learn and recall orally presented narrative passages. He demonstrated weakness in his performance on a verbal paired-associate task. He was above average on a facial recognition test and in the average range on a task demanding free recall of family pictorial stimuli. Mr. Morgan showed a low-average ability to retain and recall previously learned narrative passages after a delay (70% retention). Immediate learning and reproduction of visual designs placed his performance at the 25th percentile. He showed a good ability to retain and reconstruct previously learned visual designs after a delay (83% retention).

Mr. Morgan was administered the California Verbal Learning Test–2 (CVLT-2), a repetitive word list learning task. His total recall score after five administrations of the word list placed him at the 75th percentile compared to age-related peers. Observation of his test performance revealed a good initial learning trial as well as an ability to profit from repetitive administrations. Mr. Morgan demonstrated an adequate ability to retain word list information in a short delay, free recall process. He was mildly below expected performance on a long delay, free and cued recall process. Assessment of learning characteristics revealed poor recall from the primacy region of the word list; there were mildly excessive intrusive errors. Mr. Morgan's performance on a recognition test revealed a good ability to discriminate target from nontarget words, though he made a high rate of false-positive errors (13). Mr. Morgan was errorless in his performance on a long delay, forced-choice recognition test consistent with our observation of providing good effort.

VISUAL–SPATIAL/VISUAL CONSTRUCTIONAL FUNCTIONS

There was no evidence of visual inattention, constructional difficulties, or neglect. Mr. Morgan's performance on WAIS-III tasks assessing perceptual/organizational skills placed his score at the 27th percentile. He demonstrated variability in his performance across visual–spatial tasks. He was above average on a task demanding attention to visual detail in the tangible environment. In contrast, he demonstrated weakness in his performance on the matrix reasoning test, a test demanding nonverbal planning and sequencing of meaningful stimuli, and a test demanding analysis and construction of spatial relations. Mr. Morgan's performance on a test demanding fine discriminations of lines in space placed his score at the 9th percentile. Yet, the pattern of his errors suggested that concentration difficulties, rather than spatial impairment, were the likely causes.

On a visual–graphic sequencing test involving the serial processing of numbers, Mr. Morgan was slow in his completion of the test but did not make any confusional errors. When the task became more demanding, involving alternation between numbers and letters in sequential fashion, his performance was suggestive of mild to moderate impairment and he was noted to make several confusional errors.

HIGHER REASONING/PROBLEM-SOLVING SKILLS

Mr. Morgan had no difficulties inhibiting and sequencing fine motor movements on go/no-go types of tasks. He was below average in his performance on a word generativity test. He also demonstrated difficulties meeting the set shifting requirements of the Trail Making Test B, which is suggestive of mild executive dysfunction.

Mr. Morgan was administered the WAIS-III classifying his intellectual functioning to be in the low average to average range with a Full Scale IQ of 89, a Verbal IQ of 88, and a Performance IQ of 91. His Full Scale IQ places him at the 23rd percentile compared to age-related peers. WAIS-III analysis revealed Mr. Morgan to be efficient in his performance on tests assessing processing speed. He scored in the low range of average on WAIS-III tasks assessing working memory, perceptual organizational skills, and verbal comprehension skills.

Analysis of separate WAIS-III subtests revealed significant weakness on a verbal task demanding the finding of a common construct between disparate items (5th percentile). Mr. Morgan demonstrated strengths on tests demanding rapid psychomotor coding of symbolic stimuli as well as attention to visual detail in the environment.

Mr. Morgan was administered the Wechsler Test of Adult Reading (WTAR) to attain a prediction of his premorbid intellectual/memory functioning. His score on the WTAR provided a provision of WAIS-III scores that were consistent with that obtained in the current evaluation. The WTAR-predicted WMS-III scores were also consistent with the scores obtained in the current evaluation.

Mr. Morgan was administered the Wisconsin Card Sorting Test (WCST). He demonstrated difficulties in his capacity to methodically generate and discover the correct hypotheses as well as to shift the basis of his responding when the externally imposed demands of the task necessitated this. Mr. Morgan attained only one of the expected six categories with a significant rate of perseverative errors (32%) and one failure to maintain set.

Mr. Morgan was administered the Tactual Performance Test (TPT), which demands keen kinesthetic/proprioceptive abilities as well as organizational/planning skills. His initial dominant-hand performance was suggestive of mild impairment and he had difficulties profiting from the initial learning trial during his second trial, nondominant hand performance as well as his third trial, both-hands performance. His incidental memory score as well as his location score were suggestive of mild to moderate impairment.

EMOTIONAL/PSYCHOLOGICAL FUNCTIONING

Mr. Morgan reports continuing cervical and lower back pain. He was described by his wife as having a change in his emotional/personality functioning with low frustration tolerance, impatience, and increased irritability. During the interview, he acknowledged some recent episodes of sadness secondary to the loss of significant people in his life. He expressed concern regarding the persistence of sleep disturbance in the middle of the night due to the interfering effects of pain. He also acknowledged increased irritability as well as a tendency toward social withdrawal and reduced interest in interpersonal relations.

Mr. Morgan completed the Personality Assessment Inventory (PAI) to further assess his psychological functioning. His response set indicated that he presented himself in an honest, straightforward fashion. He reported significant suspiciousness and hostility in his relations with others. He also reported that he occasionally experiences, to a mild degree, maladaptive behavior patterns aimed at controlling anxiety. This appears related to his increased fearfulness and vigilance when in close proximity to tractor-trailer trucks. Self-concept was reported to be stable and generally positive. Interpersonally, Mr. Morgan is likely to be a rather unassuming individual who generally prefers to avoid leadership roles in social interactions and relationships. He denied being disturbed by thoughts of self-harm. His responses to the PAI did not suggest highly disruptive depression, anxiety, or being overly complaining of pain difficulties.

Mrs. Morgan provided further information regarding her husband via completion of the Post Mild Traumatic Brain Injury Symptom Checklist. She noted that at times. Mr. Morgan has episodes of dizziness and a loss of balance. There was also a report of severe (frequently present and disrupts activities) difficulties with concentration, making decisions, slowed thinking, fatigue, sleep disturbance, irritability/easily annoyed, and poor frustration tolerance.

Mr. Morgan completed multiple cognitive symptom checklists identifying internal distractors to his ability to attend and concentrate. Internal distractors include fatigue, headache, pain, and physical discomfort, as well as episodic dizziness. He also complained of the manner in which he "gets angry quickly." He is overly stressed and at times experiences intrusive recollections of the traumatic MVA. There was a significant endorsement of being easily distracted because of difficulties with sustained, divided, and simultaneous attentional capacities. Mr. Morgan also complained of significant memory difficulties and executive dysfunction in day-to-day pursuits affecting his processing speed and reaction time, initiating and following through on tasks, planning, sequencing, and organizational skills. With regard to language functions, there was not a high rate of complaints other than difficulties organizing speech and talking at a speed that others can understand easily. There was also report of memory difficulties in his day-to-day pursuits.

Summary/Integration

Mr. Morgan is a 40-year-old married male who is status postconcussion and multiple traumas sustained in an MVA (11 months prior to this evaluation). He has returned to employment capacities but is experiencing persistent difficulties as a result of injuries sustained in the MVA.

Neuropsychological evaluation revealed results consistent with Mr. Morgan's complaints with evidence of a decreased capacity to sustain his attention/concentration, particularly manifesting on multiprocessing tasks. Indeed, Mr. Morgan's decreased capacity for attention/concentration appears to be his primary deficit leading to the experience of decreased memory functioning in his everyday pursuits. Neurocognitive evaluation revealed intellectual functioning to be in the low-average range. Generally, Mr. Morgan's performance on tests assessing anterograde memory was consistent with his intellectual abilities. He demonstrated weakness in his performance on visual–spatial tasks, though this was viewed as likely secondary to the interfering effects of attention/concentration deficits. There was no evidence of receptive or expressive language dysfunction, sensory–perceptual disturbance, or motor difficulties, though Mr. Morgan does have complaints of episodic dizziness/vertigo that result in balance problems.

Mr. Morgan continues to experience multisite pain, particularly affecting the cervical region as well as the neck/shoulder and lower back. I am in agreement with the recent evaluation by the pain management doctor regarding the residual negative impact associated with these chronic pain difficulties. Headaches persist and are posttraumatic in origin and also likely result from radiating pain from the cervical region. Cervical discomfort is particularly triggered by Mr. Morgan's employment capacities as a truck driver. In addition to chronic pain and discomfort, he is experiencing a significant sleep disturbance that is worthy of formal intervention. There are also social executive changes common to the postconcussive and chronic pain syndrome including increased irritability, low frustration tolerance, and impatience.

It appears that Mr. Morgan is experiencing neurocognitive impairments due to the interfering effects of his chronic pain syndrome as well as the residuals of a concussive head injury. Relative to the effects associated with a severe TBI, his neurocognitive impairments are minor and primarily interfere with his capacity to sustain his attention/concentration and effectively meet the demands of multiprocessing tasks. Table 7.4 presents the neuropsychologist's diagnostic impressions.

With regard to treatment, the following recommendations are offered:

1. Mr. Morgan is in need of continuing care as proposed by the pain management doctor to assist with his ongoing pain difficulties. Improved management could involve injections or a return to physical therapy.

2. Mr. Morgan is in need of assistance with regard to his sleep disturbance and excessive fatigue. It is likely that he would profit from placement on a soporific agent to assist him in attaining a healthier sleep pattern.

3. Mr. Morgan is experiencing neurocognitive impairments primarily affecting his attentional capacities. Improved management and relief from pain as well as improved sleep could allow for an improvement in his attentional capacities. If attentional difficulties persist with improvement in pain and sleep disturbance, he would be an appropriate candidate for consideration of a sustained release psychostimulant such as Concerta or Adderall XR or use of a nonstimulant such as Strattera or Provigil to assist with his residual attentional difficulties as"the result of a concussive head injury.

TABLE 7.4. Multiaxial Diagnoses of the Evaluating Neuropsychologist Based on the *Diagnostic and Statistical Manual of Mental Disorders—Fourth Edition* (DSM-IV)

Axis I
294.90 cognitive disorder not otherwise specified secondary to the interfering effects of chronic pain, fatigue, and residuals of a concussive head injury 307.89 pain disorder associated with both psychological factors and a general medical condition

Axis II
V71.09 No diagnosis

Axis III
Cervical/lower back pain; posttraumatic headache; episodic dizziness/vertigo; status post head injury; hypertension; gastroesophageal reflux disease

Axis IV
Need for improved management of pain; workers' compensation

Axis V
GAF = 62 (current)

Analysis

The following text is based on the summary from my written review of this case that I submitted to defense counsel. The text has been modified slightly and supplemented (the section on pain) for this chapter but is essentially unchanged from the original.

Issues Related to Mild Traumatic Brain Injury

Mr. Morgan suffered a blow to the head and was initially diagnosed with a concussion. Later, this was characterized as a mild head injury, which is a roughly synonymous term (Iverson, 2005). His GCS score at the scene was 15/15 and he was found to be fully alert. It appears that he had a brief period of posttraumatic amnesia but there is no independent, objective evidence of any loss of consciousness. However, even if he was unresponsive for 5 minutes, the classification of the severity of this injury would not change, nor would the expected outcome. In short, Mr. Morgan suffered a blow to the head and suffered a brief alteration of consciousness.

According to the criteria of the Mild Traumatic Brain Injury Committee of the Head Injury Interdisciplinary Special Interest Group of the American Congress of Rehabilitation Medicine (1993), patients are considered to have suffered a mild TBI (concussion) if the following are present: (1) posttraumatic amnesia (PTA) not greater than 24 hours; (2) after 30 minutes, an initial GCS score of 13–15; (3) loss of consciousness of approximately 30 minutes or less. Thus, it is clear that Mr. Morgan suffered a concussion.

The research literature on simple concussion is extensive (see Iverson, 2005, for an excellent summary). Deficits following such an injury usually involve attention, concentration, and slowed cognitive speed. Cognitive impairment due to concussion gradually resolves over time with the direct neurological and cognitive effects resolving in 3 months or less (Belanger, Curtiss, Demery, Lebowitz, & Vanderploeg, 2005). Delayed onset or worsening of deficits is not consistent with the expected pattern of recovery following a concussion (Alexander, 1995). At 1 year, for most of these patients, performance on neuropsychological testing is no different from patients who only suffered physical trauma but no head injury (Dikmen et al., 1994). In the absence of objective brain pathology, symptoms persisting for more than a year are often associated with premorbid psychological factors, emotional problems, pain, stress, litigation, and/or malingering (Belanger et al., 2005; Carroll et al., 2004).

It is important to recognize that problems with attention, concentration, and processing speed are nonspecific (as are the symptoms attributed to postconcussion syndrome) (Iverson, 2005). This means that their presence is not diagnostic of any particular condition. This was acknowledged by the neuropsychologist when he concluded that Mr. Morgan's test performance was affected by his chronic pain syndrome.

It is worth pointing out that cognitive test performance can be adversely impacted by suggesting to a patient that a mild brain injury can cause persistent, or even permanent, cognitive problems (Ferguson et al., 1999; Mittenberg et al., 1992; Suhr & Gunstad, 2005). This finding is supported by the work of Mittenberg and colleagues (2001) who noted that advising patients that their concussions would produce initial problems that should resolve resulted in a lower rate of postconcussive complications. The implication was that the patient's expectation of outcome could significantly influence that outcome. Unfortunately, this means that the pain management doctor, by incorrectly suggesting to Mr. Morgan the possibility that the concussion could have caused permanent brain damage, may have unwittingly contributed to his persistent symptoms.

The scientific literature (cf. Iverson, 2005) suggests that any cognitive impairment due to the effects of a concussion even when neuropsychologically evaluated 11 months postinjury, had resolved. Therefore, it would be incorrect to attribute any cognitive deficits to the direct neurological effects of that injury. It was correct, however, to suggest that pain (Eccleston, 1994; Kewman, Vaishampayan, Zald, & Han, 1991), pain medications (Eccleston, 1994, 1995; Ravnkilde et al., 2002), lack of sleep (Menefee et al., 2000), and psychological distress (Brown, Glass, & Park, 2002; Fishbain, Cutler, Rosomoff, & Rosomoff, 1999; Iezzi, Duckworth, Vuong, Archibald, & Klinck, 2004) may have adversely affected his test performance and his day-to-day functioning.

Issues Related to Malingering

It is important to recognize the potential for malingering in a case like this. Indeed, it is well established that financial incentive is related to outcome following brain injury, with the effect of money being the strongest at the mild end of the severity continuum (Bianchini, Curtis, & Greve, 2006; Binder, 1986; Binder & Rohling, 1996; Paniak et al., 2002; Price & Stevens, 1997; Reynolds, Paniak, Toller-Lobe, & Nagy, 2003; Youngjohn, Burrows, & Erda, 1995). A similar effect is observed in chronic pain (Harris, Mulford, Solomon, van Gelder, & Young, 2005; Rohling, Binder, & Langhinrichsen-Rohling, 1995). One might tend to discount the possibility of malingering because Mr. Morgan demonstrated grossly intact cognitive, especially memory, function and because he passed the TOMM. Yet, two points are relevant here.

First, the examination of malingering in Mr. Morgan's evaluation was incomplete. A negative finding on any malingering test, especially any one malingering test, cannot be used to rule out the presence of malingering (Greve & Bianchini, 2004; Millis & Volinsky, 2001; Slick, Sherman, &

Iverson, 1999). In particular, a negative finding on the TOMM cannot be used in this way. Indeed, there is significant information in the public domain regarding the TOMM so it may be easy to obtain enough information about this test to avoid detection (Bauer & McCaffrey, 2006). Also, empirically, the TOMM may fail to identify between 40 and 60% of malingerers at the standard cutoffs (Greve, Bianchini, & Doane, 2006). At the same time, it appears that the neuropsychologist failed to consider a range of other empirically studied and published scores and indicators of malingering that can be derived from the clinical tests he gave (e.g., WAIS, WMS, CVLT, and WCST) and that could have informed his conclusions about the presence of malingering and symptom exaggeration.

Second, because Mr. Morgan's symptom presentation is largely related to chronic pain, it is possible that he did not malinger or exaggerate cognitive symptoms but has exaggerated pain-related (emotional, somatic) problems. A review of issues in the detection and diagnosis of pain-related malingering is available in the literature (Bianchini, Greve, & Glynn, 2005). Regarding exaggeration or malingering of pain-related problems, this evaluation is also incomplete. The neuropsychologist used the PAI to assess psychological issues. While this is a psychometrically sound instrument that is very popular among neuropsychologists, it is not well validated for the detection of malingering and lacks scales that are sensitive to malingered somatic complaints. In contrast, there is a research literature for the Minnesota Multiphasic Personality Inventory–2 (MMPI-2) in this regard (e.g., Greve, Bianchini, Love, Brennan, & Heinly, 2006; Larrabee, 1998, 2003; Lees-Haley, English, & Glenn, 1991). Moreover, there is a general chronic pain literature on the MMPI-2, which makes it extremely valuable for the assessment of patients with chronic pain, particularly in identifying psychological involvement in pain complaints and obstacles to effective physical and behavioral management of pain (e.g., Block, Gatchell, Deardorff, & Guyer, 2003).

Issues Related to Chronic Pain

Mr. Morgan reported persisting pain and continuing medical pain management was recommended by the evaluating neuropsychologist. There are a number of psychosocial factors known to complicate recovery in pain-related conditions. Among these are the presence of (1) childhood trauma, neglect, or loss; (2) current psychosocial stressors independent of the accident/injury for which compensation was being sought; (3) previous psychiatric illness and treatment; (4) previous problems with pain and pain-related problems; (5) surgery for the current pain problem; (6) other factors that might complicate recovery but that are not easily placed in one of the foregoing categories (Proctor, Gatchel, & Robinson, 2000; Schofferman, Anderson, Hines, Smith, & White, 1992).

Mr. Morgan presented with pain attributed to soft tissue injury; it had persisted for over a year, and it had not responded to medical treatments. He reported to the neuropsychologist that he had a father who "used to drink excessively," which raises the possibility that this patient is what is referred to as a "high risk" or "psychologically complicated" pain patient (an MMPI-2 would have been illuminating for this reason). Recent research has shown that the presence of psychological complication can meaning-fully impact outcome, including response to treatment, in patients with pain (Block et al., 2003; Gatchel & Gardea, 1999; Linton, 2000).

The psychologically complicated pain patient has a number of obsta-cles to successful outcome (Gatchel, 2004) but may be effectively treated if functional restoration programs address their psychological issues (Bailey, Freedenfeld, Kiser, & Gatchel, 2003; Block et al., 2003; Gatchel, Adams, Polatin, & Kishino, 2002). Functional restoration (e.g., Mayer et al., 1998) represents an important departure from more traditional, purely medical/physical approaches to the treatment of pain and pain-related disability.

Functional restoration approaches feature a combination of rehabilita-tion practices combined with careful assessment of how psychological factors are impacting symptom reports and thus treatment. Lebovits (2000) has pointed out that the management of chronic pain includes both a careful psy-chological screening to ensure patient appropriateness for medical proce-dures and the use of more conservative treatments such as cognitive-behav-ioral interventions implemented within a multidisciplinary approach. Thus, when practiced properly (see Gatchel, 2005), this approach helps to identify patients who are at high risk for psychological complications and uses inter-vention strategies that consider those complicating psychological factors. In keeping with the rehabilitation tradition, there is also typically an explicit em-phasis on rehabilitating function and less focus on simply treating symptoms.

Summary

What were the major points made to the retaining attorney to guide his ne-gotiations with the plaintiff's attorney?

1. The available records indicate that Mr. Morgan suffered a concus-sion in the accident in question. The brain dysfunction associated with con-cussion resolves naturally and completely. Persisting cognitive deficits fol-lowing concussion are due to other factors, which include psychopathology (including preexisting conditions), medical illness, and malingering.

2. Persisting cognitive problems following concussion can be pre-vented or minimized simply by providing accurate information about the normal course of recovery following concussion; they can be created or ag-gravated by the provision of inaccurate information regarding that course. It is thus possible that some of Mr. Morgan's clinicians contributed to his

persisting complaints by providing that kind inaccurate information and creating negative expectations regarding his injury (an iatrogenic effect).

3. It is reasonable to conclude that a pain syndrome and related problems (e.g., insomnia) can produce the kinds of attention/concentration problems reported by the patient and documented on formal cognitive testing. If Mr. Morgan's attention and concentration problems were a consequence of his chronic pain, then effective management of that chronic pain (e.g., functional restoration) may reasonably be expected to reduce those problems.

4. Given inconsistencies in subjective pain report and objective findings described in the records, questions of whether Mr. Morgan was continuing to experience pain and the extent to which that pain was causing functional disability remained unresolved.

5. The potential for symptom exaggeration/fabrication (including malingering) must be considered and thoroughly examined. This had not been done, so exaggeration/fabrication could not reasonably be ruled out as a factor in this patient's test performance and functional complaints.

Epilogue

Discussion of the information outlined previously was part of settlement negotiations. The plaintiff attorney found the cited literature to be persuasive and all parties agreed to a final award that was less than the original demand.

ACKNOWLEDGMENTS

I would like to thank Kevin Bianchini for his important contributions to my professional development and to our joint research activities. Kevin taught me how to do pain psychology and how to survive in the forensic environment. He is also the driving force conceptually behind our pain research program. Much of this chapter was inspired by his creative conceptual insights.

REFERENCES

Alexander, M. P. (1995). Mild traumatic brain injury: Pathophysiology, natural history, and clinical management. *Neurology, 45*, 1253–1260.

Bailey, B. E., Freedenfeld, R. N., Kiser, R. S, & Gatchel, R. J. (2003). Lifetime physical and sexual abuse in chronic pain patients: Psychosocial correlates and treatment outcomes. *Disability and Rehabilitation, 25*, 331–342.

Bauer, L., & McCaffrey, R. J. (2006). Coverage of the Test of Memory Malingering, Victoria Symptom Validity Test, and Word Memory Test on the Internet: Is test security threatened? *Archives of Clinical Neuropsychology, 21*, 121–126.

Belanger, H. G., Curtiss, G., Demery, J. A., Lebowitz, B. K., & Vanderploeg, R. D. (2005). Factors moderating neuropsychological outcomes following mild traumatic brain injury: A meta-analysis. *Journal of the International Neuropsychological Society, 11*, 215–27.

Bianchini, K. J., Curtis, K. L., & Greve, K. W. (2006). Compensation and malingering in traumatic brain injury: A dose–response relationship? *The Clinical Neuropsychologist, 20,*
831–847.

Bianchini, K. J., Greve, K. W., & Glynn, G. (2005). On the diagnosis of malingered pain-related
disability: Lessons from cognitive malingering research. *The Spine Journal, 5,* 404–417.

Binder, L. M. (1986). Persisting symptoms after mild head injury: A review of the postconcussion
syndrome. *Journal of Clinical and Experimental Neuropsychology, 8,* 323–346.

Binder, L. M., & Rohling, M. L. (1996). Money matters: A meta-analytic review of the effects of financial incentives on recovery after closed-head injury. *American Journal of Psychiatry, 153,* 7–10.

Block, A. R., Gatchell, R. J., Deardorff, W. W., & Guyer, R. D. (2003). *The psychology of spine
surgery.* Washington, DC: American Psychiatric Association.

Brown, S. C., Glass, J. M., & Park, D. C. (2002). The relationship of pain and depression to cognitive function in rheumatoid arthritis patients. *Pain, 96,* 279–284.

Carroll, L. J., Cassidy, J. D., Peloso, P. M., Borg, J., von Holst, H., Holm, L., et al. (2004). Prognosis for mild traumatic brain injury: Results of the WHO Collaborating Centre Task Force on
Mild Traumatic Brain Injury. *Journal of Rehabilitation Medicine, 43*(Suppl.), 84–105.

Cassidy, D. C., Carroll, L, J., Cote, P., Lemstra, M., Berglund, A., & Nygren, A. (2000). Effect of
eliminating compensation for pain and suffering on the outcome of insurance claims for
whiplash injuries. *New England Journal of Medicine, 342,* 1179–1186.

Dikmen, S. S., Temkin, N. R., Machamer, J. E., Holubkov, A. L., Fraser, R. T., & Winn, H. R. (1994).
Employment following traumatic head injuries. *Archives of Neurology, 51,* 177–186.

Dvir, Z., & Keating, J. (2001). Reproducibility and validity of a new test protocol for measuring
isokinetic trunk extension strength. *Clinical Biomechanics, 16,* 627–630.

Eccleston, C. (1994). Chronic pain and attention: A cognitive approach. *British Journal of Clinical Psychology, 33,* 535–547.

Eccleston, C. (1995). Chronic pain and distraction: An experimental investigation into the role
of sustained and shifting attention in the processing of chronic persistent pain. *Behavior
Research and Therapy, 33,* 391–405.

Ferguson, R. J., Mittenberg, W., Barone, D. F., & Schneider, B. (1999). Postconcussion syndrome following sports-related head injury: Expectation as etiology. *Neuropsychology, 13,* 582–589.

Fishbain, D. A., Cutler, R., Rosomoff, H. L., & Rosomoff, R. S. (1999). Chronic pain disability
exaggeration/malingering and submaximal effort research. *Clinical Journal of Pain, 15,*
244–274.

Frymoyer, J. W., & Cats-Baril, W. L. (1991). An overview of the incidence and costs of low back
pain. *Orthopedic Clinics of North America, 22,* 263–271.

Gatchel, R. J. (2005). *Clinical essentials of pain management.* Washington, DC: American Psychological Association.

Gatchel, R. J., Adams, L., Polatin, P. B., & Kishino, N. D. (2002). Secondary loss and pain-asso-
ciated disability: Theoretical overview and treatment implications. *Journal of Occupational Rehabilitation, 12,* 99–110.

Gatchel, R. J., & Gardea, M. A. (1999). Psychosocial issues: their importance in predicting disability, response to treatment, and search for compensation. *Neurologic Clinics, 17,* 149–166.

George, C. (2002). The six-month incidence of clinically significant low back pain in the
Saskatchean adult population. *Spine, 27,* 1778–1782.

Greve, K. W., & Bianchini, K. J. (2004). Setting empirical cut-offs on psychometric indicators of
negative response bias: A methodological commentary with recommendations. *Archives
of Clinical Neuropsychology, 19,* 533–541.

Greve, K. W., Bianchini, K. J., & Doane, B. M. (2006). Classification accuracy of the Test of
Memory Malingering in traumatic brain injury: Results of a known-groups analysis. *Journal of Clinical and Experimental Neuropsychology, 28,* 1176–1190.

Greve, K. W., Bianchini, K. J., Love, J. M., Brennan, A., & Heinly, M. T. (2006). Sensitivity and
specificity of MMPI-2 Validity scales and indicators to malingered neurocognitive dysfunction in traumatic brain injury. *The Clinical Neuropsychologist, 20,* 491–512.

Guo, H. R., Tanaka, S., Cameron, L. L., Seligman, P. J., Behrens, V. J., Ger, J., et al. (1995). Back pain among workers in the United States: national estimates and workers at high risk. *American Journal of Industrial Medicine, 28,* 591–602.

Guo, H. R., Tanaka, S., Halperin, W. E., & Cameron, L. L. (1999). Back pain prevalence in US industry and estimates of lost workdays. *American Journal of Public Health, 89,* 1029–1035.

Hardin, J. G., & Halla, J. T. (1995). Cervical spine and radicular pain syndromes. *Current Opinion in Rheumatology, 7,* 136–140.

Harris, I., Mulford, J., Solomon, M., van Gelder, J. M., & Young, J. (2005). Association between compensation status and outcome after surgery: A meta-analysis. *Journal of the American Medical Association, 293,* 1644–1652.

Hazard, R. G., Reeves, V., & Fenwick J. W. (1992). Lifting capacity: Indices of subject effort. *Spine, 17,* 1065–1070.

Iezzi, T., Duckworth, M. P., Vuong, L N., Archibald, Y. M., & Klinck, A. (2004). Predictors of neurocognitive performance in chronic pain patients. *International Journal of Behavioral Medicine, 11,* 56–61.

Iverson, G. L. (2005). Outcome from mild traumatic brain injury. *Current Opinions in Psychiatry, 18,* 301–317

Kewman, D. G., Vaishampayan, N., Zald, D., & Han, B. (1991). Cognitive impairment in musculoskeletal pain patients. *International Journal of Psychiatry in Medicine, 21,* 253–262.

Larrabee, G. J. (1998). Somatic malingering on the MMPI and MMPI-2 in personal injury litigants. *The Clinical Neuropsychologist, 12,* 179–188.

Larrabee, G. J. (2003). Exaggerated MMPI-2 symptom report in personal injury litigants with malingered neurocognitive deficit. *Archives of Clinical Neuropsychology, 18,* 673–676.

Lebovits, A. H. (2000). The psychological assessment of patients with chronic pain. *Current Review of Pain, 4,* 122–126.

Lees-Haley, P. R., English, L. T., & Glenn, W. J. (1991). A fake bad scale on the MMPI-2 for personal injury claimants. *Psychological Reports, 68,* 203–210.

Linton, S. J. (2000). A review of psychological risk factors in back and neck pain. *Spine, 25,* 1148–1156.

Mayer, T., McMahon, M. J., Gatchel, R. J., Sparks, B., Wright, A., & Pegues, P. (1998). Socioeconomic outcomes of combined spine surgery and functional restoration in workers' compensation spinal disorders with matched controls. *Spine, 23,* 598–605.

Menefee, L. A., Cohen, M. J. M., Anderson, W. R., Doghramji, K., Frank, E. D., & Lee, H. (2000). Sleep disturbance and nonmalignant chronic pain: A comprehensive review of the literature. *Pain Medicine, 1,* 156–172.

Mild Traumatic Brain Injury Committee of the Head Injury Interdisciplinary Special Interest Group of the American Congress of Rehabilitation Medicine. (1993). Definition of mild traumatic brain injury. *Journal of Head Trauma Rehabilitation, 8,* 86–87

Millis, S. R., & Volinsky, C. T (2001). Assessment of response bias in mild head injury: Beyond malingering tests. *Journal of Clinical and Experimental Neuropsychology, 23,* 809–828.

Mittenberg, W., Canyock, E. M., Condit, D., & Patton, C. (2001). Treatment of post-concussion syndrome following mild head injury. *Journal of Clinical and Experimental Neuropsychology, 23,* 829–836.

Mittenberg, W., DiGiulio, D. V., Perrin, S., & Bass, A. E. (1992) Symptoms following mild head injury: Expectation as aetiology. *Journal of Neurology, Neurosurgery, and Psychiatry, 55,* 200–204.

Morken, T., Riise, T., Moen, B., Bergum, O., Vigeland-Hauge, S. H., Holien, S., et al. (2002). Frequent musculoskeletal symptoms and reduced health-related quality of life among industrial workers. *Occupational Medicine, 52,* 91–98.

Navin, F., Zein, S., & Felipe, E. (2000). Road safety engineering: An effective tool in the fight against whiplash injuries. *Accident Analysis and Prevention, 32,* 271–275.

NIH Consensus Development Panel on Rehabilitation of Persons with Traumatic Brain Injury.

(1999). Rehabilitation of persons with traumatic brain injury. *Journal of the American Medical Association, 282,* 974–983.

Novack, T. A., Bush, B. A., Meythaler, J. M., & Canupp, K. (2001). Outcome after traumatic brain injury: Pathway analysis of contributions from premorbid, injury severity, and recovery variables. *Archives of Physical Medicine and Rehabilitation, 82,* 300–305.

Paniak, C., Reynolds, S., Toller-Lobe, G., Melnyk, A., Nagy, J., & Schmidt, D. (2002). A longitudinal study of the relationship between financial compensation and symptoms after treated mild traumatic brain injury. *Journal of Clinical and Experimental Neuropsychology, 24,* 187–193.

Picavet, H. S., & Schouten, J. S. (2003). Musculoskeletal pain in the Netherlands: Prevelences, consequences and risk groups, the DMC3–study. *Pain, 102,* 167–178.

Price, J. R., & Stevens, K. B. (1997). Psycholegal implications of malingered head trauma. *Applied Neuropsychology, 4,* 75–83.

Proctor, T., Gatchel, R. J., & Robinson, R. C. (2000). Psychosocial factors and risk of pain and disability. *Occupational Medicine, 15,* 803–812

Rainville, J., Sobel, J. B., Hartigan, C., & Wright, A. (1997). The effect of compensation involvement on the reporting of pain and disability by patients referred for rehabilitation of chronic low back pain. *Spine, 22,* 2016–2024.

Ravnkilde, B., Videbech, P., Clemmensen, K., Egander, A., Rasmussen, N. A., & Rosenberg, R. (2002). Cognitive deficits in major depression. *Scandinavian Journal of Psychology, 43,* 239–251.

Reynolds, S., Paniak, C., Toller-Lobe, G., & Nagy, J. (2003). A longitudinal study of compensation-seeking and return to work in a treated mild traumatic brain injury sample. *Journal of Head Trauma Rehabilitation, 18,* 139–147.

Rohling, M. L., Binder, L. M., & Langhinrichsen-Rohling, J. (1995). A metal-analytic review of the association between financial compensation and the experience and treatment of chronic pain. *Health Psychology, 14,* 537–547.

Rose, J. M. (2005). Continuum of care model for managing mild traumatic brain injury in a workers compensation context: A description of the model and its development. *Brain Injury, 19,* 29–39.

Schofferman, J., Anderson, D., Hines, R., Smith, G., & White, A. (1992). Childhood psychological trauma correlates with unsuccessful lumbar spine surgery. *Spine, 17*(6, Suppl.), S138–S144.

Slick, D. J., Sherman, E. M. S., & Iverson, G. L. (1999). Diagnostic criteria for malingering neurocognitive dysfunction: Proposed standards for clinical practice and research. *The Clinical Neuropsychologist, 13,* 545–561.

Suhr, J. A., & Gunstad, J. (2005). Further exploration of the effect of "diagnosis threat" on cognitive performance in individuals with mild head injury. *Journal of the International Neuropsychological Society, 11,* 23–29.

Tate, D. G. (1992). Worker's disability and return to work. *American Journal of Physical Medicine and Rehabilitation, 71,* 92–96.

Vaccaro, A. R., Ring, D., Scuderi, G., Cohen, D. S., & Garfin, S. R. (1997). Predictors of outcome inpatients with chronic back pain and low-grade spondylolisthesis. *Spine, 22,* 2030–2034.

van Tulder, M. W., Koes, B. W., & Bouter, L. M. (1995). A cost-of-illness study of back pain in the Netherlands. *Pain, 62,* 233–240.

Walker, B. F. (2000). The prevalence of low back pain: A systematic review of the literature from 1966 to 1998. *Journal of Spine Disorders, 13,* 205–217.

Woodwell, D. A., & Cherry, D. K. (2004). National Ambulatory Medical Care Survey: 2002 summary. *Advance Data, 26,* 1–44.

Wrona, R. M. (2006). The use of state workers' compensation administrative data to identify injury scenarios and quantify costs of work-related traumatic brain injuries. *Journal of Safety Research, 37,* 75–81.

Youngjohn, J. R., Burrows, L., & Erda, L. K. (1995). Brain damage or compensation neurosis?: The controversial post-concussion syndrome. *The Clinical Neuropsychologist, 9,* 112–123.

Part II
Forensic Case Analysis from Opposing Perspectives

8

Mild Head Injury Case from a Treating Neuropsychologist

NEUROPSYCHOLOGICAL EVALUATION

Name: Mrs. Patient
Date of birth: 8/12/57
Education: 12 years
Occupation: School teacher
Handedness: Right
Dates of exam: 9/13 and 9/20/03
Referral: Family physician

Identifying Information/Reason for Referral

Mrs. Patient is a 46-year-old, married, right-handed, Caucasian woman who was in a motor vehicle accident (MVA) on February 12, 1998 (almost 6 years ago). Her car was struck from behind and then it hit the vehicle in front of hers. There is no reported loss of consciousness, but she recalls "seeing stars," feeling lightheaded and nauseous. She also reports the immediate onset of headache and pain in her neck, low back, left knee, foot, and right thumb. She was seen in the emergency room (ER) at a local hospital the next day; results of X-rays were normal and she was discharged to the care of her primary physician and prescribed muscle relaxants, pain killers, and physical therapy. Mrs. Patient's primary persistent complaints include headache; problems with concentration, memory, and word retrieval; and pain in her knee and foot. She underwent a previous neuropsychological in October 1998 (8 months post-MVA). The present evaluation was for the purpose of assessing her current neurocognitive and emotional difficulties. The results are to be used to assist her physician in treatment planning.

Interview Information

The following information was obtained through an interview with Mrs. Patient. Emphasis is directed toward information relevant to understanding her current neurocognitive and emotional status. Accident-related and acute treatment information is contained in other records and was not available for review.

When asked about her current symptoms and complaints, Mrs. Patient reported that since the accident she has had persistent physical, cognitive, and emotional difficulties. Physically, she complains of pain in her left foot, left knee, back, and neck. She also reported that she has severe headaches once every several weeks, especially at times of heightened stress; yet, they are not as bad as they were nor do they occur as often as they used to. Cognitively, her complaints include forgetting simple things and difficulties with concentration and word retrieval. She noted that these deficits are not as bad as they were early on after the accident. She feels that she has regained about 90% of her prior abilities and hopes for further improvement. Emotionally, she reported that she feels frustrated and angry and is under a lot of stress because of ongoing litigation associated with the accident. She is disappointed that the case has not yet settled and wondered why things have had to take so long before resolution.

Mrs. Patient returned to work as an elementary school teacher within 1 year following the accident. She noted that because she is a single mother she had to force herself to return to work even though she was still experiencing pain at that time. She currently works full time and reports an increase in her wages since the accident, yet she feels as if she is unable to do things with the same degree of focus she had prior to the accident. Mrs. Patient does not presently participate in any medical, rehabilitative, or psychiatric treatment related to the accident and she did not follow up with the recommended treatments because she said that she did not have health insurance. Her current medical consultations include routine checkups with her primary care physician. She does not currently take any medications and she denied regular use of alcohol or tobacco products.

Previous Neuropsychological Test Results

Mrs. Patient was evaluated by Dr. Neuropsyche in September 1998 (8 months post-MVA). This was upon referral of Dr. Practitioner, the physician who first evaluated her a few weeks post-MVA. At the time, she complained of headaches, memory problems, irritability, frustration, fatigue, back and neck pain, foot swelling, and mental slowing. Results of the evaluation were felt to reflect mild to moderate cognitive and emotional dysfunction including deficits on tasks measuring problem solving, memory, and attention. Emotionally, she evidenced signs of ongoing psychosocial stress. It was the opinion of the examining neuropsychologist that the identified changes represented a change in functioning for Mrs. Patient. She likely had problems in certain areas (e.g., problem solving and mental efficiency) before the MVA, but the mild injury may have exacerbated these weaknesses to the point whereby they resulted in functional deficits. A brief course of cognitive rehabilitation and supportive psychotherapy was recommended.

A neuropsychological follow-up in February 1999 (1 year post-MVA) showed ongoing complaints of headache and trouble with time management. Mrs. Patient reported minimal improvement in her symptoms and also indicated that she had not complied with the treatment recommendations because of financial constraints. Results of the brief screening revealed objective improvements in cognitive functions but little improvement in self-reported physical or emotional symptoms. Headache was the most prominent difficulty for her; interventions to address her headache complaints were recommended. Of note, Drs. Practitioner and Neuropsyche did not have a complete account of Mrs. Patient's medical history at the time they saw her.

Relevant Medical/Psychosocial History

A review of records indicates that Mrs. Patient had a number of physical symptoms and complaints preceding the accident in 1998 and other car accidents pre- and post-1998 with litigation. Primary physical conditions and complaints included mitral valve prolapse, pain in the low back, right shoulder, and right side of her neck; headaches, dizziness, temporomandibular joint (TMJ) pain, tinnitus, recurring gastric problems, panic-like symptoms and a "stress reaction" associated with an assault, problems with memory in 1989, and episodes of confusion while driving. She was in an MVA in August 1995 with associated cervical and shoulder strain and also in an MVA in December 2000 that included pain in the right side of her neck and right rib cage and low back pain. Educationally, Mrs. Patient completed high school and had no further schooling after that. She described herself as an average student and said that she was "easily distracted" as a young girl. She was married and is divorced and has raised two daughters who live with her.

Behavioral Observations

Mrs. Patient arrived late and was unaccompanied to the testing. She was adequately groomed, alert, and responsive. She was fully oriented to place and person but missed the day of the month by 1 day. She ambulated without apparent difficulty and there were no obvious motor abnormalities. Her speech was normal in terms of rate, volume, and prosody and there was no evidence for expressive or receptive language impairments. Her ability to provide information about personal past life events suggested intact remote memory. Thought processes appeared intact, coherent, and goal directed. She seemed somewhat guarded and stated that she has no clear recollection when asked about any previous litigation related to other MVAs. Throughout the testing day she appeared motivated to perform well on all tasks presented to her and demonstrated adequate frustration tolerance on the more difficult tests items and appropriate use of time limits. A separate discussion of effort testing follows later.

Mrs. Patient's affect was generally positive, yet throughout the day she maintained an edge of defensiveness and came across as rather tense and skeptical about the objectivity of the test results and subsequent interpretation. She expressed frustration about having to undergo the current evaluation and regarded the evaluation as taking place too late and including tests that were not included in the previous one, especially those that emphasize psychological issues (e.g., the Minnesota Multiphasic Personality Inventory–2 [MMPI-2]). She stated that she doubts if the current evaluation would be a valid comparison to the previous one she had in 1998. Toward the end of the testing day, she reported that she was very fatigued and refused to complete the MMPI-II and Post-Concussion Symptom (PCS) Checklist—Revised that remained. She requested that another appointment be scheduled so that she could complete these measures and called to speak with her attorney about her concerns. He subsequently contacted this examiner and expressed concern about his client even having to take the MMPI-2. When he was informed that this was an important and standard component of the neuropsychological examination, he requested to have his client return on another day the following week. This was agreed to, with the expectation that she not be "coached" about the content of this inventory. An appointment date was scheduled with Mrs. Patient for 1 week later.

Tests Administered

The following tests were administered: Wechsler Adult Intelligence Scale–III (WAIS-III, selected subtests); Wechsler Test of Adult Reading (WTAR); Wechsler Memory Scales–III (WMS-III, selected subtests); California Verbal Learning Test–2 (CVLT-2); Brief Visuospatial Memory Test—Revised

(BVMT-R); Rey Complex Figure Test (RCFT); Wisconsin Card Sorting Test (WCST-64); Trail Making Test A/B; Brief Test of Attention (BTA); Boston Naming Test (BNT); tests of verbal fluency; Judgment of Line Orientation (JLO) Test; Finger Tapping Test; Grooved Pegboard; Grip Strength; Beck Depression Inventory–II (BDI-II); Post-Concussion Symptom (PCS) Checklist— Revised; Minnesota Multiphasic Personality Inventory–2 (MMPI-2); Rey 15-Item Memory Test (recall and recognition); Test of Memory Malingering (TOMM); and Victoria Symptom Validity Test (VSVT).

Response Bias/Symptom Validity Considerations

On tests designed to assess effort, motivation, and potential response bias on cognitive testing, and on measures sensitive to malingering and erratic performance patterns, Mrs. Patient's performances were variable. For instance, she performed within the valid range on the TOMM (Trial 1 = 46/50, Trial 2 = 49/50, Delayed Recall = 46/50), the Rey 15-Item Free Recall trial (15/15), and the forced-choice section of the CVLT-II (Hits = 16/16). In contrast, on the VSVT (Easy Items 23/24, Difficult Items 13/24), and Rey 15-Item Recognition trial (Hits 13/15, 5 commission errors) she scored below the range considered within normal limits, indicating suboptimal effort. In fact, her score on the VSVT difficult items was almost at chance (50%) level, and closer to that of groups of patients seeking compensation and instructed to feign memory deficits than it was to that of patients who are non–compensation seeking. Her scores were also well below the scores of groups of patients with documented mild and severe head injuries not in litigation. She scored at the cutoff (7) on Reliable Digit Span, another measure of insufficient effort. Taken together, the obtained results on formal measures of cognitive effort along with her observed test-taking behavior suggest that Mrs. Patient exerted variable levels of effort throughout cognitive testing. As such, any impaired scores should be interpreted with caution as they may not reflect reliable and valid impairments in functioning.

Intellectual Functions

Mrs. Patient was administered selected subtests of the WAIS-III to assess her current intellectual abilities. She obtained an estimated Verbal IQ (VIQ) of 78 (Borderline impaired range), a Performance IQ (PIQ) of 94 (average range), and a Full Scale IQ of 83 (low-average range). Her current Full Scale IQ (FSIQ) is consistent with the score obtained in the 1998 evaluation (FSIQ = 84), suggesting that the previous score did not reflect a decline in cognitive abilities and her current scores represent fairly stable intellectual functions. Individual WAIS-III subtest scores varied from the borderline impaired to average range (4–10). Her highest subtest scores were on tasks requiring visual–motor coordination and speed, visual alertness, verbal concept formation, visual–spatial analysis and synthesis, and visual discrimination. Low-average performances were obtained on measures of working memory, verbal attention span, and general fund of knowledge. Her lowest score (borderline impaired) was on a measure of mental arithmetic. Mrs. Patient's Processing Speed Index score of 93 (32nd %ile) fell in the average range; her Working Memory Index score of 73 (4th %ile) was borderline impaired range. The difference between these indices is considered significant, with working memory a relative weakness compared to processing speed, a pattern that is not especially consistent with that seen among patients with mild head trauma.

Mrs. Patient was administered the WTAR as a measure of estimated premorbid intellectual functioning. She obtained a reading score (90) in the low-average/average range and a demographically predicted score of 99. Thus, her current FSIQ is less than her estimated premorbid abilities as measured by both of these indices. In addition, her current borderline impaired VIQ score was below her predicted average score (WTAR predicted = 93, demographic predicted = 100), whereas her PIQ was essentially at predicted levels. Her VIQ and overall FSIQ were clearly brought down by her low score on Arithmetic and Digit Span. Because there were no raw data to compare to, it is unknown to what degree these represent a decline in performance compared to the previous evaluation.

Orientation and Attention/Concentration

Mrs. Patient was alert yet only partially oriented to time because she missed the day by one. Behavioral observation yielded no evidence of impairment in her attention/concentration skills. She scored in the low-average range on a measure of verbal attention span (Digit Span = 6) and on a more challenging verbal attention span test requiring immediate recall of both letters and numbers (Letter–Number Sequencing = 7). Her performances declined to the borderline impaired range on a mental arithmetic test, with significant attentional demands (Arithmetic = 4). Similarly, she performed in the borderline impaired range on a measure of selective attention (BTA = 2nd–9th %ile). She demonstrated variable performances on measures of processing speed and efficiency. For instance, she performed in the average range on WAIS-III subtests assessing visual–motor coordination and speed (Digit Symbol = 10, Symbol Search = 8) and in the borderline impaired range on another measure of processing speed that requires visual scanning and sequencing skills (Trail Making Test A, $T = 36$).

Learning and Memory

On a test of auditory verbal learning and memory (CVLT-2), Mrs. Patient demonstrated a mild to moderately impaired ability to learn a list of 16 words across five trails (4, 7, 7, 8, 8). Her performance on both short and long delayed free recall trails was in the mildly impaired range and did not appreciably improve with semantic cues. Her performance on a recognition paradigm was indicative of a liberal response bias, as she tended to identify most items as target items, thus, correctly identifying 16 words with 17 false positives. Such a high number of false positives has been regarded by some as a sign of poor/suspicious effort on this task. Mrs. Patient's immediate and delayed memory appreciably improved to the average range when information was presented in a story format: Her performance also improved on the recognition paradigm (28/30). On measures of visual learning memory, her performances ranged from moderately impaired to moderately to severely impaired. For instance, on the BVMT-R she performed in the moderately impaired range across the three learning trials and in the mildly to moderately impaired range on the delayed recall trial. On the recognition paradigm, she correctly identified five of the target figures with no false positives. Similarly, her immediate and delayed free recall performances on the RCFT were in the moderately to severely impaired range, while her score on the recognition paradigm was average.

Executive Functions

On all the different measures of executive functioning, Mrs. Patient exhibited intact performances. For instance, she scored within the normal range on a WAIS-III subtest assessing verbal concept formation abilities (Similarities = 9). Similarly, she performed within normal limits on a measure of nonverbal concept formation/problem solving and set-shifting abilities in response to external feedback (WCST). An average score was also obtained on a task requiring sequencing, set-shifting and mental flexibility (Trail Making Test B, $T = 52$: this was better than her score on the easier Trail Making Test A, $T = 35$).

Other Neuropsychological Functions

Mrs. Patient's conversational speech was fluent and her thought processes lucid and goal directed throughout the evaluation. On task of semantic verbal fluency, she performed in the average range ($T = 48$); her performance declined to the low-average range on a phonemic verbal fluency task ($T = 37$). On a confrontation-naming task, she performed in the average range (BNT $z = -.13$). Thus, results do not reflect any language impairments.

Mrs. Patient's performances on measures of visual–spatial–constructional abilities varied from average to severely impaired. On WAIS-III Block Design, a measure of visual–spatial analysis and synthesis, she performed in the average range (scaled score = 8). Her performances declined to the borderline impaired range on a task of visual–spatial perception and judgment (JLO 9th %ile). Her lowest score was on a visual–constructional task where she was required to reproduce a complex two-dimensional design (RCFT Copy < 1st %tile). Her visual–spatial skills were judged to be intact in the previous evaluation; as such, the present scores represent an unexpected decline in functioning. Variable performances were seen on upper-extremity motor tests. On a test of grip strength, Mrs. Patient scored in the mildly impaired range with her dominant right hand ($T = 34$) and in the average range ($T = 44$) with the left. Her scores on a measure of fine motor speed was low average, bilaterally (right hand $T = 39$; left hand $T = 39$). Bilateral mildly impaired performances were noted on a measure of speeded fine motor dexterity (right hand $T = 34$; left hand $T = 32$).

Emotional Functioning

Mrs. Patient obtained a score of 6 on the BDI-II, which does not reflect symptoms of depression. But, she endorsed sleep disturbance, irritability, concentration difficulty, and tiredness/fatigue. On the PCS Checklist, she rated 24/83 items in the moderately to severely impaired range (3 to 5 on a 1- to 5-point scale). Those rated as most severe (5) were largely physical in nature, including back pain and foot pain; she also rated "involved in a lawsuit" as a 5. Items rated as 4 included concentration problems, fatigue, irritability, memory problems, neck pain, trouble finding the right word to say, and trouble remembering things. Importantly, controls and patients with other psychological and medical conditions also endorse a number of items on this questionnaire.

Mrs. Patient's responses to the items of the MMPI-2 generally reflected a balance between positive self-evaluation and self-criticism, but she showed a tendency toward mild defensiveness and hesitancy to admit to psychological difficulties. Her score on the Fake Bad Scale (FBS; 22) was right at the cutoff used to identify individuals who tend to exaggerate or magnify their symptoms. The overall profile does not include significant ($T > 65$) elevations on any of the clinical scales (although Hypomania was right at 65). The pattern on Scales 1, 2, and 3 represent a "conversion V" pattern. Whereas the elevations on these scales is not clinically significant, it suggests that Mrs. Patient reports functioning at a reduced level of efficiency. Physical symptoms are endorsed, many of which increase in times of stress, and often there is clear secondary gain associated with them. Importantly, given that Mrs. Patient did not complete this inventory the first day and had to come back on another occasion to complete it, the effects of coaching cannot be completely ruled out. In fact, her responses to a number of items completed on the first day (items 1–45) were different and endorsed in a manner that reflects more social desirability and poorer health the second time.

Summary and Impressions

Results of the present evaluation conducted almost 6 years post-MVA without reported loss of consciousness do *not* provide evidence of prominent changes in neurocognitive functions secondary to the accident. Indeed, Mrs. Patient performed at, or very close to, her estimated premorbid level on the majority of tests; any weaknesses that were present appear to be largely a product of normal variability or psychological or motivational factors. In fact, her scores on several of the symptom validity measures raise a serious concern about the validity of any identified deficits. Whereas this may not reflect a conscious attempt to feign or exaggerate deficits, there are clearly some other factors besides brain-based disturbances in functioning that are influencing the test results and ongoing subjective complaints. Her score on one of the tests (VSVT hard items) was almost at chance level, which raises a serious concern about the validity of her complaints of impaired memory.

The fact that Mrs. Patient's current scores closely approximate the scores from the first evaluation suggests that they reflect relatively stable cognitive abilities and are essentially consistent with her estimated premorbid abilities and are not a product of injury. In cases of significant brain injury, scores from the first postaccident evaluation would likely be the most impaired and then show objective improvement over time. Mrs. Patient reports ongoing subjective difficulties, characterized most prominently by infrequent headaches, leg pain, and inefficient processing of information. Given the period of time that has passed from the onset of injury, it is highly unlikely that brain-based disturbances in functioning account for such changes. In fact, many of her current complaints are not at all different from the complaints she reported to her physician prior to February 1998.

Looking at all the data (medical records, clinical interview, test results) in combination, it appears that Mrs. Patient most likely sustained a cervical sprain/strain injury in the February 1998 accident. At worst, she may have had a very mild concussion with no loss of consciousness; the length of her posttraumatic amnesia was very short and she showed purposeful behavior immediately after the impact. Also, she did not complain of any cognitive difficulties during the course of acute treatment with her primary physician. Symptoms associated with concussion are transient, lasting anywhere from 1 to 3 months, and those that persist beyond that period of time cannot be explained by the effects of brain damage. Indeed, other factors such as depression, headaches, feelings of victimization, and the effects of secondary gain can more adequately account for the symptoms and complaints. Mrs. Patient's current complaints are rather nonspecific (i.e., they occur in normal controls and in patients with a variety of other psychological and/or medical conditions): Cervical sprain/strain injuries can also cause many post-concussive-like symptoms.

Mrs. Patient's preinjury history of stress, depression, headaches, and other prominent physical symptoms makes it very difficult to opine with any certainty the degree to which her current symptoms are a direct result of the accident in February 1998. Moreover, the effects of misattribution to brain damage may also lead her to believe that her symptoms are a product of a traumatic brain injury as a result of the MVA. But, research and clinical evidence suggest that accident events can act as a conduit or means for expressing chronic emotional distress in certain individuals and that misattribution of preexisting symptoms to the accident may cause and maintain dysfunctional behavior. Given that Mrs. Patient is and has been working full time for a number of years, I do not anticipate any detriment to her capacity to continue in this manner for the months and years to come. She would probably benefit from some time-limited psychological intervention to assist her in coping with her symptoms. This might include cognitive restructuring to help her correctly identify and reframe the cause(s) of her symptoms and complaints as well as a component directed toward stress management to lower her overall level of stress and demand.

Reginald B. Clinical, PhD
Licensed Psychologist

APPENDIX 8.1

Neuropsychological Test Scores for Mrs. Patient

Name: Mrs. Patient   **Date of Exam:** 9/13, 9/20/03   **Educ:** 12 years
Age: 46 years old   **Gender:** Female   **Hand:** Right

Intellectual/Achievement

WAIS-3: Short form (9)

		SS		SS
FSIQ:	83	Similarities: 9	Pic. Comp.	9
VIQ:	78	Arithmetic 4	Digit Symbol	10
PIQ:	94	Digit Span 6	Block Design	8
WMI:	73	Information 7	Symbol Srch	8
PSI:	93	Letter–Number 7		

WTAR: FSIQ (Reading): 93   (Demographic): 99

Learning and Memory

WMS-3:	SS	CVLT-2:	Raw	Z score	BVMT-R	Raw	%ile
LM1	9	Trial 1	4	−1.5	Trial 1	1	1
LM2	10	Trial 5	8	−2	Trial 2	4	1
%Ret.	8	Total	34	T = 33	Trial 3	7	4
LM1 1st rec	8	S Free	6	1.5	Total	12	1
LM1 LS	18	S Cued	7	−1.5	Learning	6	90
		L Free	7	−1.5	Delay	6	4
		L Cued	7	−2	%Reten.	85.7	11–16
		Hits	16	.5	Hits	5	11–16
		FP	17	−4.5	FP	0	> 16
		Discrim.	1.8	−1.5	Discrim.	5	11–16
					RB	.25	> 16

127

Attention & Executive Functions

WCST: (1 deck)	Raw	SS	T	%ile	Trail Making Test	Time	SS	T
Category	4			> 16	A	44"	6	36
Errors	14	73	45	32	B	66"	10	52
Psv Responses	6	94	46	34				
Psv Errors	6	94	46	34				
Conceptual	48	95	47	37	BTA	Total	%ile	
Level Responses						10	2–9	
1st Category	11			> 16				
Learn to Learn	–2.1			> 16				

Language

BNT:	Raw	z score	Fluency:	Total	SS	T
	55	–.13	Phonemic	27	7	37
			Semantic	20	10	48

Visual–Spatial & Sensory–Motor

JLOT:	Raw	%ile
	19	9

Tapping	Raw	T	Pegs	Raw	T	Grip	Raw	T
Dominant	34.8	39	Dom	80	34	Dom	21	34
Nondominant	38.2	39	Nondominant	90	32	Nondominant	21	44

Effort

Rey 15-Item			TOMM:	1st	2nd	Retention
# Correct:	15/15			46	49	46
Recognition:	28/30					

VSVT:	Easy	Hard
# Correct	23/24	13/24
Latency	2.11	2.57

Personality/Emotional

MMPI-2 (T scores)   BDI-II   6 (Normal)

L	56	Pa	58
F	40	Pt	44
K	56	Sc	46
Hs	58	Ma	65
D	44	Si	30
Hy	62	FBS	22 (raw)
Pd	44		
Mf	56		

9

Plaintiff Expert's Analysis of the Case

Wilfred G. van Gorp

GENERAL COMMENTS AND OVERVIEW

The first step for the neuropsychologist serving as an expert witness or consultant to an attorney or the court in a personal injury case, regardless of which opposing side has retained him or her, is to review the materials forwarded by the retaining attorney, including any prior neuropsychological evaluations, medical records, and ambulance and emergency technician reports. The next step is to undertake an analysis and conceptualization of the case. The attorney should be informed of the strengths and limitations of any neuropsychological or mental health reports that have been rendered. Some key elements that I often consider in reviewing various neuropsychological and/or mental health reports include:

• When was the evaluation I am reviewing performed in relation to the date of injury? This relates to issues such as ongoing recovery that may be occurring, what recovery may still be expected, or the permanence of any impairments that may be present. For instance, if the data were collected soon after an injury, it is possible that considerable recovery could still occur. On the contrary, if—as we have here—the data were collected many years after the accident, any impairments (if valid) would be more likely to represent permanent sequelae from an accident.

• Were the neuropsychological tests that were administered appropriate for this person and this situation, and do they demonstrate good sensitivity and/or specificity related to the alleged injury or condition? Obviously, the tests selected must take into account any physical limitations or peripheral injuries the person may have sustained, and they must be current tests with demonstrated sensitivity, specificity, reliability, and validity.

• Were cultural and/or language factors taken into account? Were appropriate measures selected and norms utilized for this person's demographic background?

• Were standard procedures followed, such as informed consent, appropriate testing conditions/methods, and so on? Some of us have encountered situations in which tests such as the Trail Making Test A/B were administered in a group format, violating standardized test procedures, and by persons not formally trained in clinical neuropsychology or test administration.

• Do the results make "neuropsychological sense" in light of the claimed injury? If not, are there behavioral and/or motivational factors that can explain the discrepancy? With test takers becoming more informed about neuropsychological testing procedures through the Internet, via their own research, or from coaching by their attorney, they may "pass" validity tests while obtaining noncredible performance on standard clinical measures. Is there evidence of this type of pattern in what I am reviewing?

• Did the neuropsychologist or mental health expert consider all reasonable or likely causes for the findings in his or her examination? Were premorbid factors (such as preexisting educational difficulties) explored and taken into account? Were factors such as depression and anxiety assessed and thereby taken into account in interpreting the cognitive test results?

• Finally, was an attempt made to obtain and review all relevant prior medical, educational, and employment records? If not, would knowledge of their contents potentially change the neuropsychologist's opinion or conclusions?

UNIQUE ISSUES WHEN RETAINED
BY A PLAINTIFF ATTORNEY

As a principle and in practice, the retained neuropsychologist should perform the same type of analysis and conduct the same type of evaluation whether retained by counsel for the plaintiff, the defendant, or the court. Tests of motivation should routinely be utilized regardless of who retained the expert in any circumstance in which there is the potential for secondary gain from a specific outcome in the assessment. A colleague once commented to me, "No, I won't utilize 'malingering tests' here—I'm retained by the plaintiff" (presumably because some examinees might "fail" such tests). Such a bias has no place in the competent and ethical practice of the neuropsychologist. In fact, some neuropsychologists seem to believe it is their role to see the case from the retaining attorney's point of view. This is a bad practice. As one attorney said in an initial conversation, "I want your candid opinion. I am not retaining a cheerleader." The reply was that I had a duty to him and his client to provide my honest and candid opinion.

Many plaintiff attorneys must make practical and strategic decisions based on the outcome of the neuropsychological evaluation, often with ethical and financial implications for their client and themselves. When I am retained by a plaintiff attorney but the outcome of the examination may not be viewed as "favorable" by him or her (such as the examination revealed no impairment), I usually preface my summary of findings with the following caveat: "I feel I have a responsibility to you and your client to tell you both the 'good' and the 'bad' so that you can make informed decisions as to how (or not) to proceed." Reputable plaintiff attorneys are usually appreciative and typically acknowledge the importance of having an accurate picture of the merits and weakness of their case in order to decide how to move forward and to what extent they should or should not include cognitive impairment in their damages claim. As one plaintiff attorney said, "Including the claim of brain damage will add approximately $100,000 to my cost. If it is not warranted, you have just saved my client and myself this expense. If it is not valid, I don't want to include it because it will involve a lot more time and expense on my part only to be proved wrong later."

One of the most important implications for the retained expert, of course, is to "do no harm." The attorney's client, your examinee, should not wrongly be given the message that he or she is "brain damaged" or cognitively impaired if the test results and other data do not firmly support that conclusion. This is the ultimate and most important responsibility of the neuropsychologist. Years beyond any litigation and monetary award and long after the neuropsychologist has been paid his or her fee for the evaluation, examinees will more likely remember that the "doctor" said they were "brain damaged" than what was written in a legal complaint filed on their behalf by their attorney. If providing feedback to an examinee referred to me by his or her attorney, I usually preface my feedback (especially in cases in which there is little or no neuropsychological impairment) with the comment: "Remember, before we review your findings—let's hope there is no impairment—the best news would be if you were normal on our tests, right?" It helps put the test results in context.

OVERVIEW OF THE CASE OF MRS. PATIENT AS SEEN BY PLAINTIFF NEUROPSYCHOLOGIST

This case recounts a frequently encountered—some might even say "classic"—scenario for the clinical neuropsychologist engaging in forensic activities regarding tort matters. Ms. Patient is alleging a mild traumatic brain injury (TBI) secondary to a motor vehicle accident in which her car was struck from behind; there was no loss of consciousness but she "saw stars." No Glasgow Coma Scale (GCS) score was reported in the records available for review but posttraumatic amnesia was brief at most. Records revealed that neuropsychological testing had been performed twice after the accident in addition to the current testing; the current testing available for our review is almost 6 years after the accident. Results for all assessments were reported to be quite similar (with a few exceptions), though on the current testing, Mrs. Patient exhibited variable results on tests of effort with some scores falling in the valid range and some not. The evaluation revealed poor performance on several cognitive tests as well as the presence of some reported emotional difficulties.

KEY ISSUES RAISED IN THE CASE

In this matter, my role is to consult to the plaintiff attorney who is my client. Here are some thoughts I would think about, and share with the retaining attorney.

1. *There was no loss of consciousness (LOC), but there was minimal posttraumatic amnesia (PTA) as well as report of some alteration of consciousness ("she saw stars").* Mild TBI *can* occur even without a loss of consciousness, if there is a clear presence of alteration of consciousness. Without loss or alteration of consciousness, there is no clear indication that a brain (as opposed to head) injury has actually occurred. A few years ago, I (retained by the defense) reviewed testing on a plaintiff who had been hit while crossing the street by a truck. The plaintiff did not sustain LOC, but both emergency room and inpatient hospital records documented prolonged mental confusion, with nursing notes indicating he repeatedly asked what had happened to him and could not consistently or accurately recount specific details such as his telephone number, and so on. Testing documented cognitive deficits consistent with a brain injury and both I, and the neuropsychologist for the plaintiff concluded a brain injury had occurred. However, in the case of Mrs. Patient we do not have such clear or convincing documentation definitively indicating that a brain injury actually occurred. The records that we have been provided indicated that Mrs. Patient "saw stars" but that she did not lose consciousness, and there is no indication of prolonged alteration of consciousness. In addition, PTA is strongly related to prognosis (e.g., de Guise, LeBlanc, Feyz, & Lamoureux, 2006), with PTA beyond 2 to 3 weeks indicating poor prognosis. As Mrs. Patient's PTA was minimal (minutes) at most, we do not have a constellation of factors that would document that a significant or credible brain injury has occurred that would be expected to produce lasting neuropsychological impairment.

Regarding this issue, I would inform the plaintiff attorney that the facts of the case would support at most the possibility that a mild TBI has occurred. In this instance, a mild TBI could produce a constellation of symptoms consistent with "postconcussion syndrome" that would be expected to resolve in most people in a matter of weeks or months. Mrs. Patient's complaints of headache, concentration problems, distractibility, issues with word recall, and pain are characteristic of postconcussion syndrome, though it would be extraordinary for these to persist up to 6 years postinjury. Mrs. Patient does state that she believes that she has improved 90% since accident.

Bottom line: I would tell the attorney that a mild TBI may have occurred, but that it is not certain at this juncture based on the lack of LOC and absence of clear-cut mental confusion beyond her simply "seeing stars."

2. *History of prior accidents.* This, of course, could be viewed from two perspectives. Mrs. Patient has a history of multiple accidents, some of which have led to prior litigation. Thus, do we have a "serial litigant" here? Or, has Mrs. Plaintiff sustained multiple prior brain injuries that might have left her more vulnerable to a mild TBI, which she may have sustained in this case? As written, the history provided in the neuropsychological report available for review is unclear. Further inquiry would be undertaken; if it were to show that she has sustained credible, multiple prior LOCs, this could explain why Mrs. Patient may have sustained a more significant brain injury in this accident compared to a person without such a history. I would advise the plaintiff attorney that it is very important to obtain and review all prior medical and legal records related to her prior accidents. If past medical records document that a brain injury occurred, then Mrs. Patient may well have been more susceptible to the effects of a mild TBI than had she not had this history.

3. *Mrs. Patient's subjective complaints.* Though the recount by Mrs. Patient of her cognitive symptoms indicates numerous problems, research has shown (Moore et al., 1997) that one's own sense or appraisal of one's cognitive function is often not correlated to actual neuropsychological test performance but rather to one's mood state. The higher the level of depressed mood, the more one's subjective sense of cognitive dysfunction. Thus, although I am not dismissing Mrs. Patient's self-report, I do not want to automatically attribute it to a brain impairment and would inform the retaining attorney that self-report is often inaccurate and related to mood state. This is, of course, the reason we administer formal cognitive tests rather than rely on self-report as an indicator of cognitive dysfunction. Again, although not dismissing Mrs. Patient's report of her symptoms, the plaintiff attorney should not be encouraged to put undue weight on Mrs. Patient's report as a definitive measure of absolute cognitive impairment.

4. *Comment on tests selected by the treating clinical neuropsychologist.* The tests administered by Dr. Neuropsyche are, in general, commonly

used tests in the field and ones that, overall, have good sensitivity, specificity, reliability, and validity. Dr. Neuropsyche administered and interpreted multiple tests of effort, especially important in the context of litigation regarding the current injury. However, one test (Rey 15-Item Memory Test) has been criticized (Vallabhajosula & van Gorp, 2001) for not demonstrating sufficient sensitivity and specificity to detect noncredible performance and could be vulnerable to a legal challenge for admissibility as scientific evidence, especially if the legal *"Daubert* standard" of admissibility of scientific testimony is applicable. The Victoria Symptom Validity Test (VSVT) was also administered. This is a solid, commonly used test, though it was one of the first tests of effort developed, and has become somewhat known to plaintiff attorneys and litigants in these types of proceedings (I have been told that some clients are informed: "If they give you a test with only two choices, be sure you get at least more than half right"), thereby limiting their sensitivity.

The clinical tests selected by Dr. Neuropsyche appear generally appropriate and have demonstrated validity and reliability. However, at least one study (Stuss, Stethem, Hugenholtz, & Richard, 1989) has indicated that the Auditory Consonant Trigrams (ACT; sometimes known as the Brown–Peterson Distracter Technique) test may be particularly sensitive to the lingering cognitive effects of mild TBI and, as such, might have been included in Dr. Neuropsyche's battery of tests to increase sensitivity in detecting lingering sequelae from any brain injury.

5. *Results of motivational tests administered to Mrs. Patient.* Here, we have variable and discrepant findings. Mrs. Patient "passed" the TOMM, the Rey 15-Item Memory Test, and the California Verbal Learning Test–2 (CVLT-2) forced-choice component. These (except for the Rey 15-Item Memory Test, which I would not rely on), all support good effort on her part. However, she performed below the published cutoff score on the VSVT, and in fact, she performed essentially at chance level (i.e., randomly) on the hard items of the test. Such a performance in a case of, at most, a mild TBI is noncredible and suggests inadequate effort on her part. Though I would not rely on the Rey 15-Item Memory Test, the examining neuropsychologist found performance below the cutoff score (according to his interpretation in the report) on the recognition portion of the Rey 15-Item Memory Test (see Boone, Salazar, Lu, Warner-Chacon, & Razani, 2002), and I would inform the plaintiff attorney this will be used, most probably, by the defense to indicate poor effort. More convincing of variable effort was the report that Mrs. Patient's performance on Reliable Digit Span was below the cutoff score of 7 and therefore suggested poor effort (Axelrod, Fichtenberg, Millis, & Wertheimer, 2006). Even if we do not rely on the Rey 15-Item Memory Test findings (both "for" and "against" full effort), there is clear-cut evidence from the VSVT and the Reliable Digit Span that Mrs. Patient did not *consistently* exert full effort across tests of

motivation and effort. Though multiple measures of effort were administered, hence increasing the potential of false-positive findings (akin to an inflated alpha level, requiring a Bonferroni or other type correction), the nature of the findings (near-chance performance on the hard items of the VSVT) indicates that the remainder of the tests cannot be relied on as necessarily valid indicators of Mrs. Patient's true level of cognitive functioning because she did not appear to consistently apply full effort. In my opinion, this finding is reasonably conclusive and much more probable than not.

In a situation such as this, what would I tell the plaintiff attorney who had retained me? I would inform him or her that some of the validity indicators were unmistakably out of the range of valid performance, thus rendering most of the neuropsychological tests of questionable validity, and that they cannot necessarily be relied on as true indicators of his or her client's "true" or maximal abilities. Though Mrs. Patient's level of effort seems variable, we cannot ascertain on which clinical measures she tried her best and on which she did not, though her "best performance" on the tests indicates she has at least that level of ability on those tests (i.e., one can perform lower on tests than he or she really is, but one cannot artificially perform better than he or she really is). Indeed, some results on the clinical tests are simply not credible. Mrs. Patient has worked, and is currently working, as a schoolteacher. It is not credible that she has an interpolated Verbal IQ (VIQ) of 78 given the nature of the demands of her work. Though the VIQ score is derived from only some of the Verbal Wechsler Adult Intelligence Scale–III (WAIS-III) subtests, the resulting overall score in the borderline range is not a credible finding and supports the finding of invalidity of the overall results. The same is true of her Working Memory Index (WMI) finding of 73. Unless this is the product of an acute confusional state (and hence, also responsible for variable effort on the validity tests), a finding of the WMI in the borderline range is simply not credible or consistent with the demands of Mrs. Patient's employment or daily functioning. The same can be said of Mrs. Patient's performance on the CVLT-2. In my opinion, these clinical findings do not comport with someone who can live independently and return to work as a schoolteacher.

Although some of the findings reflect inadequate effort on the part of Mrs. Patient, we cannot conclude from these findings that her poor effort was the product of conscious factors (i.e., malingering) versus other factors (such as depression or psychiatric factors). Insufficient, variable, or poor effort does not necessarily indicate conscious intent. Although we have all seen our share of probable malingerers, I have also encountered numerous cases of persons with demonstrable brain impairment (evidence without dispute on magnetic resonance imaging [MRI] scans, for example) who did not exert full effort in order to produce valid neuropsychological test scores. In those cases, no (conscious) malingering is occurring; rather, we have poor or insufficient effort despite an actual brain injury present.

Given these findings, I would inform Mrs. Patient's attorney of four things: First, the conclusions I have reached regarding the test scores are quite standard and that most bona fide neuropsychologists would likely come to the same conclusion. To conclude otherwise would not only be inaccurate and misleading but would be effectively rebutted on cross-examination. Second, this invalidity does not equate, necessarily, with "malingering." Invalid test performance is not always the result of a conscious attempt to distort the results—it simply documents inconsistent effort (i.e., only performance "below chance" indicates purposeful intent to perform poorly). Third, other information—observations, history, reports from other observers and sources—that is not the product of Mrs. Patient's tested ability can be relied on to reach an ultimate conclusion as to the nature of her injury and any sequelae from it. Finally, I would inform the retaining attorney that—regrettably—the noncredible findings in this testing will no doubt have a negative impact on Mrs. Patient's credibility regardless of whether or not they are the product of conscious factors, and that he or she should be aware of this as the case proceeds. In my experience, cases in which this type of finding has occurred are more likely to reach a settlement rather than be litigated in open court. If litigated, it is at risk for an adverse or reduced verdict based on credibility issues due to the finding of variable effort regardless of whether it is the result of conscious factors or not.

6. *I disagree with Dr. Neuropsyche's conclusions from comparison of prior testing on Mrs. Patient.* Dr. Neuropsyche states: "The fact that Mrs. Patient's current scores closely approximates [sic] the scores from the first evaluation, suggest that they reflect relatively stable cognitive abilities and are essentially consistent with her estimated abilities and are not a product of injury."

I disagree with Dr. Neuropsyche's statement and its essential conclusion. In my opinion, the results are *not* consistent, overall, with her premorbid abilities, including Verbal (prorated) IQ and her CVLT-2 performance. Dr. Neuropsyche's statement also seems to overlook Mrs. Patient's invalid performance on select tests of motivation. Rather, my view (and feedback to the retaining plaintiff attorney) is that the results are most probably *not* representative, overall, of Mrs. Patient's ability. This is a point I would concede at the beginning for the reasons listed previously. One cannot conclude, at the same time, that the results are invalid but reflect her premorbid ability. Such a position is illogical and internally inconsistent.

7. *Mrs. Patient's Minnesota Multiphasic Personality Inventory–2 (MMPI-2) and emotional factors in this case.* Mrs. Patient's MMPI-2 is generally valid, and if anything, there is the suggestion of an *underreporting* of emotional symptoms (F–K = –17) with no clinical scale above 65T. This bolsters her credibility in that there is no suggestion that Mrs. Plaintiff has "malingered" or amplified any psychiatric symptoms.

We have very little specific information on Mrs. Patient's preaccident psychiatric history or a recount of her current array of psychiatric symptoms (if any), but we are told that in the past, Mrs. Patient had panic-like symptoms and a "stress reaction" associated with an assault. This history may be significant in relation to her current situation and complaints. More information on her history is clearly needed and I would advise the attorney that we need to obtain this information as Mrs. Patient may be an "eggshell"—especially vulnerable to emotional distress because of her history.

CASE CONCEPTUALIZATION AND WHAT I WOULD TELL AND ADVISE PLAINTIFF ATTORNEY

There are a number of key elements in this case. First, it seems that Ms. Patient has a history of several other automobile accidents (one in 1995 and one in 2000) though we do not have information if either of these included LOC. There was also an assault, perhaps in 1989 (the report, as written, is somewhat unclear on this), but we know there were reported problems with memory then and presumably these were associated with the assault. We also know that Mrs. Patient exhibits a range of cognitive complaints that she attributes to the current accident at issue.

I have reached the following conclusions based on my review:

1. I do not see evidence that a significant brain injury has occurred in this accident that would be expected to lead to significant, long-lasting cognitive impairment. That Mrs. Patient has returned to work and, indeed, is earning more now than before the accident is consistent with this conclusion. In my opinion, this is not a "brain injury"–type case, Mrs. Patient's prior accidents or injuries notwithstanding.

2. Mrs. Patient produced variable results on tests of motivation/effort, indicating that the current test results are not valid and should not be relied on to form an opinion. Though this could have a negative impact on her credibility, it does not indicate a conscious attempt to feign or exaggerate impairments, and the MMPI-2, in fact, seems valid or, if anything, minimizing of Mrs. Patient's emotional symptoms, thereby indicating she is not feigning or amplifying any psychiatric symptoms.

3. Mrs. Patient may be an "eggshell" based on her prior accidents and report of psychiatric symptoms, which appear to have resurfaced at this time. It could be that the accident has rekindled emotional symptoms of either posttraumatic stress or some other type of anxiety disorder. This should be evaluated more fully, as it is inadequately explored in this assessment. This could either be done through a more extensive psychological interview and more thorough review of prior psychiatric symptoms by myself

or through a referral to a psychiatrist to perform this evaluation. An emotional or psychiatric component could also contribute to Mrs. Patient's poor performance on selected tests of effort in the battery, as she may be distracted by symptoms of anxiety or distress.

In terms of a tort action, if Mrs. Plaintiff is an eggshell, emotionally, then this accident may have produced a cascade of new or reemerged psychiatric symptoms that now need to be more fully explored and treated. Thus, tort damages in this case may be in the psychiatric more than the cognitive domain and must be fully worked up and explored. To me, this is the direction the case should take. To push the claim of significant brain injury and damage (other than emotional factors) would be both inaccurate and ill advised, both to the attorney and to the examinee.

CLOSING COMMENTS

This case illustrates the role of the neuropsychologist in dealing with the plaintiff and defense attorney. My overall assessment is that the examinee exerted variable effort and only *possibly* sustained a concussion, with symptom complaints akin to what is often seen in postconcussion syndrome. Nevertheless, this usually resolves in weeks to months. My guidance to the attorney is to explore psychiatric factors that may be accounting for the examinee's complaints rather than attempting to substantiate that a brain injury occurred.

REFERENCES

Axelrod, B., Fichtenberg, N. L., Millis, S. R., & Wertheimer, J. C. (2006). Detecting incomplete effort with Digit Span from the Wechsler Adult Intelligence Scale—Third Edition. *The Clinical Neuropsychologist, 20*, 513–523.

Boone, K. B., Salazar, X., Lu, P., Warner-Chacon, K., & Razani, J. (2002). The Rey 15-item recognition trial: A technique to enhance sensitivity of the Rey 15-Item Memorization Test. *Journal of Clinical and Experimental Neuropsychology, 24*, 561–573.

de Guise, E., LeBlanc, J., Feyz, M., & Lamoureux, J. (2006). Prediction of outcome at discharge from acute care following traumatic brain injury. *Journal of Head Trauma Rehabilitation, 21*, 527–536.

Moore, L. H., van Gorp, W. G., Hinkin, C. H., Stern, M. J., Swales, T., & Satz, P. (1997). Subjective complaints versus actual cognitive performance in predominantly symptomatic HIV-seropositive individuals. *Journal of Neuropsychiatry and Clinical Neurosciences, 9*, 37–44.

Stuss, D. T., Stethem, L. L., Hugenholtz, H., & Richard, M. T. (1989). Traumatic brain injury: A comparison of three clinical tests, and analysis of recovery. *The Clinical Neuropsychologist, 3*, 145–156.

Vallabhajosula, B., & van Gorp, W. G. (2001) Admissibility of scientific evidence on malingering of cognitive deficits, post-*Daubert. Journal of the American Academy of Psychiatry and the Law, 29*, 207–215.

10

Defense Expert's Analysis of the Case

Wiley Mittenberg

Neuropsychological examination is the established method of assessing cognitive and emotional status following mild head trauma, and it is considered essential in cases in which litigation concerns the presence of cognitive or emotional impairment (American Academy of Neurology, 1996). Metanalyses suggest that approximately 95% of patients recover from any initial cognitive impairment within 3 months of sustaining mild head trauma. Speed of thought process and memory ability are most often affected when cognitive reduction is present in association with a history of mild head injury. (Binder, Rohling, & Larrabee, 1997; Schretlen & Shapiro, 2003). Postconcussion syndrome is the most common emotional disorder following mild head trauma. The incidence in consecutively hospitalized patients is approximately 38% at 6 weeks and about 28% at 6 months after injury (Mittenberg & Strauman, 2000). Persistent symptoms are often related to anxiety and stress rather than to impairment in brain functions (Mittenberg & Strauman, 2000). The possibility that apparent cognitive or emotional symptoms are exaggerated or malingered must also be considered in cases that involve personal injury litigation. A survey of the membership of the American Board of Clinical Neuropsychology (ABCN) indicated that approximately 40% of mild head injury claims involved probable malingering or symptom exaggeration based on a sample of 11,400 litigating- or compensation-seeking cases (Mittenberg, Patton, Canyock, & Condit, 2002).

This chapter demonstrates a typical review of case material from the perspective of a neuropsychologist consulting with a defense attorney. The patient was previously examined by a neuropsychologist involved in the initial treatment; it is unknown whether the patient's attorney prompted the evaluation. Most often the defense attorney typically receives a report of the neuropsychological examination as part of the documents that are presented in support of a claim for compensation. He or she may then consult with an independent neuropsychologist in order to obtain an objective opinion about the cause of deficits, extent of impairment, and eventual prognosis.

PROFESSIONAL APPROACH

Independent examinations in personal injury cases constitute about 15–20% of the average neuropsychological practice, with the majority of consultations being referred by defense attorneys (Essig, Mittenberg, Petersen, Strauman, & Cooper, 2001; Sweet, Nelson, & Moberg, 2006). Practice demographics information is typically requested by attorneys in an attempt to discredit an expert during a deposition or trial by inferring unfair bias due to dependence on legal referrals for too large a proportion of income, or as demonstrated by consulting solely on defense or plaintiff cases. An expert may also be asked how frequently he or she has seen cases at the request of the referring attorney for similar reasons and can be required to provide copies of tax documents that indicate the amount of income gained via forensic work.

Performing an initial record review at no cost is a gracious means of maintaining professional objectivity. A preliminary opinion can usually be formed after about 2 hours of record review. This time is well compensated in that it spares both the neuropsychologist and referring attorney involvement in a conflict of interests, as the attorney is free to contact another doctor if the preliminary opinion does not appear to be useful to his or her case. An opinion based on record review in a personal injury litigation case would typically have to be confirmed by subsequent independent examination of the patient. Records for preliminary review should include an ambulance report, chart notes from the hospital emergency room, head computed tomography (CT) or magnetic resonance imaging (MRI) reports, and reports from subsequent hospitalization, treatments, and/or examinations. Educational transcripts (for use in estimating premorbid level of function) and copies of test forms or scores from previous examinations may be obtained and reviewed prior to the independent examination.

Copies of neuropsychological test forms should be sent from one psychologist to another rather than to an attorney in order to preserve the security of test content (National Academy of Neuropsychology, 2000).

Florida codified this recommendation by enacting legislation that prohibits psychologists from releasing raw test data, test protocols, test questions, or written answer sheets to anyone other than another licensed psychologist (Florida Administrative Code, 1997). Nevertheless, a court may still order that copies of test forms, test questions, test manuals, and even the tests themselves be provided to an attorney. In some cases a court may also order that an expert provide the attorney with copies of all his or her publications and presentations. In such instances the expert should request advance payment for the considerable time involved to locate and copy these documents. Photocopying companies may refuse to duplicate copyrighted material such as test manuals without a court order directing them to do so.

CASE BACKGROUND

The patient is described in the neuropsychological examination report as having a 12th-grade education and as being employed as an elementary school teacher both before and after her 1998 motor vehicle accident. Her occupation and educational level appear to be potentially inconsistent, in that elementary school teachers typically have a college education. The report also notes that the patient did not follow up with recommended medical treatments because she did not have health insurance, which is unusual for an elementary school teacher. Educational transcripts and employment records might be obtained in order to resolve this inconsistency. Exaggeration of occupational or educational attainment is sometimes noted to be a correlate of symptom exaggeration in personal injury litigation cases (Greiffenstein, Baker, & Johnson-Greene, 2002; Johnson-Greene & Binder, 1995).

Preaccident medical history is significant for neck pain, back pain, headaches, memory difficulty, confusion, and distractibility, symptoms that the patient currently attributes to the 1998 motor vehicle accident. Individuals who have sustained a mild head injury often misattribute preexisting symptoms to their accident (Mittenberg & Strauman, 2000). History is also significant for an assault in 1989, a prior motor vehicle accident in 1995, and another motor vehicle accident 2 years after the 1998 incident that is the subject of the current lawsuit. It is therefore possible that any current cognitive or emotional symptoms were caused by injuries sustained before or after the one in 1998. Records from these accidents should be reviewed and the patient interviewed regarding any disability related to these other accidents. The patient reported that she returned to work full time and that her wages increased after the 1998 accident. This history is potentially inconsistent with the patient's reported cognitive symptoms and with some of the current neuropsychological test results. Employment records might be reviewed in order to resolve this discrepancy.

The patient appears to have sustained a mild or minor head injury 6 years prior to the examination based on the limited history provided in the report. She did not report loss of consciousness, did not have to be taken to the hospital by ambulance, and did not report any period of posttraumatic amnesia. She apparently went to the emergency room the next day, but it appears that she did not report symptoms that would indicate that a CT scan or MRI of the head was necessary. Given the available accident history, no persisting cognitive impairment would typically be expected. Hospital records should be reviewed to substantiate these impressions. Opinions about the patient's complaints of pain would be deferred to an orthopedist or another physician.

Medical history indicates that muscle relaxers and pain medications were prescribed by the primary care physician immediately following the 1998 accident. It is important to note the use of potentially sedating medications such as these that might reduce performance on cognitive tests or in the patient's day-to-day life. The neuropsychologist who examined her in 1998 reported mild to moderate decline in cognitive function but may not have considered potential medication effects because a complete medical history was not available at that time. This doctor also believed that the patient may have had preexisting cognitive difficulties. A review of educational transcripts would be useful in this case to determine if a history of learning disability or attention-deficit disorder were present that might account for the patient's test performance. Cognitive rehabilitation and psychotherapy were recommended. The fact that the patient did not seek treatment suggests that her symptoms may not have been as troublesome as she reported them to be.

The patient appeared guarded when asked about litigation related to the other motor vehicle accidents. Review of documents related to other litigation is often useful to determine if the current symptoms are related to other injures, and occasionally shows a history of symptom embellishment.

CASE ANALYSIS

Behavioral observations from the current neuropsychological examination indicate the patient was oriented to person and place but missed the day of the month by 1 day. This performance is normal (Benton, Sivan, Hamsher, Varney, & Spreen, 1994).

Examination of effort with the Victoria Symptom Validity Test (VSVT) yielded performances of 13/24 difficult items and 36/48 total items. The examining neuropsychologist concluded that the patient's performance on the difficult items indicated insufficient effort, and that apparent impairment in neuropsychological test performance might therefore be invalid. The VSVT manual (Slick, Hopp, Strauss, & Thompson, 1997) classifies the difficult item score as reflecting questionable but not clearly invalid performance. Subsequent studies have suggested that no patients with severe head trauma or other medically documented central nervous system disorders obtain scores lower than 18/24 difficult items or 38/48 total items (Grote et al., 2000; Macciocchi, Seel, Alderson, & Godsall, 2006). However, 12% of nonlitigating cognitively impaired patients obtained difficult item scores below this cutoff in another study (Loring, Lee, & Meador, 2005). Current results are therefore equivocal, and a definitive conclusion would await independent examination. Tests such as the Portland Digit Recognition Test (Binder, 1993) or the Computerized Assessment of Response Bias (Allen, Conder, Green, & Cox, 1997) would be useful in clarifying if the patient intentionally attempted to display cognitive impairment that was not actually present. Performance was variable across other effort measures (e.g., the Test of Memory Malingering and the Rey 15-Item Memory Test), with indications of both sufficient and insufficient effort. The current report concludes that apparently impaired test scores may reflect variable effort rather than actual impairment. Repeated examination might clarify the patient's actual levels of function.

Intelligence testing showed significant reductions in Full Scale IQ, Verbal IQ, and Working Memory Index (WMI) compared to premorbid levels as estimated by educational attainment and reading vocabulary. In contrast, Performance IQ and Processing Speed Index (PSI) were intact. As noted in the report, this pattern is not consistent with the intellectual consequences of traumatic brain injury. The PSI is the most sensitive to neurological disorders generally and traumatic brain injury in particular (Psychological Corporation, 2002; Van der Heiden & Donders, 2003). Intellectual impairment caused by head trauma would therefore be characterized by impairment in processing speed. Performance IQ is also typically more sensitive to head trauma than Verbal IQ, which recovers more completely (Rawlings & Crewe, 1992). The patient's 16 point Verbal–Performance IQ difference is therefore in the direction opposite that which generally characterizes intellectual impairment secondary to head trauma. These anomalous index and IQ score patterns in the context of particular weakness on the Arithmetic and Digit Span subtests suggest that the patient's measured intelligence may have been reduced by preexisting attention-deficit disorder, learning disability, or insufficient effort. The patient reported that she was easily distracted in school, and a review of educational transcripts might clarify the cause of her reduced test scores. Patterns of cognitive test performance that are inconsistent with the condition also often suggest symptom exaggeration (Mittenberg et al., 2002).

The patient's scores on memory tests was somewhat variable, with average recall of paragraphs but impaired recall for word lists and visually presented information. The degree of apparent impairment noted on the California Verbal Learning Test and Rey Complex Figure Test recall is not consistent with the chronic consequences of mild head injury or the patient's current ability to work as a schoolteacher. Potential explanations include distraction caused by pain, fatigue during the examination, or insufficient effort. Severity of cognitive impairment that is inconsistent with the condition is the most frequent indication of symptom exaggeration reported by neuropsychologists (Mittenberg et al., 2002). The cause of these lowered scores might be further clarified by comparison with the test scores obtained in prior testings and by a repeated independent examination.

The patient showed normal performance on measures of executive functioning that are quite sensitive to impairment caused by traumatic brain injury (Trail Making B, Wisconsin Card Sorting Test). These results are consistent with the conclusion that prominent changes in neurocognitive functions secondary to the accident are not present. Impaired scores on visual–spatial tasks are noted to have been absent in the previous neuropsychological examination and therefore cannot be attributed to the consequences of the 1998 motor vehicle accident. T-scores below 40 are reported on measures of grip strength and fine motor speed (finger tapping). Reduction of motor function is not typically associated with the chronic presentation of mild head trauma (Arnold et al., 2005; Binder, Kelly, Villanueva, & Winslow, 2003) but could be the result of orthopedic injuries. Conclusions about this would be deferred to an orthopedist, a physiatrist, or a neurologist. Apparent motor impairment may also be due to poor effort (Arnold et al., 2005; Binder et al., 2003).

Examination of emotional functioning showed no evidence of depression or other psychiatric disorder on the Beck Depression Inventory or Minnesota Multiphasic Personality Inventory–2. These results suggest that the patient does not display an Axis I disorder that would account for her symptoms or that resulted from the 1998 accident. Although the examining neuropsychologist believed that the patient may have been coached or attempted to exaggerate symptoms, this inference is not supported by the normal inventory results obtained. The patient did report a variety of symptoms consistent with postconcussion syndrome on another symptom checklist. These symptoms may be the result of injuries sustained either before or after the 1998 accident, or they may be due to misattribution of and overreaction to normal "symptoms" that are unrelated to the accident as is noted in the report (Mittenberg & Strauman, 2000). Brief cognitive-behavioral treatment that supports reattribution of symptoms such as that recommended by the examining neuropsychologist is effective in alleviating postconcussive syndrome. Analgesic or antidepressant medication may also be effective treatments (Mittenberg, Canyock, Condit, & Patton, 2001). The fact that the patient did not previously pursue recommended treatment for these symptoms diminishes the extent to which they could be viewed as causing current impairment. From a legal perspective, it can be said that she "failed to mitigate" the damages.

CONCLUSIONS

This 45-year-old woman appears to have sustained mild head trauma about 6 years prior to the current examination. History is significant for reported attentional difficulties during high school and motor vehicle accidents associated with orthopedic injuries before and after the 1998 incident. She currently complains of orthopedic pain, headache, reduced memory efficiency, and poor concentration that she attributes to the 1998 accident. Review of current examination results suggests the preliminary opinion that the patient does not display cognitive or emotional impairment caused by head trauma, and the apparent reductions in cognitive function are most likely due to insufficient effort. Potential alternative causes include symptom exaggeration, symptoms due to orthopedic injuries, preexisting cognitive limitations, and/or the effects of her motor vehicle accident 2 years later. Independent neuropsychological and medical examinations would be recommended to clarify these initial impressions. These would include a review of educational and employment records and reviews of the patients complete medical records.

REFERENCES

Allen, L. M., Conder, R. L., Green, P., & Cox, D. R. (1997). *CARB 97 manual for the Computerized Assessment of Response Bias.* Durham, NC: CogniSyst.

American Academy of Neurology. (1996). Assessment: Neuropsychological testing of adults: Considerations for neurologists. Report of the Therapeutics Technology Assessment Subcommittee of the American Academy of Neurology. *Neurology, 47*, 592–599.

Arnold, G., Boone, K. B., Lu, P., Dean, A., Wen, J., Nitch, S., et al. (2005). Sensitivity and specificity of finger tapping test scores for the detection of suspect effort. *Clinical Neuropsychologist, 19*, 105–120.

Benton, A. L., Sivan, A. B., Hamsher, K. D., Varney, N. S., & Spreen, O. (1994). *Contributions to neuropsychological assessment* (2nd ed.). New York: Oxford University Press.

Binder, L. M. (1993). *Portland Digit Recognition Test manual.* Beaverton, OR: Author.

Binder, L. M., Kelly, M. P., Villanueva, M. R., & Winslow, M. M. (2003). Motivation and neuropsychological test performance following mild head injury. *Journal of Clinical and Experimental Neuropsychology, 25*, 420–430.

Binder, L. M., Rohling, M. L., & Larrabee, G. J. (1997). A review of mild head trauma. Part 1: Meta-analytic review of neuropsychological studies. *Journal of Clinical and Experimental Neuropsychology, 19*, 421–431.

Essig, S. M., Mittenberg, W., Petersen, R. S., Strauman, S., & Cooper, J. T. (2001). Practices in forensic neuropsychology: Perspectives of neuropsychologists and trial attorneys. *Archives of Clinical Neuropsychology, 16*, 271–291.

Florida Administrative Code, Rule 64B19–18. 004[3], [6] (amended 1997).

Greiffenstein, F. M., Baker, J. W., & Johnson-Greene, D. (2002). Actual versus self-reported scholastic achievement of litigating postconcussion and severe closed head injury claimants. *Psychological Assessment, 14*, 202–208.

Grote, C. L., Kooker, E. K., Garron, D. C., Nyenhuis, D. L., Clifford A., Smith, C. L., et al. (2000). Performance of compensation seeking and non-compensation seeking samples on the Victoria Symptom Validity Test: Cross-validation and extension of a standardization study. *Journal of Clinical and Experimental Neuropsychology, 22,* 709–719.

Johnson-Greene, D., & Binder, L. M. (1995). Evaluation of an efficient method for verifying higher educational credentials. *Archives of Clinical Neuropsychology, 10,* 251–253.

Loring, D. W., Lee, G. P., & Meador, K. M. (2005). Victoria Symptom Validity Test Performance in non-litigating epilepsy surgery candidates. *Journal of Clinical and Experimental Neuropsychology, 27,* 610–617.

Macciocchi, S. N., Seel, R. T., Alderson, A., & Godsall, R. (2006). Victoria Symptom Validity Test performance in acute severe traumatic brain injury: Implications for test interpretation. *Archives of Clinical Neuropsychology, 21,* 395–404.

Mittenberg. W., Canyock, E. M., Condit, D., & Patton, C. (2001). Treatment of postconcussion syndrome following mild head injury. *Journal of Clinical and Experimental Neuropsychology, 23,* 829–836.

Mittenberg, W., Patton, C., Canyock, E. M., & Condit, D. (2002). Base rates of malingering and symptom exaggeration. *Journal of Clinical and Experimental Neuropsychology, 24,* 1094–1102.

Mittenberg, W., & Strauman, S. (2000). Diagnosis of mild head injury and the postconcussion syndrome. *Journal of Head Trauma Rehabilitation, 15,* 783–791.

National Academy of Neuropsychology. (2000). Test security: Official position statement of the National Academy of Neuropsychology. *Archives of Clinical Neuropsychology, 15,* 383–386.

Psychological Corporation. (2002). *WAIS-III and WMS-III Technical manual.* San Antonio, TX: Harcourt Assessment.

Rawlings, D. B., & Crewe, N. M. (1992). Test–retest practice effects and test score changes on the WAIS-R in recovering traumatically brain injured survivors. *The Clinical Neuropsychologist, 6,* 415–430.

Schretlen, D. J., & Shapiro, A. M. (2003). A quantitative review of the effects of traumatic brain injury on cognitive functioning. *International Review of Psychiatry, 15,* 341–349.

Slick, D., Hopp, G., Strauss, E., & Thompson G. B. (1997). *Victoria Symptom Validity Test. Professional manual.* Odessa, FL: Psychological Assessment Resources.

Sweet, J. J., Nelson, N. W., & Moberg, P. J. (2006). The TCN/AACN 2005 salary survey: Professional practices, beliefs, and incomes of U.S. neuropsychologists. *The Clinical Neuropsychologist, 20,* 325–364.

Van der Heiden, P., & Donders, J. (2003). WAIS-III factor score patterns after traumatic brain injury. *Assessment, 10,* 115–122.

Part III
Special Topics

11

Anoxic Brain Injury
Daubert *Challenge,*
Fixed versus Flexible Battery

Erin D. Bigler

I have been a practicing neuropsychologist since 1975 and an academic, research, and training director of clinical neuropsychology subspecialty curriculum at American Psychological Association (APA)–approved clinical PhD programs since 1977—first at the University of Texas–Austin, where I established the program and directed it until 1990, and since then at Brigham Young University. Even before the "Houston model" (Hannay, 1998) became the standard for training in clinical neuropsychology, it was the training method I used, continue to use, and endorse. I have always approached neuropsychological assessment from the perspective that a patient's history, clinical presentation, and symptoms guide the type of consultation performed, including the selection of neuropsychological tests administered—clearly a "flexible-battery" approach (Benton, 1992). I had already been licensed and practicing for a year when, in 1976, the first edition of Lezak's *Neuropsychological Assessment* became the standard that guided my original approach to teaching and evaluating neuropsychological problems. In the beginning of my career, I also used the Halstead–Reitan Neuropsychological Battery (HRNB; see Reitan & Davison, 1974) because it provided, within a single-battery approach, methods for what then was termed *lesion localization, lateralization* of cerebral dysfunction, and detection of *organic brain damage* or *organicity*—important referral questions by 1970s standards. There have been recent surveys that have assessed the flexible versus fixed battery (i.e., HRNB) approach in clinical neuropsychological practice. While a fixed battery was in common use in the 1970s and 1980s, the most recent surveys show that its usage constitutes less than 15% in contemporary clinical practice (Rabin, Barr, & Burton, 2005; Sweet, Nelson, & Moberg, 2006).

In the early days of clinical neuropsychology, these were important concepts. Much of clinical psychology of the 1950s and 1960s was entrenched in psychodynamic theory of behavior and neuropsychology was demonstrating that some differences in behavior were not because of unconscious motives but because of brain dysfunction. Beginning in the 1950s the HRNB method could demonstrate "brain impairment" by use of standardized psychological instruments. Since this predated all the tremendous advances in neuroimaging, neuropsychology was showing that behavior could be measured in a way that inferred brain function. Indeed, my role in some of the earliest cases that I saw in the 1970s was to assist neurologists and neurosurgeons with "lesion localization" to infer the location and extent of damage in presurgical cases, especially with vascular or neoplastic disease. However, by the 1980s two distinct problems in neuropsychological assessment and consultation became evident with the fixed-battery approach exemplified by the HRNB: Performance on the HRNB could be entirely normal in individuals with indisputable neuroimaging and neurosurgical findings of brain damage (Bigler, 1988) and insurance reimbursement began to change and limit the amount of time that could be devoted to neuropsychological assessment, incompatible with daylong test administration required by the fixed-battery HRNB approach. When simple detection of "organicity" and/or lateralization/lesion localization were no longer the primary province of neuropsychological assessment, replaced largely by neuroimaging, along with the introduction of excellent, well standardized tests of a multitude of cognitive and neurobehavioral functions that came available in the 1980s and 1990s, the flexible-battery approach became much more suited to the targeted referral questions addressed by neuropsychologists (i.e., a patient referred for memory assessment, rather than whether he or she had "organic" dysfunction) and how I practiced clinical neuropsychology. Thus, from the 1970s until now, tremendous growth occurred in the number of tests and normative data available to assess and study the neurological bases of behavior. As an example of this growth, Lezak's first edition (1976) had 549 pages; the fourth edition has 1,016 (Lezak, Howieson, & Loring, 2004).

The aforementioned factors were followed by the emergence of functional neuroimaging and cognitive neuroscience methods that opened up entirely new approaches to assessing brain function, particularly cognitive abilities. Gazzaniga's (1995) text, titled *The Cognitive Neurosciences,* was the first to attempt to integrate this new field of studying the "mind" not just in clinical populations but in so-called normal individuals. Important for neuropsychology was/is that cognitive neuroscientists were not necessarily psychologists and therefore not beholden to past or even contemporary psychological theory, where theory in cognitive neuroscience was more biologically and medically driven. HRNB theoretical underpinnings, on the other hand, date back to the 1930s and 1940s, with nothing all that new since then. So, while early in its development the HRNB may have been "state of the art," in my opinion, the HRNB quickly became outdated by advances in clinical neuroscience including neuroimaging along with increased availability of "flexible" approaches for assessing cognitive deficits (Lezak et al., 2004; Mitrushina, Boone, Razani, & D'Elia, 2005; Strauss, Sherman, & Spreen, 2006). So given that background, one day I received a fax outlining a challenge to my testimony as a retained plaintiff expert in a case of hypoxic brain injury, because of my use of a flexible-battery approach to neuropsychological assessment. The identified patient had documented hypoxia with magnetic resonance imaging (MRI) indicating the classic signs of anoxic brain injury (i.e., bilateral symmetric basal ganglia lesions, deep white matter lesions, bilateral hippocampal atrophy, and hypothalamic lesions; see Hopkins & Bigler, 2001). However, this was not a fax merely stating that the neuropsychologist retained by the defense disagreed with my conclusions. Rather, it implied that my entire approach to neuropsychological assessment and my test data and testimony should be summarily dismissed; not allowed whatsoever in the courtroom because the flexible-battery approach was *not valid*! The legal issues of this attempt to exclude testimony have already been published elsewhere (Bigler, 2007) and what follows herein are additional clinical and forensic details.

PREAMBLE

In neuropsychology, what eventually becomes a legal case involving neuropsychological expert opinion often begins as a routine "clinical" case for someone, where various clinicians see and evaluate a patient with some type of neurological or neuropsychiatric presentation. In fact, this represents an important legal distinction between a clinician who was/is a "treater" versus a "forensic expert" (see discussion in Bigler, 2006). Most view the clinical record and the patient's history as key to understanding the disorder and making an accurate diagnosis (Dames, Tonnerre, Saint, & Jones, 2005). This initial clinical information is assumed to be unfettered by subsequent legal issues that may obscure the patient's assessment, care and treatment. Thus, this initial period of symptom onset and potential injury provides key baseline information about the patient and his or her level of initial impairment. When a case switches from just a clinical case to one that involves litigation, the prelitigation clinical record becomes a matter of intense scrutiny, as well as any other pertinent preincident history, dissected to find clues that may contribute to understanding the diagnosis.

What may be earnest disagreement between two clinicians interpreting the same neuropsychological data often becomes something quite different in a highly contested legal case. When plaintiff attorneys file a case, they often use the initial clinical record to support their contentions. If there is legal agreement on the defense side as to what happened and the potential sequelae, typically, litigation goes no further and the case is resolved through some mutually agreeable solution. However, if the defense side, after reviewing these same clinical and historical records, comes to different conclusions from what treating clinicians have already established and diagnosed, then the adversarial litigation process begins. Thus legal sides are chosen and irrespective of the side, from the attorney's perspective, each major point made by one side has to be addressed or countered by the other. As this point/counterpoint process progresses, often multiple experts across many disciplines are retained for specific legal purposes, completely separate from any clinical reason.

In an ideal world, it should not matter whether the neuropsychologist is retained by the plaintiff or the defense. Regardless of the side of retention, neuropsychologists should carry out their assessment as they would in any clinical setting, by simply applying the best in contemporary research and practice standards to their assessment, diagnosis, and prognosis of any patient. In theory, that is how it should be and is advocated by at least one of our major neuropsychology organizations (see American Academy of Clinical Neuropsychology, 2007), but, forensic neuropsychology has many pressures, one of which is beyond the role of the clinician. When some attorneys retain an expert, they also see that neuropsychological expert as a "consultant" for their side, a consultant that will help them *win* their case. The consultant role has many trappings that may be very different than what happens in clinical practice; it is also different from the purely expert role.

Attorneys are unlikely to retain a neuropsychologist whose professional opinions about the case are not likely to match their own. Therefore, from the plaintiff side that typically means that the retained expert's opinions support the presence of neuropsychological sequelae associated with the injury or disorder in question. Typical positions taken by the defense, however, are quite opposite and include that "no injury or deficit" is present, the problem has resolved (i.e., recovered), or the problem can be attributed to other factors (i.e., premorbid conditions) or factors other than the one in question (patient is actually depressed and not brain damaged, patient is malingering, etc.), or that the problems are less severe than concluded by the plaintiff's side. These aforementioned approaches are commonplace and occur at some level in the defense of every case. However, what happened in this case—the implication that *anyone* who uses a flexible battery is using an invalid measure inadmissible in court—I had not experienced in the 30+ years I have been in practice.

Attorneys can challenge an expert's opinions by various legal maneuvers. One method is a *Daubert* challenge (Masten & Strzelczyk, 2001), often colloquially referred to as the junk science defense. In brief, this means that one side challenges the other on using methods not up to the scientific standards for the profession. In the present case, the defense-retained neuropsychologist critiqued the work of the original clinical psychologist, who in his role as a treater conducted a flexible-battery approach as did I in evaluating this patient with an anoxic brain injury. In such a scenario for neuropsychology, the methods of assessment become the centerpiece of the defense expert's attack of the clinical record. In this case, the defense argued that *all* neuropsychological tests from a flexible-battery approach were invalid for forensic purposes and, therefore, any diagnostic conclusions made and testimony based on such procedures should be thrown out.

CASE STUDY

This was a case in which the plaintiff experienced an anoxic brain injury as a consequence of errors in postsurgical management. As shown in Figure 11.1, bilateral basal ganglia lesions, as well as deep white abnormalities and presence of bilateral hippocampal atrophy, were documented on postincident imaging. Given these objective findings at the time I was retained to be the plaintiff's expert, this appeared to me to be a straightforward case.

As might be expected, as a result of this anoxic injury, the plaintiff developed neuropsychiatric symptoms, and before any litigation was filed, the treating psychiatrist requested a psychological assessment conducted by a clinical psychologist, who had some background in neuropsychological testing. This was done before the MRI findings. Prior to litigation being filed, the private practice clinical psychologist saw the patient for a comprehensive evaluation and administered a broad spectrum of psychological measures, including neuropsychological screening tests. Results reflected lower than expected (patient had 4 years of college and professional level employment prior to the anoxic injury) memory and speed of processing scores (Digit Symbol scaled score of 5 on the Wechsler Adult Intelligence Scale–III [WAIS-III], and a slow Trail Making Test B of 108 seconds, with a

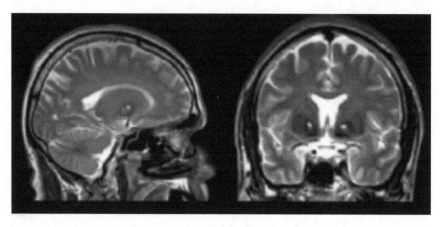

FIGURE 11.1. Left: T2 sagittal MRI cut through the left basal ganglia at the level of the globus pallidus showing significant signal change in that region of the brain. Right: Coronal T2 MRI at the level of the basal ganglia showing bilateral globus pallidus lesions. These objective neuroimaging abnormalities are the typical changes seen in hypoxic brain injury.

standard score of 91 on both the Wechsler Memory Scale–III (WMS-III) General Memory Index and the Working Memory Index along with poor performance on the Booklet Category Test (81 errors). The clinical psychologist also diagnosed depression and recommended psychotherapy and further medication review.

Defense's Initial Response

The defense initially retained a neurologist and another clinical psychologist/ neuropsychologist to review the records but not to formally examine the plaintiff; the records review occurred before the MRI was performed. Both of these defense experts acknowledged the medical evidence of hypoxia but discussed the reversibility of anoxic conditions, emphasizing that most of the psychological testing done by the treating clinical psychologist demonstrated "average" ability level and, therefore, "no specific impairment nor deficit" was evident. Both agreed that the patient was depressed.

Plaintiff's Response: Case Formulation and Conclusions

The plaintiff side retained a clinical neurologist who examined the patient but also had an MRI performed, with the abnormalities as described in Figure 11.1. It was at this point that I was contacted by the plaintiff side. I was asked to first review the various medical records, the MRI findings along with the testing data of the treating psychologist who had seen the patient, and also the position being put forth by the defense. I have been involved in an ongoing anoxic brain injury research program here in Utah for over 15 years, so I had seen many hypoxic/anoxic patients and have published numerous studies over the years (see Hopkins & Bigler, 2001; Hopkins, Tate, & Bigler, 2005). Upon reviewing these records, an immediate impression I had was that this patient's depression and affective changes may be the most prominent sequelae of the anoxia. Indeed, there is a subgroup of anoxic patients who have dramatic neuroimaging findings, yet it is not so much the cognitive deficits as it is the emotional/affective changes that result in disability. This is because of the vulnerability of basal ganglia and limbic structures to the effects of anoxia. My impression during the clinical interview was that the emotional/affective changes were probably the primary neurobehavioral sequelae of this case.

In cases of anoxic brain injury, dramatic disorders of memory may not be seen, but what is commonly observed is that cognitive measures assessing working memory tend to be below levels of expectation. Thus, neuropsychological testing in such patients does not reveal amnesia but, rather, inefficiency in memory, which may also affect executive functions. In this patient, based on all examinations performed, all validity indicators, including the ones I used (i.e., 100% correct on the Tests of Neuropsychological Malingering; see Pritchard, 1998); 15/15 on the Rey 15-Item Memory Test; 16/16 on the Recognition trial of the California Verbal Learning Test; see Delis, Kramer, Kaplan, & Ober, 1994), were within normal limits (WNL) suggesting that appropriate effort was present yielding a valid profile of neuropsychological test results, the type typically observed in anoxia (Hopkins & Haaland, 2004). During various stages of this case, the patient underwent four separate psychological/neuropsychological evaluations, with Full Scale IQ (FSIQ) scores ranging from a low of 102 to a high of 116. The overall average across these four assessments was 108. The patient had almost enough hours to graduate from college but had not completed a degree but had maintained responsible, professional-level employment prior to the anoxic incident. So, given that the IQ test results were average to above average, my estimate of premorbid ability was that before the anoxia this patient was at least high average to above average in cognitive function. Consequently, a standard score of 94 on the Delayed Memory component of the Repeatable Battery for the Assessment of Neuropsychological Status (RBANS; Randolph, 1998), along with an Attention standard score of 85, were ~1.0–2.0 standard deviations below expected IQ, when I examined the patient. There were similar findings on the Working Memory Index of the WMS (standard score 91; overall General Memory Index was 104). Likewise, although the overall California Verbal Learning Test T-score was 57 and, hence WNL, the first two trials were 7 and 8, slightly below expectations (recognition memory was 16/16; as already indicated). The Rey Complex Figure Test Design score was 34/36 for copy but 15-minute recall was 17, below expectation given IQ and premorbid ability level (a score higher than ~22 would have been predicted; see Mitrushina et al., 2005). Four errors where present on the Benton Visual Retention Test, whereas only two would have been expected given age and IQ. My view of these findings was that the patient's attentional system was less than optimal, common in individuals with documented subcortical basal ganglia damage (Chudasama & Robbins, 2006; Werring et al., 2004). Responses to psychological inventories indicated significant endorsement of symptoms of depression (Beck Depression Inventory raw score of 23, with T-scores of 72 on the Symptom Check List 90-R and 96 on the Minnesota Multiphasic Personality Inventory [MMPI] Depression Scales). As already mentioned, clinical depression was evident on mental status examination. Depression is a common a sequelae of anoxia (Jasper, Hopkins, Duker, & Weaver, 2005). Taking all of this together—a well-documented anoxic episode, MRI documentation of signature abnormalities consistent with anoxia, clinical presentation of depression and neuropsychological tests implicating inefficient memory and attentional systems—my assessment was that this was a rather straightforward case of neurobehavioral sequelae associated with hypoxic brain injury.

My deposition was tendered and there were lots of questions about my approach to, and philosophy of, how clinical neuropsychological assessment should be done. At the time I did not think much about the line of questioning, because it seemed fairly routine, except the defense attorney kept asking and having me reaffirm that I used the flexible-battery approach to everything I did. In my deposition I emphasized both the emotional and cognitive problems but gave what I considered a "fair and balanced" deposition indicating that there were things that could be done to treat the emotional and cognitive residuals from this hypoxia. When the deposition concluded, I felt satisfied that I had appropriately addressed the issues in the case and provided a detailed overview of how hypoxia can produce neuropsychological and neuropsychiatric sequelae. At the time, however, I thought nothing more about what might actually be behind that line of questioning.

Defense Recounters: Third Neuropsychological Evaluation Ordered

The defense retained a neuropsychologist to critique my evaluation as well as the original treating clinical psychologist's assessment. Initially, this defense-retained neuropsychologist did not see the patient but only reviewed records and issued a report with the following conclusions: The patient "does not demonstrate neurocognitive impairment that would be consistent with hypoxic brain injury. In fact, neuropsychological test performance appears to reflect average abilities that are within expectation given educational and vocational background. The effects of non-neurological factors such as chronic pain and psychological/psychiatric disorder are likely explanations for the variability in test performances and for the difficulties the patient is having in function." This defense-retained neuropsychologist also raised the specter of the invalidity of the treating psychologist's and my use of a *flexible*-battery approach because we used a "research" version of the Category Test (the HRNB purist only should use the original back-lit carousel slide projector Category Test, from which the original norms were established). This defense-retained neuropsychologist specifically stated that a booklet or computerized version of the Category Test were "inappropriate" and its "clinical significance unknown." This defense-retained neuropsychologist was also critical that a full "original" HRNB was not administered.

The defense sought and was granted a court order to have the defense neuropsychologist examine the patient. The examination was performed 7 months after my examination and approximately 3 years after the anoxic incident. The plaintiff was examined for 2 days, back to back, and was administered the original HRNB, Wechsler Adult Intelligence Scale (again HRNB purists only use the Wechsler–Bellevue or the original WAIS), the Wide Range Achievement Test—Revised, the Personality Assessment Inventory (PAI), the Victoria Symptom Validity Test, the Test of Memory Malingering, Rey 15-Item Memory Test, Mini-Mental State Examination, and a clinical interview; with the results of what constitutes the core components of the HRNB Impairment Index presented in Table 11.1. The defense neuropsychologist concluded the following after conducting this examination:

> Examination of this patient's neuropsychological functioning indicates generalized and specific neuropsychological functioning that is within normal expectation. Some mild sensorimotor deficits were evidenced. This pattern of results is not suggestive of any significant neurocognitive impairment or significant residual neuropsychological impairment. In fact, the patient demonstrates many intact higher neurocognitive abilities. Psychologically, the patient presents with significant psychological difficulties that are likely contributing to problems in function.

Motion to Exclude

With the report of the second defense-retained neuropsychologist in hand, along with my multiple and repeated deposition statements that I *relied* on

TABLE 11.1. HRNB Defense Expert Results

			Original Reitan cutoff	Impaired range	GNDS	Rating
Category Test						
Number of errors			42	> 51	—	26–45	1
Tactual Performance Test						
Dominant Hand (R)	8.7	Total time	15.6	> 15.6	—	15.1–25.0	2
Nondominant Hand (L)	3.7	Memory	9	≤ 6	*	8–10	0
Both hands	3.2	Localization	4*	≤ 4	—	3–5	0
Seashore Rhythm Test						
Number correct	29		29	> 5 errors	—	28–30	0
Speech Sounds Perception Test						
Number of errors			7	> 7 errors	—	7–10	1
Finger Tapping Test						
Dominant Hand (R)	50.8		51	< 50	—	50–54	1
Nondominant Hand (L)	41.4						
Impairment index				≥ 0.5	0.1		

Note. HRNB, Halstead–Reitan Neuropsychological Battery; GNDS, General Neuropsychological Deficit Scale.

a flexible-battery approach for interpreting neuropsychological test results in forming my conclusions, the defense immediately filed a formal "motion to exclude" my evaluation and testimony along with the treating clinical psychologist's. To offer the reader a flavor of this legal argument, following are verbatim excerpts from the motion written by the lawyers defending the case:

> When it comes to neuropsychological testing, reliability equals validity. There are two different types of neuropsychological test batteries: (1) the fixed battery (2) and the flexible battery. One is scientifically validated (the fixed battery), while the other, by definition, cannot be scientifically validated (the flexible battery). Unless the neuropsychologist's choice of test batteries is scientifically validated for the purpose of specifically demonstrating the causation of cognitive deficits, their opinions cannot meet the reliability standards of scientific methodology in [state deleted] *courts.*
>   The flexible batteries used by the plaintiff's experts "have never been scientifically validated to show brain injury, and therefore both

the methodology of these experts and their opinions based on this methodology cannot pass muster under *Robinson*[1] [because] these *individual* [emphasis added] tests have never been scientifically validated to demonstrate cognitive deficits vs. normal variation or another cause for poor performance, and therefore these opinions cannot survive a Robinson analysis.

A more complete review of this motion can be found in Bigler (2007). In my opinion, this was an astonishing move by the defense, a legal maneuver inspired by what some neuropsychologist's have published and argued, as discussed below.

Rejoinder

In the past, the fixed-battery approach with its use of cut-points was selected to detect the presence or absence of "organicity" or "organic brain damage"—brain damage that affected the person's behavior (Benton, 1994). This approach, taken by the defense neuropsychologist, says that if a patient surpasses a cut-point he or she is neurologically impaired (i.e., "brain damaged"). But, if the cut-point is not reached, the patient is neurologically intact (i.e., "not brain damaged"). Using the fixed-battery approach in this manner focuses the clinical decision making on detecting "brain damage" not the relative performance within a cognitive or behavioral domain compared to normative data or in reference to the patient's estimated premorbid ability. In fairness to this approach, the authors of the fixed battery HRNB method do discuss borderline, mild, moderate, and severe categories of impairment (Reitan & Wolfson, 1993; Russell, Neuringer, & Goldstein, 1973) but for the HRNB purist the problem is that a patient's performance *must* reach the set-point of impairment as defined by a cutoff score before any classification or label of brain damage or dysfunction is made. So, the defense neuropsychologist pointed out that the HRNB Impairment Index in this patient was just 0.1, well below the 0.5 cut-point for diagnosing brain damage and, therefore, WNL. When using this approach, any score below the cut-point is considered WNL regardless of how *close* it comes to being "abnormal." Reitan and Wolfson (1985) have also published cutoff scores for the General Neuropsychological Deficit Scale (GNDS), which I have expanded in Table 11.1, but the GNDS was never mentioned or reported by the defense neuropsychologist. Reviewing Table 11.1 shows that in both the original cutoff scores as well as the GNDS the patient comes very close to performing in the "abnormal" range

---

[1]*Robinson* is a reference to state case law similar to the more generally known *Daubert* standard (Hollingsworth & Lasker, 2004).

as denoted by asterisks. As Reitan and Wolfson (1993) have stated, a GNDS score of 1 means the score is still "within the normal range, but represents a performance that was not quite as good as might be ideally expected" (p. 350). Reitan and Wolfson also state that an Impairment Index of "0.4 is considered borderline" (p. 92). As shown by the asterisks in Table 11.1 using Reitan and Wolfson's (1985) GNDS gradations, this patient's scores are in the border zone between normal and impaired on three of the tests and in the impaired range on two of the tests, a fact never mentioned by the defense neuropsychologist. So, instead of pointing this out, the patient's scores were merely interpreted as being WNL because they fell below the cutoff. Reitan and colleagues have argued against using age and education adjusted normative data (Reitan & Wolfson, 1997, 2005; Russell, Russell, & Hill, 2005) and therefore the defense neuropsychologist argued against the use of anything like the Heaton, Grant, and Matthews (1991) norms and merely classified this HRNB performance as "normal," never acknowledging the GNDS ratings and dismissing any argument for how close this patient came to being classified as impaired.

For the defense-retained neuropsychologist, an HRNB Impairment Index below the cut-point meant normal brain function, *period*. So, despite the well-known relationship between basal ganglia lesions and motor slowing and diminished coordination (Aparicio, Diedrichsen, & Ivry, 2005; Monza et al., 1998; Schwarz, Fellows, Schaffrath, & Noth, 2001; Shin, Aparicio, & Ivry, 2005), the defense neuropsychologist only mentions that "some mild sensorimotor deficits" were observed but dismisses the clinical significance by stating that "significant psychological difficulties . . . are likely contributing to problems in function." The defense neuropsychologist makes no mention whatsoever of basal ganglia lesions as documented in the MRI or how such lesions might affect motor performance, memory, or mood. In fact, the defense neuropsychologist at the time of deposition could not cite even one study where the HRNB was used in evaluating anoxic brain injury in patients with MRI-defined basal ganglia lesions, but that did not deter the defense neuropsychologist from reaffirming the normalcy of HRNB performance based on the 0.1 Impairment Index. However, as shown in Table 11.1, motor slowing on the Tactual Performance Test (TPT) was evident where the patient gets a total score of 15.6 (cutoff 15.7) minutes. Thus, the patient missed the brain-damaged cut-point by one-tenth of a minute or *6 seconds!*—a fact never pointed out in the report or alluded to in any way.

The patient's TPT localization score was 4, the only impaired HRNB score, which of course is a measure of memory. A serious criticism of the HRNB has long been its lack of any systematic assessment of memory (Bigler & Clement, 1997). Again, the HRNB purist will supplement the HRNB with the original WMS (Wechsler, 1945), the rationale being that the original WMS would have been the only memory test available when the original standardization of the HRNB occurred in the 1950s and 1960s, although some renorming of the original WMS has occurred with the HRNB (see Russell, 1988). Even with its shortcomings, the WMS nonetheless was sensitive to memory impairment (Bigler, 1984; Bigler & Clement, 1997), but this defense neuropsychologist only looked at a "retention coefficient" of the WMS rather than percentile performance in comparison to a normative sample (Russell, 1988). Thus, only the Logical Memory (LM) stories of the original WMS were administered. The patient recalled 17.5/47 on immediate recall and 15.5/47 on the delay component. The retention coefficient used by the defense neuropsychologist divided the delayed score by the immediate retention score (15.5/17.5), yielding an approximate retention coefficient of 90%. Such an approach, in my opinion, was highly misleading and ignores how this patient's memory performance is in reference to any normative sample. What also struck me from the initial assessment of the clinical psychologist who originally evaluated this patient as well as my evaluation was that while the patient's memory performance was technically within the average range, many of the individual scores appeared subpar to me, given that the job skills required to perform the work premorbidly would have been demanding, requiring strong working memory skills. In my opinion, retaining less than half of the material on the WMS LM subtest was consistent with the patient's memory complaints, not how the defense neuropsychologist used this to show "good retention" over time of what was initially recalled. Of course, memory problems could also be influenced by depression and other neuropsychiatric aspects of the patient's clinical presentation, but these too, in my opinion where all related to the anoxic injury.

Finally, the patient's Category Test score was 42 on the defense neuropsychologist's examination. The GNDS gives this score a rating of 1, indicating a less than optimal score. This was never mentioned by the defense neuropsychologist. From the perspective of this patient's premorbid status, the patient's job required complex decision making and one would have expected better performance on the Category Test. Furthermore, when I assessed this patient's difficulties with the Wisconsin Card Sorting Task (completed only three categories, making 22 perseverative errors) were encountered. While the copying of the Rey Complex Figure Test was well within normal limits (two minor errors resulting in a score of 34), the patient's retention was not. The Rey Complex Figure Test not only assesses memory but is thought to tap aspects of executive functions (Knight, 2003); yet for the fixed-battery traditionalist the only acceptable approach to assessing executive function is based on the HRNB, and the original 1940s method of administration of the Category Test. Returning to Table 11.1, based on the GNDS of the defense neuropsychologist's own data (not mine or the other treating clinical psychologist) the patient shows motor slowing, borderline memory on one measure (TPT Localization) and borderline performance on, the Category Test, all findings that are consistent with the types of motor, executive, memory, and emotional dysfunction associated with hypoxia (Hopkins & Haaland, 2004; Lim, Alexander, LaFleche, Schnyer, & Verfaellie, 2004). However, looking at the same data this defense neuropsychologist concluded "no deficits present."

It is well established that the emotional sequelae associated with hypoxic brain injury can result in depression (Jasper et al., 2005), particularly when bilateral basal ganglia lesions are present (Miller et al., 2006). Basal ganglia lesions can also result in apathy (Levy & Dubois, 2006), features of which were also present in this patient. In fact, the patient told all evaluators that something was emotionally "wrong" and often he "just didn't feel anything anymore." Interestingly, none of the retained defense experts ever mentioned that the basal ganglia are critical structures in regulating mood and the perception of emotion (Caligiuri et al., 2006; McEwen, 2005; Sheline, 2000), that MRI-determined basal ganglia abnormalities are associated with depression (Foncke, Schuurman, & Spellman, 2006; Kanner, 2004) and that acquired basal ganglia lesions, specifically as in this case, may induce severe depression (Foncke et al., 2006; Miller et al., 2006). In fact, Miller and colleagues (2006) present a case study of a patient with acquired bilateral lesions from hypoxia that essentially has *normal* neuropsychological findings but life-altering anhedonia after the hypoxic injury. Clinically, in my assessment, mood changes secondary to hypoxic injury in this patient with what appeared to be acquired bilateral globus pallidus lesions make sense, and that was my conclusion. In fact, I considered these neuropsychiatric abnormalities to be of equal or greater importance to the cognitive deficits.

Another important point, discussed by none of the defense experts, is the potential delayed effects of hypoxic injury (Kwon, Chung, Ha, Yoo, & Kim, 2004; Lee & Lyketsos, 2001; Tamura et al., 2002). In both animal and human literature, it is well documented that a delayed, most likely an excitotoxic, cascade can occur days to weeks postinitial hypoxic injury. As a result of these delayed effects, the full manifestation of the original hypoxic injury may take months to evolve, and how the patient appears immediately upon recovery from hypoxia may not be predictive of outcome.

Defense Deposition

My deposition was tendered shortly after I examined the patient, likely part of the defense tactic to get on the record my use and reliance on a flexible-battery approach. Specific answers to defense cross-examination questions during my deposition were used in the motion to exclude, so clearly that was one of the defense strategies from the beginning. However, before the motion could be decided on by the judge, the plaintiff side had the opportunity to take the defense neuropsychologist's deposition, who had performed the face-to-face HRNB assessment. Obviously, the plaintiff side was interested in this neuropsychologist's statement about what kind of HRNB findings would be expected in cases of subcortical damage from hypoxia, because when the defense neuropsychologist performed the evaluation, it was done knowing that the patient had bilateral basal ganglia, medial temporal lobe abnormalities and signal changes in the deep white matter and hypothalamus verified on two independently performed MRI studies. However, the defense neuropsychologist was unable to cite any literature showing sensitivity and specificity of the HRNB in detecting subcortical damage of the type typically seen in hypoxic brain injury. Recall that this neuropsychologist's initial report stated that neither my assessment nor the treating clinical psychologist's initial evaluation showed any "impairment that would be consistent with hypoxic brain injury." However, although there is abundant literature showing memory and executive function deficits associated with hypoxic brain injury, particularly when positive basal ganglia and/or medial temporal lobe damage is present (Hopkins et al., 1995; Hopkins & Haaland, 2004; Hopkins, Myers, Shohamy, Grossman, & Gluck, 2004), the defense neuropsychologist could not cite a single study using the HRNB that had been conducted in patients with hypoxic brain injury with documented abnormal imaging findings. So, the defense neuropsychologist merely adhered to the position that the HRNB performance was technically normal, the Impairment Index "was below" the cut-point, ergo "no brain damage."

Plaintiff Prevails in the Motion

The defendant's motion to exclude was denied by the judge, shortly after which the case settled. This is not the first case to receive this type of challenge (McKinzey & Ziegler, 1999; Reed, 1996) and by some of the literature being published in clinical neuropsychology as I write this chapter; this is likely not to be the last one. The entire issue of admissibility of testimony based on neuropsychological assessment is likely to be ongoing and one with which clinical neuropsychology will have to deal (Hollingsworth & Lasker, 2004; Kaufmann, 2005; Masten & Strzelczyk, 2001; Vallabhajosula & van Gorp, 2001).

COMMENT: FIXED- VERSUS FLEXIBLE-BATTERY APPROACH

The plaintiff attorneys asked that I provide them a historical background to the defense's position. The idea that psychometric measures could be used to reliably assess human behavior, in many respects, defines the very beginnings of clinical psychology. Naturally, because brain disorders alter behavior, psychologists began applying such psychometric methods in evaluating humans with some known neurological condition. Classic examples of this involve some of the most important names of 20th-century psychologists, including Hebb's (1939) paper on applying intellectual testing in the evaluation of lobectomy patients, Teuber's (1964) evaluation of World War II soldiers with penetrating head injury and Halstead's (1947) seminal contribution on intelligence in man. Simultaneous with these early developments were Lashley's (1929) animal work of mass action and equipotentiality of cortical lesions in rats and Lauretta Bender's (1938) human work, influenced by Lashley as well as the gestalt movement in sensation and perception, that led to a "unifying" concept of detecting brain damage or organicity, championed by her visual–motor gestalt test—a test taught to every clinical psychology student from the 1950s through the 1970s. *Organicity* was a dichotomous concept—one was either organic, meaning some type of brain dysfunction/damage, or not. However, prior to the 1970s (and really not until the 1990s), few of the so-called mental disorders were considered to be related in any way to brain dysfunction (see Page, 1947). When brain damage was not detected with these crude methods the patient's problems where then categorized as "functional" or "supratenorial" (i.e., above the tentorium, or "it's all in your head," medical slang for a psychological disorder). So, in the early days of the emerging field of clinical neuropsychology, the HRNB became a so-called gold standard (Russell et al., 2005) of psychometric methods for some to detect organicity because Reitan included some neurosurgical patients who had tissue extirpation, thereby incontrovertible proof of brain damage (Reitan, 1955). Thus, if someone performed on the HRNB like someone with known brain damage, then the inference was made that the individual's HRNB test performance was reflective of brain damage.

The era of standardization of the HRNB (1950s through the early 1980s) as the *only* validated fixed battery occurred during an era where only the most basic of brain–behavior assumptions were known, the issue of organicity dominated the clinical literature, and contemporary neuroimaging did not exist. Furthermore, none of the standardizations were done where consensus panels were independent of those standardizing the test, a common practice in today's research world. The HRNB became a commercial product, and therefore any promotion of its merits by those who benefit from its sale or training of its use (i.e., putting on workshops) raises issues of conflict of interest for it being the "only" standard to be used in the courtroom. Finally, in this case the defense neuropsychologist adhered to Reitan's initial normative data, as detailed in Reitan and Wolfson (1985), which had just 50 brain-damaged subjects and 50 matched controls, to establish the cut-points defining for what is normal and abnormal brain function.

In earlier publications (Bigler, 1984), I have written extensively on the merits of using the HRNB in neuropsychological assessment and have no problem with clinicians who use it, as long as they do so knowing its limitations. However, in my opinion the argument that the HRNB is *the only set of neuropsychological tests that can be used in forensic assessments* is simply baseless. Accordingly, the following quote from Russell and colleagues (2005), which was one of the centerpiece arguments for the motion to exclude, is, in my opinion, simply incorrect given the current status of clinical neuroscience: "In summary, in forensic situations, the expert witness using a standardized battery is the *only* [italics added] psychologist who can provide dependable testimony interpreting psychometric test data as a whole to the court. The expert witness who utilizes a flexible battery *cannot* [italics added] provide dependable evidence derived from the battery as a whole . . . " (p. 792). During my deposition I put forward my opinion that contemporary clinical neuroscience has moved far beyond the HRNB and that these were but dying arguments based on a historical footnote from the beginnings of clinical neuropsychology.

Finally, in this case the medical record demonstrated that a significant hypoxic/anoxic event had occurred and two independent MRI examinations had demonstrated the presence of abnormalities most consistent with hypoxic/anoxic brain injury. In my opinion, the issue of whether or not brain damage was present was not the question for neuropsychology—it clearly had already been answered by the patient's medical history and the positive imaging findings. Neuropsychology's role here was to provide data about the neurobehavioral and neurocognitive sequelae of the injury and a flexible-battery approach nicely portrayed the kinds of problems that occurred in this case.

CONCLUSIONS

In legal disputes there are always two sides to every argument. To accept the defense's position one would first have to accept that no untoward lasting effect whatsoever could have injured the brain from a medically well-documented generalized hypoxia. Then, one would have to reject the idea that the patient's subjective complaints of mood and cognitive changes after this hypoxic event had no neurological basis. Furthermore, one would have had to reject the patient's early clinical presentation as evaluated by a psychiatrist and clinical psychologist (before any legal action) was unrelated to the hypoxic injury and positive imaging findings. The abnormal imaging findings, considered to be hallmark abnormalities of hypoxic–ischemic injury in otherwise normal individuals, would have to be considered just a chance finding and unrelated to the documented hypoxia. Finally, one would have to conclude that the profile of impairments documented in the neuropsychological tests of both the plaintiff-retained and defense-retained psychologists were also unrelated to any hypoxia or imaging findings. From my perspective, such conclusions were specious and untenable. My impression was that the patient had suffered a hypoxic brain injury that left him with residual impairments, as described previously. Adherence and overreliance to a fixed-battery approach ignores the underlying clinical issues critical in determining the relationship between history, neuropsychological presentation, and neuroimaging findings.

REFERENCES

American Academy of Clinical Neuropsychology. (2007). Practice guidelines for neuropsychological assessment and consultation. *The Clinical Neuropsychologist, 21*, 209–231.

Aparicio, P., Diedrichsen, J., & Ivry, R. B. (2005). Effects of focal basal ganglia lesions on timing and force control. *Brain and Cognition, 58*(1), 62–74.

Bender, L. (1938). A visual motor Gestalt test and its clinical use. *American Orthopsychiatric Association, Research Monograph, No. 3.*

Benton, A. (1992). Clinical neuropsychology: 1960–1990. *Journal of Clinical and Experimental Neuropsychology, 14*(3), 407–417.

Benton, A. L. (1994). Neuropsychological assessment. *Annual Review of Psychology, 45*, 1–23.

Bigler, E. D. (1984). *Diagnostic clinical neuropsychology.* Austin: University of Texas Press.

Bigler, E. D. (1988). Frontal lobe damage and neuropsychological assessment. *Archives of Clinical Neuropsychology, 3*, 279–298.

Bigler, E. D. (2006). *Mild traumatic brain injury: Causality considerations from a neuroimaging and neuropathology perspective.* New York: Springer-Verlag.

Bigler, E. D. (2007). A motion to exclude and the "fixed" versus "flexible" battery in "forensic" neuropsychology: Challenges to the practice of clinical neuropsychology. *Archives of Clinical Neuropsychology, 22*(1), 45–51.

Bigler, E. D., & Clement, P. (1997). *Diagnostic clinical neuropsychology* (3rd ed.). Austin: University of Texas Press.

Caligiuri, M. P., Brown, G. G., Meloy, M. J., Eberson, S., Niculescu, A. B., & Lohr, J. B. (2006). Striatopallidal regulation of affect in bipolar disorder. *Journal of Affective Disorders, 91*(2–3), 235–242.

Chudasama, Y., & Robbins, T. W. (2006). Functions of frontostriatal systems in cognition: comparative neuropsychopharmacological studies in rats, monkeys and humans. *Biological Psychology, 73*(1), 19–38.

Dames, S., Tonnerre, C., Saint, S., & Jones, S. R. (2005). Don't know much about history. *New England Journal of Medicine, 352*, 2338–2342.

Delis, D. C., Kramer, J. H., Kaplan, E., & Ober, B. A. (1994). *California Verbal Learning Test—Children's version.* San Antonio, TX: Psychological Corporation.

Foncke, E. M., Schuurman, P. R., & Speelman, J. D. (2006). Suicide after deep brain stimulation of the internal globus pallidus for dystonia. *Neurology, 66*(1), 142–143.

Gazzaniga, M. S. (1995). *The cognitive neurosciences.* Cambridge, MA: MIT Press.

Halstead, W. C. (1947). *Brain and intelligence.* Chicago: University of Chicago Press.

Hannay, J. E. A. (1998). Houston conference. *Archives of Clinical Neuropsychology, 13*, 157–160.

Heaton, R. K., Grant, I., & Matthews, C. G. (1991). *Comprehensive norms for an expanded Halstead–Reitan Battery.* Odessa, FL: Psychological Assessment Resources.

Hebb, D. O. (1939). Intelligence in man after large removals of cerebral tissue: Report of four left frontal lobe cases. *Journal of General Psychology, 21*, 73–87.

Hollingsworth, J. G., & Lasker, E. G. (2004). The case against differential diagnosis: *Daubert*, medical causation testimony, and the scientific method. *Journal of Health Law, 37*(1), 85–111.

Hopkins, R. O., & Bigler, E. D. (2001). *Pulmonary disorders.* New York: Plenum Press.

Hopkins, R. O., Gale, S. D., Johnson, S. C., Anderson, C. V., Bigler, E. D., Blatter, D. D., et al. (1995). Severe anoxia with and without concomitant brain atrophy and neuropsychological impairments. *Journal of the International Neuropsychological Society, 1*(5), 501–509.

Hopkins, R. O., & Haaland, K. Y. (2004). Neuropsychological and neuropathological effects of anoxic or ischemic induced brain injury. *Journal of the International Neuropsychological Society, 10*(7), 957–961.

Hopkins, R. O., Myers, C. E., Shohamy, D., Grossman, S., & Gluck, M. (2004). Impaired probabilistic category learning in hypoxic subjects with hippocampal damage. *Neuropsychologia, 42*(4), 524–535.

Hopkins, R. O., Tate, D. F., & Bigler, E. D. (2005). Anoxic versus traumatic brain injury: amount of tissue loss, not etiology, alters cognitive and emotional function. *Neuropsychology, 19*(2), 233–242.

Jasper, B. W., Hopkins, R. O., Duker, H. V., & Weaver, L. K. (2005). Affective outcome following carbon monoxide poisoning: A prospective longitudinal study. *Cognitive and Behavioral Neurology, 18*(2), 127–134.

Kanner, A. M. (2004). Structural MRI changes of the brain in depression. *Clinical EEG and Neuroscience, 35*(1), 46–52.

Kaufmann, P. M. (2005). Protecting the objectivity, fairness, and integrity of neuropsychological evaluations in litigation. A privilege second to none? *Journal of Legal Medicine, 26*(1), 95–131.

Knight, J. A. (2003). *The handbook of Rey–Osterrieth Complex Figure usage: Clinical and research applications.* Odessa, FL: Psychological Assessment Resources.

Kwon, O. Y., Chung, S. P., Ha, Y. R., Yoo, I. S., & Kim, S. W. (2004). Delayed postanoxic encephalopathy after carbon monoxide poisoning. *Emergency Medicine Journal, 21*(2), 250–251.

Lashley, K. S. (1929). *Brain mechanisms and intelligence.* Chicago: University of Chicago Press.

Lee, H. B., & Lyketsos, C. G. (2001). Delayed post-hypoxic leukoencephalopathy. *Psychosomatics, 42*(6), 530–533.

Levy, R., & Dubois, B. (2006). Apathy and the functional anatomy of the prefrontal cortex-basal ganglia circuits. *Cerebral Cortex, 16*(7), 916–928.

Lezak, M. D. (1976). *Neuropsychological assessment.* New York: Oxford University Press.

Lezak, M. D., Howieson, D. B., & Loring, D. W. (2004). *Neuropsychological assessment* (4th ed.). Oxford, UK: Oxford University Press.

Lim, C., Alexander, M. P., LaFleche, G., Schnyer, D. M., & Verfaellie, M. (2004). The neurological and cognitive sequelae of cardiac arrest. *Neurology, 63*(10), 1774–1778.

Masten, J., & Strzelczyk, J. J. (2001). Admissibility of scientific evidence post-*Daubert*. *Health Physics, 81*(6), 678–682.

McEwen, B. S. (2005). Glucocorticoids, depression, and mood disorders: Structural remodeling in the brain. *Metabolism, 54*(5 Suppl. 1), 20–23.

McKinzey, R. K., & Ziegler, T. G. (1999). Challenging a flexible neuropsychological battery under *Kelly/Frye*: A case study. *Behavioral Sciences and the Law, 17*(4), 543–551.

Miller, J. M., Vorel, S. R., Tranguch, A. J., Kenny, E. T., Mazzoni, P., van Gorp, W. G., et al. (2006). Anhedonia after a selective bilateral lesion of the globus pallidus. *American Journal of Psychiatry, 163*(5), 786–788.

Mitrushina, M., Boone, K. B., Razani, J., & D'Elia, L. F. (2005). *Handbook of normative data for neuropsychological assessment* (2nd ed.). New York: Oxford University Press.

Monza, D., Soliveri, P., Radice, D., Fetoni, V., Testa, D., Caffarra, P., et al. (1998). Cognitive dysfunction and impaired organization of complex motility in degenerative parkinsonian syndromes. *Archives of Neurology, 55*(3), 372–378.

Page, J. D. (1947). *Abnormal psychology: A clinical approach to psychological deviants.* New York: McGraw-Hill.

Pritchard, D. A. (1998). *Tests of neuropsychological malingering (version 2.0).* New York: CRC Press.

Rabin, L. A., Barr, W. B., & Burton, L. A. (2005). Assessment practices of clinical neuropsychologists in the United States and Canada: A survey of INS, NAN, and APA Division 40 members. *Archives of Clinical Neuropsychology, 20*, 33–65.

Randolph, C. (1998). *Manual—Repeatable Battery for the Assessment of Neuropsychological Status.* San Antonio, TX: Psychological Corporation (Harcourt).

Reed, J. E. (1996). Fixed vs. flexible neuropsychological test batteries under the *Daubert* standard for the admissibility of scientific evidence. *Behavioral Sciences and the Law, 14*(3), 315–322.

Reitan, R. M. (1955). Certain differential effects of left and right cerebral lesions in human adults. *Journal of Comparative and Physiological Psychology, 48*, 474–477.

Reitan, R. M., & Davison, L. A. (1974). *Clinical neuropsychology: Current status and applications.* Washington, DC: Winston.

Reitan, R. M., & Wolfson, D. (1985). *The Halstead–Reitan Neuropsychological Test Battery: Theory and clinical interpretation.* Tucson, AZ: Neuropsychology Press.

Reitan, R. M., & Wolfson, D. (1997). The influence of age and education on neuropsychological performances of persons with mild head injuries. *Applied Neuropsychology, 4*(1), 16–33.

Reitan, R. M., & Wolfson, D. (2005). The effect of age and education transformations on neuropsychological test scores of persons with diffuse or bilateral brain damage. *Applied Neuropsychology, 12*(4), 181–189.

Russell, E. W. (1988). Renorming Russell's version of the Wechsler Memory Scale. *Journal of Clinical and Experimental Neuropsychology, 10*(2), 235–249.

Russell, E. W., Neuringer, C., & Goldstein, G. (1973). *Assessment of brain damage.* New York: Wiley.

Russell, E. W., Russell, S. L., & Hill, B. D. (2005). The fundamental psychometric status of neuropsychological batteries. *Archives of Clinical Neuropsychology, 20*(6), 785–794.

Schwarz, M., Fellows, S. J., Schaffrath, C., & Noth, J. (2001). Deficits in sensorimotor control during precise hand movements in Huntington's disease. *Clinical Neurophysiology, 112*(1), 95–106.

Sheline, Y. I. (2000). 3D MRI studies of neuroanatomic changes in unipolar major depression: The role of stress and medical comorbidity. *Biological Psychiatry, 48*(8), 791–800.

Shin, J. C., Aparicio, P., & Ivry, R. B. (2005). Multidimensional sequence learning in patients with focal basal ganglia lesions. *Brain and Cognition, 58*(1), 75–83.

Strauss, E., Sherman, E. M. S., & Spreen, O. (2006). *A compendium of neuropsychological tests: Administration, norms, and commentary.* New York: Oxford University Press.

Sweet, J. J., Nelson, N. W., & Moberg, P. J. (2006). The TCN/AACN 2005 "salary survey": Professional practices, beliefs, and incomes of U.S. neuropsychologists. *The Clinical Neuropsychologist, 20*, 325–364.

Tamura, D. Y., Moore, E. E., Partrick, D. A., Johnson, J. L., Offner, P. J., & Silliman, C. C. (2002). Acute hypoxemia in humans enhances the neutrophil inflammatory response. *Shock, 17*(4), 269–273.

Teuber, H.-L. (1964). *The riddle of frontal lobe function in man.* New York: McGraw-Hill.
Vallabhajosula, B., & van Gorp, W. G. (2001). Post-*Daubert* admissibility of scientific evidence on malingering of cognitive deficits. *Journal of the American Academy of Psychiatry and the Law, 29*(2), 207–215.
Wechsler, D. (1945). A standardized memory scale for clinical use. *Journal of Psychology, 19,* 87–95.
Werring, D. J., Frazer, D. W., Coward, L. J., Losseff, N. A., Watt, H., Cipolotti, L., et al. (2004). Cognitive dysfunction in patients with cerebral microbleeds on T2*-weighted gradient-echo MRI. *Brain, 127*(Pt. 10), 2265–2275.

12

A Pediatric Neuropsychologist's Lessons from "Independent Educational Evaluations"

Respect Parents, Listen to Teachers,
Do Your Homework, but Think for Yourself

Karen Wills

The role of a pediatric neuropsychologist in one type of forensic assessment, the "independent educational evaluation" (IEE), stems naturally from the clinical practice of collaborating with parents, teachers, and school psychologists to evaluate children with brain injury or developmental disability. Many children referred for neuropsychological evaluation have been tested previously by a school or clinical psychologist; therefore, reviewing, critiquing, and incorporating results of previous testing into one's neuropsychological reports may be more routine in pediatric than in adult practice. Attending and contributing to school meetings to assist in designing an IEP (individualized education plan) for a child builds relationships that may later result in referrals from school personnel to evaluate other children and, sometimes, requests for a "second opinion" when parents have disagreed with the school's evaluation of a child.

WHAT IS AN IEE?

Any evaluation of a child conducted by a qualified person who is not employed by the state or local educational agency may be called an IEE. (For brevity's sake, in this chapter I use "the school" to stand for "the state or local educational agency.") The main purpose of any IEE is to determine whether a child has a disability and to identify the educational needs of the child, under the current reauthorization of the Individuals with Disabilities Education Act (IDEA-2004, Public Law 108-446, signed in December 2004 and effective July 1, 2005, is the current version of the U.S. federal law that provides for a "free and appropriate public education" for children with disabilities, with special educational programming and services based on determination of the child's individual needs). IEEs are not limited to assessment of cognitive and academic abilities but encompass any sort of educationally relevant evaluation, such as social–emotional or functional behavioral assessments; medical examinations (including vision or hearing tests); and speech–language, occupational therapy, physical therapy, assistive technology, or augmentative communication assessments. This chapter concerns IEEs as conducted by neuropsychologists, which usually focus on cognitive and behavioral functioning associated with known or suspected brain injuries or neurodevelopmental disorders.

Before analyzing opportunities and difficulties inherent in the four different types of neuropsychological IEEs, it is worth noting that an IEE is distinguished from most other forensic neuropsychological evaluations by the *ongoing relationship* between the parents and the school. Most forensic evaluations take place in an adversarial context where the relationship between the parties is of little concern to the evaluator, although understanding and working with family relationships is important in some cases (for instance, determining competency of an elderly woman whose two children disagree about the severity of her dementia, or assessing a teenager with Down syndrome whose parents are in conflict about his independent living situation). In contrast, IEEs related to parent–school disputes nearly always involve school personnel who are *not* family members but who may have strong emotional ties and will carry on in a caregiving role with the child, regardless of the outcome of the case. The same school psychologist, or a close colleague of that person, probably will reevaluate this student in the future, and the teachers or special education staff will be seeing that child in their classrooms. It is essential, therefore, that the neuropsychologist's approach in an IEE be respectful, collegial, and educative, not contentious or arrogant, even when presenting results and opinions directly contrary to those of the school psychologist or other school personnel. Whenever possible, the educational dispute, no matter how heated, may be best viewed and treated as a process of negotiation, with the ultimate goal that the participants can carry on with caring for the child.

Experience with conducting many IEEs has led me to believe that it is critically important to distinguish among four different contexts within which a neuropsychological IEE can occur. I term these four contexts (1) the clinical IEE; (2) the consulting IEE; (3) the dispute resolution IEE; and (4) the adjudicator-ordered IEE. The four contexts, or types, of IEE represent a continuum from a primarily clinical evaluation to situations that are increasingly "court-like" or "forensic." Important differences among the four types of IEE include the nature of parent–school relationship (from consensual to adversarial); the initiator (parent, school, or hearing officer); the initiator's desired outcome of the IEE (supplementing, supplanting, refuting, or clarifying the school's evaluation); and the payer (parent or school). In the following sections, I present some examples, with analysis of the particular opportunities and difficulties each context can pose for pediatric neuropsychologists. (In case examples, all the names and details have been altered to protect individual's identities, and some examples are composites. Short of due process hearings, the proceedings of school staffings remain confidential.)

Literature pertaining to IEEs in the context of educational dispute resolution, and more general work on forensic assessment of children in school-related contexts, is limited but growing (see, e.g., Demers & Nellis, 2006; Etscheidt, 2003; Goldberg, 2005, 2006; Imber & Radcliff, 2003; Lorber & York, 1999; Waterman, 1994; Wills & Sweet, 2006). With few exceptions (see Imber & Radcliff, 2003), publications about IEEs are written for either parents or educators, not for the evaluators. It is unfortunate that the literature is so sparse, and that relatively few pediatric neuropsychologists receive any direct training or supervision in this endeavor. I find that conducting an IEE, and participating as a consultant in special education meetings, is a challenge that draws on one's training not only in neuropsychology but also in developmental, child clinical, school and organizational psychology, special education and behavioral analysis, and even courses in family therapy and divorce mediation. The shared goal of most individuals involved in an IEE is to provide a child with an appropriate education. Despite differences of opinion about how to achieve it, this shared goal makes the IEE process inherently more collaborative and respectful, most of the time, than, say, the average tort case. In one of my favorite IEE meetings, the special education administrator began by passing around a copy of the student's school picture. "This is Christopher," she said. "He's why we're all here." Even the parents, though remaining adamantly opposed to the school's proposed program, began that meeting with a nod and a smile.

THE CLINICAL IEE

In a parent-initiated, privately financed IEE, the parents choose to share results and recommendations of a clinical neuropsychological evaluation (initiated by them or by a medical provider) with the school, with the goal of supplementing or obviating the need for testing by a local school psychologist. This can occur with almost any clinical pediatric neuropsychological evaluation that documents an educational impact of cognitive, learning, or behavioral problems.

A clinical IEE provides an opportunity for a neuropsychologist to apply, and share with educators, his or her specialized knowledge about assessing and treating educational consequences of medical or neurodevelopmental conditions. Potential pitfalls include insufficient knowledge about educational policies, so that a clinical IEE may fail to meet school criteria for educational decision making. On the other hand, some school teams may overlook the federal mandate that they review and take into account the information in a clinical IEE. For example, parents frequently report that someone at school has said, "We don't have to accept the neuropsychologist's evaluation because it is medical, not educational." This shows a naive understanding of IDEA-2004. Schools are not constrained to abide by the recommendations of an IEE, but they risk financial penalties if failure to incorporate those recommendations leads to inappropriate educational programming (Imber & Radcliff, 2003).

Under IDEA, the school is required *to consider* the results and recommendations of parent-initiated, privately financed, independent evaluations in making educational decisions, but only if those evaluations match state and school district criteria for school-based assessments, as defined in state education laws. This implies that if a neuropsychologist wants school personnel to review, appreciate, and even incorporate his or her findings and conclusions, it is essential to know and utilize (1) the state education department criteria for selecting tests and other assessment procedures; (2) the specific criteria and terms used for determining whether or not a child has a disability as defined by *education* law; and (3) state-approved procedures for determining a child's needs, along with understanding the programs and services available to meet them in the educational setting.

Waterman (1994) provides a succinct overview of the school-based assessment process as outlined by IDEA. The Protection and Advocacy Offices (see, e.g., *www.pacer.org*), and the Resource and Information Centers for each state and multistate region (see the "state resource sheets" at *www.nichcy.org*) are excellent resources for learning local educational laws and guidelines. The OSERS (Office of Special Education Resources and Support) IDEA website is an invaluable resource with regard to U.S. special education law (online at *www.idea.ed.gov*).

In the clinical IEE, the child and parents are the client; the school is a third party, with which any communication must be approved in writing by the parents. Time spent in telephone or in-person participation in educational meetings is not billable to medical insurance and almost never is paid for by the school; it is either paid for by parents as an additional service not covered by insurance, by the hospital's limited philanthropy funds (e.g., via our hospital-to-school reentry programs for children with cancer or sickle cell disease), or *pro bono*.

Although I participate in this type of school meeting at the parents' invitation, most school teams seem to welcome and value the input of a pediatric neuropsychologist who, in turn, respects their expertise. Neuropsychologists are used to working "solo" whereas educational decisions are always made by a *team* of parents, teachers, and school personnel including a school psychologist. The clinical IEE will be much more readily adopted if the neuropsychologist has already gathered input from school personnel and presents the report as a source of information for team decision making, not as *the* "blueprint" for the child's education plan. IDEA provides every child with a "free and appropriate public education," with many disputes over operationalizing the word *appropriate*. "Appropriate" does not mean perfect, ideal, or optimal; it may mean something more like "necessary and sufficient, in the eyes of a reasonable person." Recommended interventions and services should be tied precisely to documented needs, follow state educational policies, and be reasonable and feasible.

School psychologists may review and accept the results of a clinical neuropsychological report as an IEE, sometimes in lieu of school-based assessment, as long as the tests and recommendations meet state educational criteria and adequately serve educational as well as medical purposes. Usually, this can be accomplished simply by including relevant educational terminology and interventions, in addition to the medical and psychosocial diagnoses and recommendations (see Appendix 12.1 for an extended case example). Indeed, if a child is undergoing neuropsychological evaluation, many schools postpone their testing until that report is received. This poses an ethical challenge to ensure that the neuropsychological evaluation, billed to medical insurance, remains focused on the clinical or medical questions and referrals and does not stray into assessing educational issues unnecessarily just because a school or parent requests such testing. Ideally, parents will consent to allow the neuropsychologist to talk with the school psychologist and "divide up" the assessment, so that the hospital-based tests focus on issues of broader medical concern, such as memory or general information processing, while concurrent school-based testing might focus on educational assessment, such as reading or math achievement.

Parental efforts to control the evaluation process or outcome, sometimes in counterproductive ways, can undermine the adequacy of an IEE.

Parents sometimes have the idea that the school and hospital should each do its own separate evaluation, without interagency communication, so that one will not "bias" the other. In most cases, the parents can be dissuaded from this notion by explaining that duplicating tests invalidates results, that any evaluation must draw on multiple informants to be useful educationally, and that it is unfair to put their child through excessive testing that requires him or her to be pulled out of class. Sometimes parents fear that if school personnel know the child is being tested, the school will somehow gain access to the results and report. Nothing in IDEA requires a family to share information from a privately funded evaluation with the school, even when school personnel contribute information (such as records of previous testing, or teacher-rating questionnaires) and are aware that the evaluation is being conducted. If parents persistently refuse to allow coordination of the components of an evaluation with the school's concurrent testing, then I postpone their appointment and ask them to complete the school evaluation *first* and send me that report, after which I can decide whether or not additional neuropsychological tests are warranted and likely to be useful.

Parents who are dissatisfied with some aspects of the child's school program may be hesitant to consent to the neuropsychologist obtaining teacher-rating questionnaires, grade reports, or other evaluative information from the teacher or other school staff. One parent gave the teacher-rating form to a child's gym instructor, instead of a classroom teacher, because "he's the only one in the school who *likes* Samuel, everybody else just runs him down." I tell parents like this that it takes a lot of trust to have someone evaluate your child; that they can trust me to gather all the facts and make up my own mind; and that if they allow me to "listen" to what school staff have to say, via interviews or questionnaires, then, when the time comes to present my opinions, the school personnel will be far more likely to "listen" to me and respect my views as well informed and fair minded.

Only once, in my recollection, did parents convince me *not* to contact the school for collateral information about the child. Their 8-year-old son had an XYY chromosomal anomaly but had not been identified as having any school difficulties, and the school did not know about his medical diagnosis. Moreover, the boy himself did not yet know of his diagnosis, which had just been confirmed. The parents were concerned that he might be stigmatized, in his highly competitive, small, private school, if staff there knew he was being evaluated by a neuropsychologist. They were concerned about idle gossip among staff, and even more so about what they might say if asked why he was being evaluated. They provided grades and narrative teacher reports indicating no academic or behavioral concerns. In this case, their legitimate and clearly articulated reasons to keep the evaluation private, amidst their struggle to accept the boy's recent genetic diagnosis, combined with their providing available school reports and records, clearly trumped my routine gathering of teacher-report forms.

THE CONSULTING IEE

In a school-initiated, publicly financed, consensual IEE, the school, with parents' informed consent, contracts with a neuropsychologist to provide an evaluation that may be outside the expertise or resources of the district's school psychologists. In my experience, this happens most often for children with low incidence or medically complex disabilities, or for children whose evaluations require special cultural or linguistic competence that may not be represented among the district's personnel.

Opportunities and pitfalls are similar to the clinical IEE initiated by the parent. In addition, this scenario, in my experience, often involves high expectations on the part of school staff for a "one woman show" that cannot possibly provide a truly comprehensive assessment of student needs. This requires the neuropsychologist to be cognizant and informed about the limits of his or her competence and to formulate a precise plan of evaluation in advance, incorporating evaluations from other professionals (e.g., speech–language pathologists, occupational therapists, and experts in assistive technology, transition planners), as indicated.

Knowing how to translate information about a child's medical condition and neuropsychological impairments into "news the school can use," that is, statements about educational needs tied to recommendations about educational interventions, is key to providing effective IEEs. A medical diagnosis or condition *per se* does not entitle a child to special education and related services, even if that diagnosis is usually associated with cognitive or behavioral impairment. Special education eligibility is based on demonstrated *educational impact* of the medical condition. As an example, for a child in Minnesota to meet criteria for eligibility under the "Other Health Disabilities" (OHD) category, the evaluation must show that the child's special educational needs are *a direct consequence* of his or her medical condition. It is critical for the neuropsychologist in this context to be well informed about the educational implications of particular disabilities. It is not enough to talk about cognitive or behavioral impairment, per se (e.g., "Susan's phonological processing, memory retention, and verbal fluency are poor."). It is essential to tie the neuropsychological impairment directly to an *educational* disability or specific educational need (e.g., "Susan lacks the phonological processing ability required to decode words with grade-level fluency. Her memory is so poor that when she reaches the end of a sentence, she cannot recall its beginning. She has trouble "calling to mind" words to express her thoughts, so that she often "draws a blank" when called on to report her knowledge.").

Sometimes, both the school and the parents actively seek a hospital-based liaison. For instance, the mother and school psychologist both called to invite me to attend a school meeting for Devon, a child with subclinical frontal lobe infarcts, whom I had seen for neuropsychological screening in the Sickle Cell Disease Clinic. His IQ scores and academic achievement tests hovered around the high 70s. The school psychologist felt Devon needed help but believed that he "didn't qualify" because his scores were neither low enough to meet educational criteria for intellectual disability (mental retardation), nor discrepant enough to meet criteria for learning disability (which requires, in 2006, that IQ significantly exceed achievement; new laws that will abandon or modify this "discrepancy criterion" are being implemented in most states). The school team was inclined to qualify him under "emotional–behavioral disabilities" in order to give him more support for prosocial behavior, but this designation would not automatically provide for his learning needs. The school psychologist was aware that Devon had sickle cell disease but did not know that this diagnosis might directly impact his ability to learn. The state educational guidelines had not yet been updated to reflect research demonstrating the risk of cerebrovascular disease, strokes, and associated neuropsychological impairment in children with this blood disorder.

On neuropsychological testing, Devon demonstrated impaired attention, memory, and executive function, with academic underachievement, compounded by defiant, disrespectful, provocative, and aggressive behavior toward teachers and peers. The neuropsychological report concluded that his sickle cell disease, by causing frontal lobe strokes, could be presumed to be a direct cause of his impaired attention, memory, and learning and a direct contributor to his behavioral disinhibition. Research references on this point were provided to the school. On the other hand, the oppositional–defiant elements of Devon's profile certainly were not directly consequent to his sickle cell disease, yet they were severe enough to require focused behavioral management in school (as well as a referral for agency-based behavioral therapy). Therefore, Devon was determined to be eligible for services under *both* the OHD category *and* the "emotional–behavioral disorders" (EBD) category, which led to his involvement with special educators who had experience in working with brain-injured children, as well as those whose experience mainly involved work with oppositional–defiant youth. The combined experience of these individuals yielded a more comprehensive plan to address Devon's cognitive and behavioral needs in school.

THE DISPUTE RESOLUTION IEE

Parents are guaranteed the right to request an IEE at public expense when they disagree with the content or process of a school evaluation (IDEA-2004, Part B, Subpart E, § 300.502). The school is obliged to pay for the IEE "in a timely manner," or to request a hearing to show that its evaluation was appropriate. In practice, most schools will agree to pay for an IEE rather than insist on the appropriateness of its initial evaluation. An IEE may cost less in time, money, inconvenience, and relationship stress than a hearing, although IEE recommendations sometimes can be costly for school districts. As noted previously, the school is mandated to *consider* the information and recommendations of an IEE, not to conform to them, but can be held accountable for failure to implement recommendations deemed necessary or appropriate to meeting the child's educational needs.

The right to a publicly funded "second opinion" IEE is a powerful tool that often helps define the nature and severity of a child's disability and identify his or her needs, via a more comprehensive assessment than many school districts can provide. Neuropsychological evaluations are too expensive for most people to pay "out of pocket," and medical insurance cannot ethically be billed for evaluations conducted for educational purposes. Therefore, the publicly funded IEE is the only route available, for many families, to obtaining a comprehensive evaluation of educationally relevant areas of functioning. This creates a peculiar situation in which the neuropsychologist's "client" is the "evaluation team"—consisting of *both* parents and school—who are not in accord. As shall be seen, this can lead to a situation in which one or both parties actively sabotages the IEE.

IDEA provides for dispute resolution procedures including mediation, impartial due process hearings, and appeals. Disputes may arise between a school and parents of a child, or group of children, in determining:

1. Whether or not a child has a disability.
2. The nature, severity, and permanence of the disability, if any.
3. Whether the disability is "educationally relevant" in that it interferes significantly with the child's educational progress and requires accommodations or modifications of the regular curricula or school environment.
4. Which "reasonable accommodations" and special education services are needed to ensure that the child has a "fair and appropriate public education" with equal access to knowledge and equal opportunity to demonstrate his or her learning.
5. Which specialized educational procedures and related services (e.g., speech therapy, occupational therapy, physical therapy, adaptive

physical education) are needed to enable the child to make adequate educational progress.

6. Whether the child is making progress over time in response to interventions, or conversely, whether there is evidence of deterioration or plateau in the child's abilities.

Imber and Radcliff (2003) summarized important parameters of IEEs in the dispute resolution context. These rights and constraints include:

1. *Consent to initial evaluation or reevaluation.* Parents can always obtain a clinical IEE and pay for it themselves, but if they want the school to pay for an IEE, then they must first allow the school to evaluate the child. The school is not obliged to pay for an IEE until it has completed an evaluation with which the parent disagrees.

2. *Timely unfettered access to IEE.* Schools must inform parents of their right to an IEE and cannot create any impediments to parents' request for an IEE. For example, parents cannot be required to give any reason or explanation for their objection to the school's evaluation (though school staff are permitted to inquire about this). In most states, parents must make the request for an IEE within 1 or 2 years after the school's evaluation, and they can request only one IEE in response to each evaluation done by the school.

3. *Quality, scope, and cost.* The IEE must conform to the same criteria that are applied to school-based evaluations, with regard to examiner qualifications, technical adequacy, scope and comprehensiveness of the evaluation (e.g., assessing all suspected areas of need and using multiple measures that are reliable and valid for the population assessed, and multiple informants, such as school records, classroom observations, and teacher interviews). The school cannot obstruct the independent evaluator's access to any sources of information that may be used in the school's own evaluations. Schools must provide parents, upon request, an exhaustive list of qualified local evaluators, though parents can identify others if they wish. The parents, not the school, select the independent evaluator. To obtain public funding for the IEE, the independent evaluator must be at least as qualified as the personnel employed by the school. (Some states and districts have attempted to limit cognitive and academic testing to licensed school psychologists, based on this "qualification" rule, but this generally has not survived the objections of licensed neuropsychologists, clinical, and counseling psychologists.) The school can limit the total cost of the evaluation to a reasonable fee range, but not a fixed sum. The school is *not* required to pay for an IEE that is done by an unqualified individual; that fails to meet state education guidelines for technical adequacy (e.g., test reliability and validity); that is inadequate in its scope or comprehensiveness (e.g.,

an evaluation that ignores major areas of need, or disregards previous test and interview data); or that fails to provide any new information beyond what was stated in the school's evaluation report.

4. *Release of information.* Parents who mistrust or disagree with the school's evaluation may obtain an IEE, without notifying the school; under federal law, schools cannot require prior notification. If they so choose, parents can review the results of the IEE with the neuropsychologist to determine whether those findings contradict, alter, or add to the school's evaluation. If not, then the parents have paid for a confirmatory second opinion; if so, then parents can state their disagreement with the school's evaluation and request that the school reimburse the neuropsychological IEE, after the fact.

As noted earlier, a privately funded clinical IEE generally remains confidential and cannot be released to the school without parents' written consent. Once parents request and accept the school's payment or reimbursement for an IEE, however, they must release the IEE report to the school and that report becomes part of the child's permanent school record. If a school has agreed in advance to pay for the IEE, the neuropsychologist must release the IEE to the school as well as to the parents. In practice, this generally is done by sending copies of the written report to both parties, simultaneously, and holding a joint feedback conference, or presenting findings at a team meeting attended by parents and school personnel.

In order to advise parents about their confidentiality rights in regard to a clinical evaluation, it is important to understand the "steps" in a special education dispute resolution process. While the details are specific to each state or commonwealth, the process typically begins with informal meetings between parents and local school personnel. If no agreement is reached, then more formal meetings, perhaps involving district, regional, or state special education representatives, may be scheduled. The next step may be a mediation process, but if no consensus is reached, then either party can request an impartial due process hearing, in which evidence will be considered and binding decisions made by a qualified hearing officer. Some cases may result in civil lawsuits decided by a judge.

If parents obtain and pay privately for a "clinical IEE," even though they may be involved in an ongoing dispute with the school, there is no obligation that they share that evaluation with the school, although they may do so at their discretion. Parents *may* present the results of any privately funded evaluations as evidence in educational disputes, but they cannot be *required* to do so by school personnel other than a hearing officer or judge. However, if the dispute is carried to the level of a due process hearing or civil trial, the parents or an independent evaluator is obligated to comply if the hearing officer or judge orders them to produce "any and all evaluations." If the parents choose to share a privately funded clinical IEE with the school, or if they are ordered to do so by a judge or hearing officer, the written report of IEE becomes part of the permanent school record and can be used as evidence, by any party, in a due process hearing or civil trial. If the clinical IEE information is disclosed during mediation, then any discussion of that information during the mediation session is sealed and confidential (along with the rest of the medication record); but still, the written report of the IEE can be subpoenaed if the case proceeds into due process hearing or civil litigation.

As mentioned earlier, in the dispute resolution IEE, although the school district pays for the IEE, the "client" is *not* the school or its attorney, however, but, rather, the school team that will determine the child's eligibility for special education services and design his or her program. By law, the team must include *both* the school personnel *and* the parents, who are viewed as equal participants in the evaluation process. This is a highly unusual situation in forensic neuropsychological assessment, as, in effect, "the client" consists of two parties who are in dispute with one another.

My experience in the case of Emma illustrates the difficulty when the school and parents have competing agendas. Ordinarily, the outcome of an educational dispute will be a compromise between the views or objectives of parents and school personnel. A refusal to compromise can stall the process for a long time, which may be precisely what one party desires, because a stalled IEP process typically results in maintaining the "status quo," with the child's placement and program remaining unchanged.

Emma was an upper-elementary-age child with multiple complex physical disabilities. A due process hearing officer had ordered an updated evaluation by a neuropsychologist to determine Emma's level of intellectual functioning. The parents had agreed to this evaluation. I did not learn of their reluctance to have the child evaluated until much later.

The school had initiated this due process hearing in order to increase Emma's services under Minnesota's "intellectual disability" category. The school team decided that Emma was "lost" in regular classes and needed more one-on-one instruction. Her parents said they believed Emma did not have an intellectual disability and preferred she remain in regular "mainstream" classes throughout most of the day. No other information about the case was volunteered. At that time, I had not yet learned to ask all the questions I currently ask, nor did I yet use the initial letter that is my standard communication now (see Appendix 12.2). Indeed, this case helped me develop the guidelines communicated in that letter.

It was evident from the beginning that someone was resistant to having a comprehensive evaluation conducted in the usual manner. Before I met Emma and her parents to begin the interview and testing process, I received a letter from the hearing officer, ordering me to constrain the neuropsychological evaluation to nothing more than a standardized IQ test. In commentary on IDEA-2004, OSERS, the federal agency responsible for implementation of special education laws, held that the IEE cannot be constrained in this way. The IEE is required to follow the same procedures and criteria that would be used in a school-based evaluation, which entails multiple measures, informants, and methods, for converging evidence of disability and a *comprehensive* assessment of the child's needs. Moreover, IDEA explicitly prohibits basing an evaluation on a single test. Emma's intellectual ability could not be adequately estimated using one standardized IQ test, given her physical disabilities; an evaluation using "converging measures" (Baron, 2004) would need to be done. I wrote a letter to the hearing officer indicating exactly what information I planned to collect, from whom, how, and why, and received the hearing officer's approval to proceed with a reasonably comprehensive assessment. At that point, I mistakenly thought that the school was trying to limit the scope of the IEE, perhaps as a cost-saving measure; much later, I learned that it was the parents who had attempted to impose this constraint, which would have disqualified the evaluation.

I requested routine information from the school, only to be told, initially, that the teachers would not provide me with any behavioral or developmental questionnaires. IDEA does not allow a school to obstruct an independent evaluator's access to any information that normally would be available to a school-based examiner. I called the special education director to complain; the teaching staff immediately called me back, with apologies, and agreed to send the requested information. I spent a day observing Emma at her school; completed her testing using modified materials and administration methods to accommodate procedures to her physical disabilities, poor vision, and short attention span; and prepared a report.

As I began to present my findings at the school staffing, the parents' attorney challenged my professional training and qualifications, testing procedures, results, and inferences, in the style of a cross-examination. The parents' attorney insisted that I had not provided a "valid, reliable, standardized" measurement of Emma's intelligence as the Minnesota statute requires. Therefore, Emma could not be categorized as having a "developmental cognitive disability" (DCD), Minnesota's current term for the special education eligibility category equivalent to the medical diagnosis of "mental retardation" or "intellectual disability," for which IQ and adaptive behavior measures are key criteria. The attorney repeatedly demanded that I produce references showing that the IQ tests used with Emma were "valid and reliable for the purposes used" and standardized for children with her various disabilities. I provided references on assessment of children with multiple physical disabilities, including the relevant sections of the test manuals that indicate allowable modifications of standard administration procedures. I described in detail how Emma had responded to various tasks, on which her tested abilities were congruent with adaptive behavior ratings obtained from parents and teachers, clearly placing her at a developmental level that would imply intellectual as well as physical disability. I provided relevant research showing that children with similar medical histories and conditions had been tested and shown to have a range of IQ scores, with Emma's scores falling toward the lower end (though not at the bottom) of this range. Emma actually had been easy to test, because she responded adeptly to a broad variety of preschool-level questions and picture puzzles. On many tests, she readily mastered the task demands; it was the content, not the format, of the tasks that baffled her, as tasks increased in difficulty. For example, she had no trouble defining "easier" vocabulary words but provided concrete, simplistic, and eventually wrong definitions as the words became more difficult.

Disregarding all arguments that supported my approach to evaluating Emma, the parents reiterated their position that "there is no reliable and valid test standardized for this population and the State requires a standardized test." This argument was used very effectively to disqualify any conceivable assessment I had, or could have, made.

Had I ascertained more clearly the full history and competing agendas of the parties involved, I probably would have declined the case, or, at least, spent far less time working on the IEE report—knowing it would likely be scrapped, as indeed, it was. I might have reported only the raw scores, in a descriptive fashion, comparing those scores to those obtained by typically developing children. I might even have recruited one or two same-age, typically developing children and administered these tests using the same modifications and accommodations that were used with Emma, to demonstrate how other children would respond to identical procedures. Any of these precautions might make sense from a clinical perspective, but they might or might not have satisfied a hearing officer that the testing procedures were sufficiently valid and reliable to meet criteria for a technically adequate IEE, from a legal perspective. In this case, a settlement was reached, and the case closed, before any judgment was rendered by a hearing officer. The 2004 revision of IDEA should make it less easy, in the future, for a talented attorney to disqualify an IEE for a child whose disabilities require carefully planned and well-documented modifications of standardized testing procedures. The new version of IDEA clearly acknowledges that serious disabilities may preclude standardized assessment in some cases, and provides for use of alternative assessments.

Emma's case can be contrasted with that of Henry, who had severe spastic quadriplegia, with no speech and no consistent, reliable, discrete, voluntary, nonverbal behavior (blinking, vocalizing, gesturing, tapping or pressing a switch, using a "sip and blow" switch, etc.) that could be trained to express an unmistakeable "yes–no" response. For Henry, I had to admit failure; I could not determine with any certainty whether or not he had intellectual deficiencies. Unlike Emma, who was marvelously responsive, it was quite impossible to measure the quality of Henry's thinking, absent any consistent, voluntary behavioral response.

Emma's and Henry's parents, by their own statements, were adamantly opposed to "labeling" these children as having significant intellectual disability. This was not motivated simply by unrealistic denial of their child's apparent intellectual limitations. Emma's mother was convinced that the intellectual disability "label" inevitably would lead to the child's being placed in a full-day, self-contained classroom where she would "learn to use the paper shredder and pick up cafeteria trays" instead of receiving academic instruction to improve her reading, computation, and general knowledge. Unfortunately, this disheartening image of the type of curriculum provided to many students with intellectual disabilities has a basis in fact (Browder & Spooner, 2006). In principle, every child is supposed to receive individual education programming in the "least restrictive environment" based on his or her unique needs and abilities. In practice, largely due to inadequate public funding of special education services, many schools compromise on programs that group together children with a range of disabilities. Children with more demanding medical needs or disruptive behaviors receive a disproportionate share of attention and time from staff. Well-socialized children may acquire inappropriate behaviors by "modeling" lower-functioning children. The "mainstreaming" alternative places the child in regular classrooms, often with a one-to-one paraprofessional aide. Without skillfully preplanned curriculum modifications, however, a child may sit through lectures that are "over her head," while the aide strives to keep her from distracting others. Quiet students may sit or sleep through class without actively participating. This situation can sometimes be *more* restrictive of the child's learning opportunities than a well-run self-contained classroom.

The neuropsychologist's role as an advisor to the IEP team can be to define the child's assets and liabilities as clearly and thoroughly as possible and recommend interventions to rehabilitate, educate, or compensate for the child's limitations; the team as a whole determines which interventions occur, when, where, how, and provided by whom. Determining the pros and cons of alternative placements requires thorough critical appraisal of all available alternatives and, sometimes, requires creating a new program rather than placing a child into an existing one. The neuropsychologist need not become a special education specialist, but it is useful to know something about major issues that influence parent and school agendas, such as the tension between "inclusion" and "self-contained" programs, described earlier. Such issues are part of the cultural subtext of any IEE, and the extent to which an evaluator understands them becomes a measure of "cultural competence" for doing this sort of work.

Another important role for a neuropsychologist involved in IEEs is as a liaison between hospital and school for children with medical disabilities. Appendix 12.2 is an excerpt from the IEE report for Theo, a boy with multiple complex disabilities, who was a recent immigrant from a Spanish-speaking country. His mother had requested an IEE and agreed with the school that I should do it. The "list of needs" from his IEE report illustrates the range of interrelated problems that must be addressed in such a child, including physiological, communicative, cognitive, sensory, motor, and social concerns. In Theo's case, these problems were complicated by the lack of bilingual staff in his school. Both the school district and the family appreciated the IEE information. Partly as a result of this IEE and related team meetings, Theo was provided with more hours per day of bilingual support and eventually transferred to a different school program, where there was a higher proportion of bilingual staff.

THE ADJUDICATOR-ORDERED IEE

Parent–school disagreements "go to due process" after less formal conferences, staffings, and mediation efforts fail. The hearing officer in charge of an impartial due process hearing can order an IEE, at public expense (i.e., paid from the school's budget), just as a judge might require a court-ordered evaluation, to provide information that may be useful to inform the hearing officer as he or she attempts to make a determination about the disputed issue(s). In this scenario, the neuropsychologist usually can follow the same guidelines that would be used in any "court-ordered" evaluation, with the hearing officer clearly functioning as both "client" and ally in facilitating or even coercing, if necessary, both parties' cooperation with the evaluation process. The main pitfall to avoid is the risk of producing yet another disputed evaluation; the IEE should adhere strictly to state and federal criteria for adequacy and thoughtfully address the hearing officer's questions, which often concern omissions or conflicts in previous evaluation reports.

Assessing a child for an IEE ordered by a due process hearing officer resembles assessing a child involved in a custody dispute. In a custody hearing, "the best interest of the child" is a standard guiding the judge; in a due process hearing, the standard guiding the hearing officer's decisions is the child's entitlement to "a free and appropriate public education" that meets his or her educational needs. A due process hearing is quite "court-like," though the level of formality may vary with the personal style of the hearing officer. Upon request by either party, the hearing officer can subpoena witnesses and require them to produce documents. Both parties usually retain attorneys skilled in special education law. A transcript of the proceedings can be made, at public expense. If a hearing officer orders an IEE in the course of an impartial due process hearing, the school district is responsible for the cost of that IEE.

An IEE will proceed much more smoothly and effectively if both parties (family and school) genuinely value the neuropsychologist's involvement, methods, and conclusions and are willing to trust and cooperate with the neuropsychological evaluation. It is common, however, for examiners in an IEE to encounter suspicion and guardedness. When parents or a hearing officer have initiated an IEE, the school may fear that the neuropsychologist will support excessive or unrealistic demands made by the parents and may not seek to understand the educators' perspectives and constraints. When a hearing officer orders an IEE, parents may not trust that the neuropsychologist will respect or understand their perspective on the child, and they may worry that the neuropsychologist's opinion will be biased because the school district is paying for the evaluation.

The potential for confusion about "who is the client" in an IEE can extend to some confusion about record review and recordkeeping. Under the Family Educational Rights and Privacy Act, parents have the right to review their child's school record in its entirety. Documents generated by, or shared with, the school become part of that permanent record. The school cannot limit access to the record by an outside evaluator conducting an IEE, but the evaluator must have parental consent to review the school record. A written report of the IEE is required, with documentation standards specified in state educational regulations. Rarely is any formal transcript made of IEP or other meetings, though individual parties often audiotape proceedings for their own informal review (if everyone present consents). Some schools routinely appoint a secretary or IEP member to document an agenda, "meeting minutes," and a summary outline of IEP proceedings, but this varies by state and district. Mediation meetings, by law, must remain confidential, and information generated as part of the mediation process *cannot* be subpoenaed as evidence if the case moves to a due process hearing. A transcript may be made of due process hearings at the request of either party.

CONCLUDING THOUGHTS

Nowadays, when I am asked to conduct an IEE, my first step is to "clarify the groundrules" in a letter (Appendix 12.1) sent to both the school administrator and the parents, as an initial effort to establish a shared understanding of my role. In the initial interviews with parents, and separately with school staff, I try to get not only a clinical history but also as much information as possible about the nature and history of the disputed issues, to ascertain the type of IEE, the agendas—open or hidden—of the parties involved, and whether my evaluation will be genuinely useful (as in Theo's case) or essentially a waste of time (as in Emma's).

To my knowledge, there is no survey of the circumstances under which an IEE has been determined to provide a more appropriate assessment of the child than the initial school evaluation. This would make an interesting and useful project, as it could be employed as a teaching tool to improve the quality of school-based assessments. Anecdotally, I would identify several areas in which professional development workshops for school psychologists might decrease the demand for neuropsychological IEEs, namely:

1. Assess the child's needs as an individual, without assuming he or she shares the same needs as an "average" child of the same diagnostic group. For example, not every child with hearing loss needs a sign language interpreter; some need other types of interpreting, such as a Cued Speech or Oral transliterator, or CART (computer-assisted real time) transcription, to follow a lecture. An appropriate evaluation must respect differences among individuals within a disability group.

2. Understand how to analyze the tasks and component skills involved in composite scores. For example, verbal abilities strongly affect most Full Scale IQ scores. A fair evaluation may require use of relatively "culture-fair and language-limited" nonverbal IQ tests, particularly for children from cultural or linguistic minority groups, and those with speech–language delays or hearing loss.

3. Don't overlook important information. Look at the child's performance overall, not just at scores on the Wechsler Intelligence Scale for Children—Fourth Edition (WISC-IV) and Woodcock–Johnson Achievement Tests (a common battery for school psychologists in my area). Measure attention, arousal, endurance, response speed, executive function, memory, language, visual–spatial, and motor functions, as they relate to educational demands and performance. Consider the response demands of various tests of reading, math, and writing in light of the child's performance on other neuropsychological tests. Consider medical, emotional, social, and behavioral, as well as cognitive and academic functioning, as these are interrelated (see, e.g., Theo's needs, in Appendix 12.2).

4. Consider disconfirmatory evidence and alternative diagnoses. For example, gaze aversion and social withdrawal, per se, do not warrant a diagnosis of autism or Asperger syndrome in the absence of pronounced social awkwardness with cognitive and emotional rigidity; in one case, social phobia was a more appropriate diagnosis, and the child did not require (or benefit from) being placed in an "autistic spectrum disorders" program. Another child whom the school had labeled "autistic" turned out to have full-blown schizophrenia with auditory hallucinations and delusions of per-

secution. A teenager whose mother challenged the determination of Asperger syndrome turned out to be severely depressed following parental divorce, a cross-country move, and intense bullying in his new school about being "gay," concurrent with his own emerging realization of his homosexual orientation.

5. Consider all the alternative "labels," in particular, consider the "physical and other health disabilities" eligibility category for children with learning problems that may be due to a health condition, and who do not fit the criteria for "severe learning disability" in reading, math, or writing, or "developmental cognitive disability" (intellectual disability).

6. Consider the environment within which the child is required to function. Every "handicap" is a product of the interaction between the child's profile of abilities and disabilities and the extent to which the social and physical environment supports or impedes his performance. A child with gifted abilities will underachieve in a stultifying environment, and a child with disabilities will achieve more when the environment facilitates his development. The most useful evaluation is one that comes closest to identifying not only the child's talents and "untalents" but also the conditions under which those talents are successfully applied.

7. Know what to look for, so you will be more likely to find it. For example, problems with executive function, attention, and hand control all contribute to a very high incidence of dysgraphia (poor graphomotor coordination for writing and drawing work) among children with hydrocephalus and spina bifida; this has been well established for a long while in the neuropsychological literature. And yet, writing disabilities are very rarely diagnosed by schools providing services to children with spina bifida because most schools do not know to expect and assess this problem. Similarly, most schools do not know to test for evidence of frontal stroke among children with sickle cell disease, or slowed speed of processing and verbal dysfluencies among children who are cancer survivors.

8. Consider the child's assets (strengths) as well as his liabilities (deficits, weaknesses), at an individual, family, and community level, in thinking about disability determination and programming interventions. A recommendation that makes sense in one child's family situation won't work for another. Useful evaluations stay focused on the needs of the *individual* child within the context of his *particular* school, family, and community. In some cases, for example, parents can afford to pay for tutoring or speech therapy outside school hours and prefer to do so rather than to have the child "pulled out" of class for these services. As long as the child's needs are adequately met, parents have the prerogative to decline services provided by the school.

9. Stay focused on the goal: "This is Christopher. He is why we are here."

REFERENCES

Baron, I. S. (2004). *Neuropsychological evaluation of the child*. New York: Oxford University Press.

Boundy, K. (2006, January–February). Examining the 2004 amendments to the individuals with disabilities education act: what advocates for students and parents need to know. *Clearinghouse REVIEW Journal of Poverty Law and Policy, 39*(9/10), 550–578.

Browder, D. M., & Spooner, F. (2006). *Teaching language arts, math, and science to students with significant cognitive disabilities*. Baltimore: Brookes.

Demers, S. T., & Nellis, L. (2006). Assessing eligibility for and appropriateness of special education services. In S. Sparta & G. Koocher (Eds.), *Forensic mental health assessment of children and adolescents* (pp. 230–244). New York: Oxford University Press.

Etscheidt, S. (2003). Ascertaining, the adequacy, scope, and utility of district evaluations. *Exceptional Children, 69*, 227–247.

Goldberg, A. L. (2005). Ethical challenges in pediatric neuropsychology, Part II. In S. Bush (Ed.), *A casebook of ethical challenges in neuropsychology* (pp. 137–146). New York: Taylor & Francis.

Goldberg, M. (2006). Examining children in personal injury claims. In S. Sparta & G. Koocher (Eds.), *Forensic mental health assessment of children and adolescents* (pp. 245–259). New York: Oxford University Press.

Imber, S. C., & Radcliff, D. (2003). Independent educational evaluations under IDEA '97: It's a testy matter. *Exceptional Children, 70*, 27–44.

Lorber, R., & Yurk, H. (1999). Special pediatric issues: Neuropsychological applications and consultations in schools. In J. J. Sweet (Ed.), *Forensic neuropsychology: Fundamental and practice* (pp. 369–418). Lisse, The Netherlands: Swets & Zeitlinger.

Simeonsson, R. J., & Rosenthal, S. L. (Eds.). (2001). *Psychological and developmental assessment: Children with disabilities and chronic conditions*. New York: Guilford Press.

Waterman, B. B. (1994). Assessing children for the presence of a disability. *NICHCY News Digest, 4*, 1–27.

Wills, K. E., & Sweet, J. J. (2006). Neuropsychological considerations in forensic child assessment. In S. Sparta & G. Koocher (Eds.), *Forensic mental health assessment of children and adolescents* (pp. 260–284). New York: Oxford University Press.

APPENDIX 12.1

Independent Educational Evaluations: Overview Letter

Dear [School District Representative]:

This letter explains my approach to conducting an Independent Educational Evaluation upon request of the parents or school district representatives. My responsibility is to behave as a fair, neutral, and unbiased expert evaluator, gathering and integrating all available relevant information, to assist in determining whether or not this child has a disability, and to identify his or her educational needs. As a pediatric neuropsychologist, there are three main differences in my approach compared to a standard school-based evaluation. First, if the child has a medical or brain condition, I expect parents to allow me to review medical records to understand relevant brain and behavior issues that impact school function, even though such records might not normally be available to the school psychologist in a regular educational evaluation. Second, if a child is "untestable" on the standard administration of age-appropriate IQ or other tests, I expect school and parents to support my modifying test procedures or selecting other tests or assessment approaches in order to estimate the child's developmental abilities, limitations, and needs. Third, the scope of evaluation may be broader than is typical in school psychology; in addition to IQ and Achievement, I may test language, visual–spatial, attention, memory, motor, executive function, or other abilities as relevant to the child.

Reimbursement Contract

The school district special education authority will sign and return to our reimbursement specialist a letter of promise to pay [the hospital where I work] for my time in evaluating the child and preparing a written report. Ethically, we cannot bill a patient's medical insurance for any part of an educational evaluation. Payment is made to compensate the hospital for my time, effort, and expertise, regardless of whether the parties agree with the conclusions and recommendations. The IEE is done in the same unbiased, neutral way regardless of whether the parents or the school district is responsible for reimbursement.

Evaluation Process

The steps involved in conducting the evaluation typically are as follows, though there are variations specific to each case:

1. I will talk briefly by telephone with parents and school representatives, separately, to understand their questions and concerns, and the reason for evaluating the child. Parents and teachers will complete some questionnaires that provide useful information about children's learning and behavior.

2. I will review relevant educational, psychological, and medical records. The school, at its expense, will copy and send me the complete school record, including any and all previous testing by psychologists, educators, occupational therapists, speech therapists, or any other specialists, with any and all outside evaluation records that may be on file, in advance of my appointment to test the child. The parents, at their expense (unless the school agrees to pay for this), will send me copies of any relevant medical records that I request including audiograms, neuroimaging reports, and reports of any evaluations done by agencies or individuals outside the school that are relevant to determining the child's educational disability or educational needs.

3. Based on the referral questions and the records, I will select tests, questionnaires, observations, or other measures that seem relevant and appropriate in order to answer the questions. If necessary, I might recommend that the child also see other specialists such as a speech pathologist, occupational therapist, or physician. If the school or parents have ideas about particular tests they want done, or areas of functioning that should be assessed, please let me know so that I can inform both parties about which tests I can do and what issues I can address.

Upon request by the school or parents, I will prepare a Plan of Evaluation indicating how much time will be needed, what I plan to do with the child, and which (if any) of the referral questions might be better answered by some other specialist or other procedure. I will send copies of this Plan of Evaluation to parents and school.

4. I will see the child in my office, brought by the parents. I will observe and test the child in a one-on-one setting with no observers or other participants. The parents will remain in a nearby waiting area unless I ask them to sit in, to reassure the child. This rarely happens; if parents do sit in, I require them to refrain from any attempt to influence the child's test performance.

5. Sometimes when I meet and work with a child, I discover that other tests are needed than those originally planned; therefore, I may substitute other tests if this is clinically appropriate, but will attempt to cover the same general area of

functioning (e.g., language, visual–spatial, academic achievement, intelligence, executive function, attention, memory, sensory–motor skills). Whenever possible, I will use tests that are standardized, reliable, and validated with a population of children similar to the one being tested. This approach to assessment is *not* always possible (nor is it informative) with children who have special needs. Therefore, I may modify standardized test administration procedures to accommodate a child's sensory or motor disability, or use snacks, toys, or rewards to maintain the child's interest and motivation. When used, all such modifications to standardized assessment procedures will be described in my written report. This approach is recognized as valid under IDEA-2004, which provides for the use of alternate assessments if doing so will yield more accurate information about the student's academic performance or achievement (see also Simeonsson & Rosenthal, 2001).

6. I will interview the parents on the day that the child comes in for testing, while the child plays or waits; or, if the child cannot tolerate waiting, then I will schedule a time to interview the parents by phone or in person on another date.

7. I will interview school staff and any other relevant providers (e.g., after-school care providers) by phone or in person, either individually or in groups (conference call).

8. In some cases, I may ask for videotape of the child at home and/or at school, or if distance and time allow, may visit the school or home to observe the child directly.

9. After scoring and analyzing the tests, and integrating that information with my direct observations, analysis of the records, and understanding of information provided in interviews, I will prepare a written report summarizing my impressions and recommendations; this report will take 3–6 weeks to prepare.

10. The parents and school representatives will meet together with me, jointly, so that I can present my report orally and in writing, elicit comments or questions, and try to answer any questions, for all parties *simultaneously*. This can be arranged in person at my office or at the school, or via conference call or videoconferencing. What matters is that all parties receive the "feedback" at the same time and in the same words. No information as to my opinions will be given to either party in advance of that "feedback conference." If the meeting requires me to travel, the school will reimburse my travel expenses at a reasonable rate to be agreed upon in advance.

11. Any further questions, comments, or concerns that the parties raise after the "feedback conference" and my responses will be summarized briefly in an addendum to my report, which also will be shared simultaneously with all parties (typically via fax).

Limits to Confidentiality

The parents and school team should understand that confidentiality of information (including test responses, questionnaires, forms, e-mails, faxes, and other correspondence) cannot be guaranteed in IEE cases. My final oral and written opinions will be shared *simultaneously* with both the school and the parents, and neither party will receive any information about my opinions separately from the other party. My *final written report* will become a permanent part of the student's school record, regardless whether or not the parents or the school agrees with my conclusions. I may quote other records, questionnaire responses, interview comments, or other information, at my discretion, in my final written report. The "raw data" test forms, questionnaires, surveys, records reviewed, and videotapes from this evaluation remain part of [the hospital's] psychological services record. The raw data do not become part of the school record, unless a judge or hearing officer orders otherwise.

Under [state] and federal laws, I am a mandated reporter, required to notify state social services authorities of any suspected neglect or abuse of a child, and in some cases may be required to intervene if a child presents serious risk of harm to him- or herself or to others. If I am ever required to make a report to child protection authorities about a child involved in an IEE, I would notify both the school representative and the parents immediately after making the report.

Use of the Report

The IEP team (parents and school) legally *must review and consider* the IEE report and its recommendations, but neither the parents nor the school representatives is required to accept and follow those recommendations (which are advisory, not mandatory). If the IEP team cannot reach an agreement, then other forms of dispute resolution may be sought by parents or school representatives. My report can be used by either party as evidence in later dispute resolution process.

If there are any questions about this process, please feel free to contact the Psychology Intake Coordinator, Ms. _____ at [number], or contact me directly.

[Signature/address/contact information]

APPENDIX 12.2

Theo's List of Needs

The following is the "list of needs" from an IEE report for Theo, a medically complex child, based on review of school records, review of medical records, interview of mother and school staff, and direct observation and individual standardized testing.

Drooling, Swallowing, and Aspiration of Food or Saliva, and Concerns about Positioning and Head Support

Having to hold up his own head may strengthen his neck muscles and prevent their atrophying; on the other hand, having the option of better head support might make it easier for him to concentrate on schoolwork and might cut down on the drooling, and perhaps also on aspiration of liquids and foods, which likely contributes to his frequent bouts of pneumonia and consequent school absences. Review of school reports indicates staff confusion (in the past, at least) about use of respiratory medications; use of nebulizer; appropriate positioning to facilitate swallowing during meals; and whether to do percussion treatments for his lungs. The new Health Care Plan should provide for the school nurse to communicate regularly with his primary care providers and clarify for other school staff how to support Theo's physical needs.

Primary Enuresis

He is 14 years old and still in diapers. He gives no signal or indication of urinary urgency. He does indicate discomfort when he is wet, quickly and clearly. Mother indicates there has never been any real, concerted, effort to toilet train or even "toilet time" him (the latter means, putting him on the toilet at about the time that he would be expected to urinate, so that the toilet comes to serve as a cue for urination). Apparently he has not had problems with urinary tract infections or skin breakdown (decubitus ulcers) or any other incontinence-related problems, but obviously this is an increasing burden as parents are aging and he is getting bigger and heavier. Some alternatives may need to be considered, such as toilet timing or clean intermittent catheterization. I am not sure whether there has ever been any question, or workup, of possible neurological problems such as a tethered cord or hydrocephalus that might contribute to enuresis. Again, the school nurse could coordinate this with his pediatrician.

Encopresis and Chronic Constipation

He has chronic constipation, which makes him more irritable and distracted. Mother gives him three enemas per week. Lack of dietary fiber may play a role, as reportedly he has no molars (per August 2003 dental report, he had only 16 teeth) and is on a soft diet with no prescribed supplements. A nutrition consult and care from a pediatric dentist specializing in children who have severe developmental disabilities are recommended. Also, he sits in his wheelchair most of the time. Increasing physical therapy and adapted physical education direct service might help him get more age-appropriate exercise, which should contribute to more normal digestion and elimination, as well as increased endurance and strength, which may help him to sustain work effort longer.

Communication Impairment, Bilingualism, and Assistive Devices

Theo expresses himself and comprehends substantially better in Spanish than in English. Affectively, he "lights up" with smiles, laughter, and alert and cheerful responsiveness when addressed in Spanish. When addressed in English he will sometimes comprehend and comply but rarely respond, and he never initiated any English speech whereas he did initiate many comments in Spanish after hearing me speak to him in that language.

Theo understood and complied with one-step direct commands such as "Toca el cuadrado azul" (Touch the blue square). He seemed confused by any longer commands, such as a two-step command, and could not consistently point to items described by more than one adjective (e.g., "Find the bunny that is BIG and BLUE"). He responded appropriately to many yes–no questions in Spanish. He appropriately said, "sí," "no," "allá," "hola," "bye-bye" (yes, no, there [pointing], hello, goodbye). He named some objects and pictures, in response to "What is this?" in terms that were comprehensible though very poorly articulated (e.g., "rota" for the word "pelota" [ball]). He responds appropriately to "Where?" by pointing, with a well-formed index point. He responds appropriately to "Whose?" by a "mine" gesture. He did not respond to "when," "how," or "why" questions. During the morning, he used a couple of phrases that were two- to three-word sentences (such as "Hambre yo" [a syntactically immature way of saying "I'm hungry"]), mostly in conversation with our Spanish interpreter who is well known to Theo from previous hospital visits. These observations suggest that his language level is roughly in the 1- to 2-year-old range; that estimate is consistent with mother's rating of his communication on a nonstandard Spanish translation of Ireton's Child Development Inventory. He is already beginning to pair some of his Spanish with English words (e.g., "Hi, Hola!") as a greeting, and it would be an appropriate IEP goal to help him do that more often. His speech goals should include functional phrases, including a phrase to indicate to an uninformed listener when he is wet or soiled. If he has such phrases in Spanish, then his aides and teachers should learn those Spanish words in order to communicate with him. Whatever phrase he uses should be reinforced consistently, when he is being changed or toilet-timed. There may be other examples throughout his day of functional communication goals that could be facilitated by a bilingual approach (help him to express when he is hungry, thirsty, doesn't understand a command or question, etc.).

In addition, he might learn to use an augmentative communication device that could bridge among pictures, Spanish words, and English words. It would be interesting to program the device to say a word both in Spanish and then in English, when the appropriate picture-icon is selected; that might let Theo practice bridging between his native language and the dominant language of his new country. Using such a device is no substitute for face-to-face interpersonal communication, especially for someone of Theo's sociable nature.

Alertness and Responsivity

Like many children with severe brain injury, Theo does not initiate much communication or activity of any sort—he is quite content to sit passively, doing nothing, if left to his own devices. That passivity is a major threat to his educational and developmental progress. Theo's educational interventions need to be proactive, stimulating, gently insistent, tightly scheduled, and closely supervised. Therefore, his IEP needs to include close attention to what he is doing throughout the schoolday, who is doing it with him, what educational goals are served by that activity, and what sort of support the family needs to keep his brain busy when he gets home in the afternoon ("homework" assignments, suggestions for occupational therapy/physical therapy or leisure activities, interagency collaboration to help make sure he has respite care support if he needs it, etc.).

Theo's alertness and accuracy fluctuated throughout the morning. From time to time he would start to look tired or "glazed" and his responses would begin to seem uncertain, or sluggish. We would pause and rest, sing a song, or just relax for a moment or two, after which he responded very appropriately to being told, "Despiértate, Theo! Siéntate bien! Vamos a trabajar!" (i.e., Wake up, Theo! Sit up nicely! Let's go back to work!) at which he would perk up, laugh, and straighten his head. This suggests that in school, at intervals, he probably will drift off and need a few moments to "zone out." It is typical for children with brain injuries to show fluctuations in arousal. Theo can rest for a minute or so and then return to his work. He does not need a prolonged rest or nap. Some staff wondered whether he has seizures. He apparently does *not* have seizures according to the medical records I reviewed. I did not witness anything that looked to me like an absence seizure. If there is any other question of seizure activity, his pediatrician might consider EEG testing.

COGNITIVE AND ACADEMIC DELAYS

As his mother indicated on a nonstandardized Spanish translation of the Child Development Inventory, Theo's thinking and reasoning abilities are very impaired relative to those of typically developing children of his same age. Currently, Theo's overall Growth Score on the Leiter International Performance Scale—Revised (LIPS-R) is 456 ± 2, which corresponds to an age-equivalent score of 4 years, 3 months (range of 4 years, 1 month to 4 years, 5 months), for the test as a whole. From a functional standpoint, his scores are in the range of developmental cognitive disability in educational terms (mental retardation or intellectual disability in medical/neuropsychological terms).

His history, physical disabilities, adaptive behavior as described and rated by his mother, and cognitive test performance, taken together, indicate that Theo has a severe, nonprogressive encephalopathy, which means an impairment of all brain functions, presumably as a result of perinatal hypoxia (a prolonged lack of oxygen to the brain, around the time of birth). Compared with standardized norms for the LIPS-R typically developing American population, Theo's scores would be considered to fall within the range of severe mental retardation; however, given his prolonged lack of exposure to any formal instruction, combined with his physical mobility limitations, and limited capacity for object manipulation and language, it is more appropriate at this time to estimate his functioning as corresponding to the range of developmental disability with level unspecified (moderate to severe range).

The pattern of LIPS-R test scores suggests that Theo is at a stage of learning simple associations or one-on-one relationships, such as "A goes with B," "A does *not* go with C," "A is bigger than B," and so forth. He does not yet "hold in mind," understand, or process more complex concepts or relationships among several things (such as an "A–B–C . . . " series, or an "A–B–A–B . . . " pattern). Development of stronger language skills would likely support verbal mediation of nonverbal cognitive tasks, and thereby support development of more complex nonverbal thinking skills. That is, if Theo could learn to communicate more effectively, he might also learn to think in more complex ways.

Socialization and Inclusion

Two of his mother's stated goals at this time were for Theo to learn to walk and to be toilet trained. I agree that these goals are critical because they will affect the quality of his care, and the breadth of his options, for eventual group home placement, as well as affecting the quality of his everyday life as long as he remains at home with family.

In addition, however, Theo is a very sociable fellow who likes to observe and imitate, if he can, what he sees other people doing. His mother would like him to have more exposure to the social behavior and experiences of typically developing children. I would suggest that enrollment in an introductory Spanish class might be an interesting inclusion opportunity for Theo, and a good chance for him to practice imitating and repeating words and phrases.

His mother also wants Theo to bring home some homework every day so that he can sit at the table with his sister and do some sort of work while she does hers. This could be drawing, copying letters or numerals, etc. I would suggest providing him with academically appropriate preschool-level activities and worksheets.

Mobility/Ambulation and Manual Dexterity

He is reportedly responding well to Botox injections, but per school and medical records, he needs stretching, physcial therapy (PT), and occupational therapy (OT), both at home *and* at school. He needs to be using his walker and standing up, not just sitting in his chair. He seems to be primarily right-handed but may neglect the left, as I observed *no* bimanual coordinated activity (such as steadying a page while writing). His mother wants OT and PT exercises to do at home. A bilingual aide would facilitate communication of OT and PT goals and exercises from home to school.

13

Through the Looking Glass
Commentary on Neuropsychological Testimony

David S. Bush

Linguists and cognitive theorists define a *semantic frame* as a mental construct that shapes the way we see the world (e.g., Fillmore, 1976; Lakoff, 2004). These frames are implicit. They can be inferred from language, actions, assumptions, beliefs, and values. As practitioners of a blend of art and science, clinical neuropsychologists operate with many kinds of semantic frames, which may or may not be rationally based. Semantic frames are pervasive and are expressed throughout clinical reports and expert testimony, albeit mostly indirectly.

For example, an expert who offers opinions concerning the presence of a permanent and disabling neuropsychological injury following an uncomplicated mild closed head trauma in the remote past, while simultaneously neglecting to consider or assess motivation to perform, exposes a number of beliefs, attitudes, and assumptions (i.e., *conceptual frames)* concerning assessment philosophy, the impact of mild head injury, his or her familiarity with head trauma outcome literature, and so on. Of course, the neuropsychologist who routinely assesses effort and responds suspiciously to clinical presentations that deviate dramatically from expectations based on controlled prospective outcome studies also betrays important aspects of his or her core professional beliefs and values.

Frames, then, refer to fundamental conceptual structures that organize language, perception, and mental content. Facts are typically adapted to fit frames, not vice versa (Lakoff, 2004). They are distinct from the narrower category of *bias*, defined as a source of influence on an opinion that may have the unintended effect of compromising objectivity and promoting error in the decision-making process. Frames reflect a basic and deeply embedded worldview, which is not usually particularly amenable to revision or modification using rational analytic methods of self-critique, such as those recommended to neuropsychologists working in an adversarial context by Sweet and Moulthrop (1999).

Reviewing neuropsychological reports and testimony with a view toward understanding underlying conceptual frames is an interesting epistemological exercise. This type of analysis can shed light on the dynamics of expert disagreements, routinely experienced by neuropsychologists involved in medical–legal or forensic work, no matter how well trained, skillful, ethically scrupulous, and hard working they may be.

In this chapter I analyze and comment on testimony by experts, made in the context of a closed head trauma claim under civil litigation. The case was evaluated in my practice when I was retained as an expert by defense counsel (see Bush, 2003, for an overview of my medical–legal work experience and approach to forensic neuropsychology practice). I was actually one of several examiners asked to evaluate the plaintiff's mental state and offer expert diagnostic opinions about the neuropsychological impact of an alleged accident, as the claim had already been adjudicated in a workers' compensation venue (for which the plaintiff had already received a monetary settlement) before he was referred to my office in conjunction with the personal injury proceeding. In keeping with standard professional practice, all identifying information has been modified to ensure the anonymity of the parties, but the essential clinical facts are unaltered. Excerpts of testimony are reproduced here verbatim, to capture the full gist of the actual communications as accurately as possible.

THE ACCIDENT FACT PATTERN

Mr. A., a 53-year-old separated man with a high school education, reported being involved in a work accident 2 years before I saw him for a compulsory neuropsychological examination. At the time of the alleged accident, Mr. A. was working as a field technician for a telecommunications company in a position he had held for less than 2 months. According to his self-report, Mr. A. and his coworker were on a railroad trestle when he heard someone shout "Train!" Initially, he thought this was a joke. When he observed an approaching train, however, he assumed he was going to die. He recalled looking over his shoulder while running away from an oncoming train, at a distance he estimated to be about 10 feet. His memory for subsequent events at the accident scene was vague and incomplete. He was under the impression that something had struck the back of his head, a sensation he likened to being hit by a sledge hammer. He was not sure whether he had jumped from the trestle or perhaps been blown off by the force of the passing train. He could not say whether he was attended by paramedics at the accident scene. (Voluminous medical records did not contain any documentation of or reference to contact with emergency medical services.) Mr. A. stated that he could not remember the names of any of the coworkers he was with on the day of the accident and no eyewitness accounts were available. He claimed to have no recall of driving himself home on the day of the accident, a distance of approximately 200 miles.

Mr. A. reported that a neighbor brought him to the local emergency room on the evening of the accident because he was acting strangely and not making sense. The emergency room records, however, did not say anything about unusual behavior or altered mentation. According to the emergency room records, more than 12 hours following a "near-death experience," Mr. A. was awake, alert, fully oriented and had a Glasgow Coma Scale (GCS) of 15. A loss of consciousness was denied. While Mr. A. complained of neck discomfort and an occipital headache, there was no reference to a head strike and a brain-imaging study was not ordered. There were no neurological deficits or overt signs of head trauma. The emergency room record did not include any documentation of the fairly dramatic evasive maneuver that Mr. A. recounted for me 2 years later. He was given nonsteroidal anti-inflammatory medication for a cervical strain and told to follow up with orthopedics.

EXPERTS' RECORDS

As already mentioned, the accident led to both a workers' compensation claim and personal injury litigation. Not surprisingly, then, Mr. A. was subsequently seen by several psychiatrists, psychologists, and neurologists. As often happens in medical–legal cases involving claims of mental damages, a careful read of the medical records reflects *evolving* history and symptom complaints. Often, the case of Mr. A. included, patients/plaintiffs provide descriptions of performance problems that are grossly incongruous with known injury fact patterns, other functional activities, clinical presentations, and behavioral test performance.

Mr. A. was first seen by a psychiatrist as part of his workers' compensation claim, about 2½ months postaccident. According to the history obtained by this doctor, Mr. A. reported jumping approximately two and a half stories to the ground below the bridge. He complained of numerous symptoms, including irritability, depression, sleep disturbance, intrusive accident-related thoughts, anxiety, crying episodes, and memory difficulty. He reported experiencing some passive suicidal thoughts. The psychiatrist's note mentioned that Mr. A. was living with his 5-year-old daughter. No objective signs of memory impairment were appreciated. He was provisionally diagnosed with posttraumatic stress disorder (PTSD) and treated with antidepressant medication. Over the course of serial visits, this psychiatrist consistently described Mr. A.'s affect and mood state as "euthymic." Some 10 months postaccident, the psychiatrist first documented word-finding difficulty. After numerous contacts, the psychiatrist characterized Mr. A.'s clinical presentation as "atypical," raising doubts about the likelihood of closed head injury as an explanation for Mr. A.'s behavior. He also opined that further use of psychotropic medications was contraindicated.

Approximately 3 months after the accident, Mr. A. was seen by a clinical psychologist (Dr. C.), who was professionally affiliated with the treating psychiatrist. Based entirely on Mr. A.'s self-report, the psychologist diagnosed PTSD, an amnestic disorder, a cognitive disorder not otherwise specified, and, later, a major depressive disorder, single episode, severe. These conditions were causally attributed to the work accident and the treatment recommendations included EMDR (eye movement desensitization and reprocessing).

Contained within the psychologist's records were notes revealing Mr. A.'s contacts with the Department of Child and Family Services (DCFS) in the months following the incident accident. Evidently, the mother of Mr. A.'s young daughter had a serious drug problem and had not been seen for several months. Even though this psychologist viewed Mr. A. as being substantially incapacitated and occupationally disabled by mental changes that were ostensibly brought on by the accident, inclusive of reportedly getting lost on several occasions and not being able to assist his daughter with her kindergarten homework, he opined that Mr. A. had excellent parenting skills. (Inasmuch as I was not able to obtain the DCFS records, I could not determine whether the state authorities were made aware of the serious mental problems that Mr. A. was alleging in the workers' compensation and personal injury venues.) In fact, this psychologist believed that Mr. A.'s mental state was too precarious to undergo neuropsychological reassessment (for a compulsory exam referred by defense counsel) more than 1 year postaccident, warning the man's workers' compensation lawyer that having to endure the stress of yet another neuropsychological exam could easily bring about further deterioration. Independent of the psychologist's impression, a number of the treatment notes indicated Mr. A.'s considerable preoccupation with litigation matters as well as his very precise recall for various details related to the lawsuit (including the dates of an upcoming mediation and the amount of a settlement demand, which was well into the seven figures!).

Records from a neurologist who saw Mr. A. about 16 months postaccident were quite interesting in that they reflected a description of the alleged accident that was more elaborate and substantially different than prior accounts, including the much more contemporaneous emergency room record. Mr. A. reported that he had jumped over a railing to avoid contact with the approaching train but that the passing train grazed his leg nevertheless, leaving a grease mark on his pants. He stated that bystanders believed he was dead at the scene of the accident and that he vaguely recalled climbing out of a canal, up an embankment. Chronic pain and multiple neuropsychological symptoms were reported. Even though his memory was not assessed, he was started on one of the newer medications (Aricept) approved for probable Alzheimer's disease. A subsequent magnetic resonance imaging (MRI) of the brain was normal. Based on a presumed brain injury, the neurologist assigned a 39% permanent impairment rating.

At approximately 5 months and at 1 year postaccident, a self-styled neuropsychologist (Dr. E.) interviewed and tested Mr. A. on referral from the clinical psychologist and neurologist referenced above. (Due to administrative reasons never fully explained to me, I was not provided with copies of test data generated by Dr. E.'s examinations of Mr. A.) Again, Mr. A. provided a fairly dramatic and elaborate description of the work accident, stating that he jumped 40 feet to avoid being hit by a train approaching at about 80 mph, coming around a blind curve. He wasn't sure but he might have been grazed by the passing train. The postaccident symptom picture included finding himself in different parts of the state, having no memory of leaving his house or driving there and having no reason to even be in these places. Other symptom complaints, such as the sensation of noxious smells and sudden episodes of intense confusion, occasioned concerns of seizure activity.

Both evaluations performed by Dr. E. included a number of very obscure measures, not listed in the indexes of major test compendia such as Spreen and Strauss (1998). Neither exam included a single symptom validity test, though Dr. E. noted that Mr. A. "passed internal checks of malingering." According to Dr. E. some of his test scores represented a decrement for a person with an engineering degree, despite the fact that Mr. A. was a high school graduate who never obtained an engineering degree. Not surprisingly, the results of the first exam led to an impression of *considerable* neuropsychological impairment, consistent with a history of traumatic brain injury. More specifically, Dr. E. found evidence of "right-hemisphere executive" impairment and diffuse axonal injury, also suggestive of "more damage to the right than the left hemisphere." Dr. E. commented on the presence of *several memory problems*, pointing out that "damage to the memory system is common after high velocity closed head injuries such as occur in some falls [sic]."

The results of the second exam were no better than the first (i.e., there was no confirmation of a cognitive recovery curve that would ordinarily be expected in the context of a traumatic brain injury assessed 5 and 12 months postaccident). In fact, several of the reported scores were significantly and unexplainably worse (e.g., Wechsler Adult Intelligence Scale–III (WAIS-III) Letter–Number Sequencing; Object Assembly). Mr. A.'s Minnesota Multiphasic Personality Inventory–2 (MMPI-2) profile was generally more elevated than it had been previously (the Fake Bad Scale was not reported for either evaluation). Again, this exam did not include a single symptom validity test. Due to a possible seizure disorder, certain visual tasks were not administered. In keeping with expectations of permanent injury documented at the time of Dr. E.'s first neuropsychological exam, the results of the second exam were judged consistent with "considerable residual impairment" secondary to traumatic brain injury, characterized by relatively greater involvement of the right hemisphere.

A second neurologist saw Mr. A. about 8 months postaccident for a compulsory exam. Mr. A. reported that he was found wandering at the accident scene. This doctor reviewed the emergency room records, commenting that he did not appreciate evidence of memory impairment or traumatic brain injury and pointing out that diffuse axonal injury was not expected with an alleged head strike that was insufficient to produce external signs of trauma.

A second psychiatrist saw Mr. A. about 10 months postaccident for a compulsory exam. The doctor felt that Mr. A. was "trying very hard to convince the examiner that he had significant memory problems." Nevertheless, he remembered 3/3 items at 5 minutes, had no trouble performing serial 7s without error, and had good recall of current national and international events. This doctor recommended neuropsychological evaluation by a board-certified neuropsychologist, implying a lack of confidence in Dr. E.'s findings and conclusions.

COMPULSORY NEUROPSYCHOLOGICAL EXAM

Mr. A. was seen in my office 2 years postaccident. He called ahead of his first appointment to apologize for running late. Even though he was brought to my office by a driver, Mr. A. wanted me to know he had gotten confused about the directions. Despite a striking absence of emotional distress, he represented himself as experiencing very dramatic memory difficulty, including not being sure of his age or marital status. For a middle-age man who claimed to be entirely unable to perform routine chores and help his young daughter with her schoolwork, I found his calm and cheerful affect and mood to be extremely odd and inappropriate. There did not appear to be any emotional expression of loss, sadness, shame, despair, or deeply felt fear and frustration. Similarly, when recounting his reportedly life-threatening accident, Mr. A. displayed no obvious sign of tension or increased psychophysiological arousal. Although he complained of severe memory difficulty and told me he had to write everything down he wanted to remember in a little notebook he kept with him at all times, he was unable produce the notebook upon request. He had no difficulty spontaneously remembering that his friend was recently laid off from his job (he knew the name of his friend's former employer) and was being paid (by the defendant) to provide him with transportation to my office.

Mr. A. had been told that he suffered brain damage as a result of the work accident ("Everybody has said that"). Sometime after the accident, however, he was granted full-time parental rights to his young daughter (born following an unplanned pregnancy). Her mother's parental rights were completely legally severed, making Mr. A. the sole custodial parent at a time in life when many men are anticipating upcoming retirement. Mr. A. was "pretty sure" the state authorities were informed about his brain injury. A network of friends, neighbors, and family members were reportedly providing substantial help with child-care activities, house chores, shopping and bill paying, and so on.

Many readers will not be surprised to learn that Mr. A. performed significantly below recommended cutoffs on symptom validity tests (Word Memory Test—Green, 2003; Test of Memory Malingering—Tombaugh, 1996). In addition, there were several atypical indicators suggesting noncredible cognitive test performance, including inordinately low scores on recognition memory measures (Recognition Memory Test; Rey Auditory–Verbal Learning Test) and contradictory motor test findings (Finger Tapping; Grooved Pegboard). A spectacularly high score (36) on the Lees-Haley Fake Bad Scale (FBS) of the MMPI-2 reflected extreme symptom exaggeration as did unusually high elevations on Hs (T90) and Hy (T114), a pattern that is not at all characteristic of clinically referred patients (Larrabee, 1998, 2003b). (See Table 13.1 for presentation of test scores.)

I concluded that there was no compelling evidence or documentation of a closed head injury secondary to the work accident. If Mr. A. did sustain a head strike, it was most likely a very mild uncomplicated closed head injury, which was not expected to produce any lasting neuropsychological problem. I commented on the presence of unequivocal evidence of motivation to perform poorly, especially in the context of memory tests and signs of extreme symptom exaggeration. The neuropsychological picture was maximally consistent with definite malingering behavior. While malingering did not necessarily preclude the co-occurrence of a legitimate injury or

TABLE 13.1. Mr. A.'s Neuropsychological Test Scores

Test name	Test result
Green's Word Memory Test	
Immediate Recall	60% correct
Delayed Recall	60% correct
Consistency	55%
Multiple Choice	30% correct
Paired Associates	30% correct
Free Recall	22.5% correct
Computerized Assessment of Response Bias	
Block 1	100% correct
Test of Memory Malingering	
Trial 1	29/50 correct
Trial 2	38/50 correct
Retention trial	40/50 correct
Wechsler Test of Adult Reading	SS = 108
Wechsler Adult Intelligence Scale–III	
Full Scale IQ	SS = 85
Verbal IQ	SS = 91
Performance IQ	SS = 79
Verbal Comprehension Index	SS = 93
Perceptual Organization Index	SS = 80
Working Memory Index	SS = 94
Processing Speed Index	SS = 86
Vocabulary	Age SS = 9
Similarities	Age SS = 8
Arithmetic	Age SS = 10
Digit Span	Age SS = 7
Information	Age SS = 9
Letter–Number Sequencing	Age SS = 10
Picture Completion	Age SS = 6
Digit Symbol–Coding	Age SS = 7
Block Design	Age SS = 8
Matrix Reasoning	Age SS = 6
Symbol Search	Age SS = 8
Wide Range Achievement Test—Revised	
Reading	SS = 112
Spelling	SS = 95
Arithmetic	SS = 92
Trail Making Test	
A	36 seconds, Heaton T44
B	106 seconds, Heaton T38
Digit Vigilance Test	
Time	372 seconds, Heaton T52
Errors	8, Heaton T46
Wechsler Memory Scale–III	
Logical Memory I—Recall	Age SS = 9
Logical Memory II—Recall	Age SS = 10

(*continued*)

Warrington Recognition Memory Test

Words	34/50 correct
Faces	36/50 correct

Rey Auditory–Verbal Learning Test

Total	$z = -1.31$
Trail 1	$z = -.75$
Trial 2	$z = -1.05$
Trial 3	$z = -1.84$
Trial 4	$z = -1.26$
Trial 5	$z = -1.48$
List B	$z = -.32$
Trial 6	$z = -1.04$
Trial 7	$z = -.91$
Recognition	7/15 correct
False Positive errors	1

Boston Naming Test	53/60 correct

Judgment of Line Orientation Test	22/30 correct

Finger Tapping Test

Dominant	Mean = 37, Heaton T28
Nondominant	Mean = 40.4, Heaton T40

Grooved Pegboard

Dominant	78 seconds, Heaton T43
Nondominant	77 seconds, Heaton T46

Letter Fluency-FAS	25, Heaton T35

Wisconsin Card Sorting Test

Categories Completed	3/6
Perseverative Errors	27, Heaton T39
Failure to Maintain Set	2

Stroop Neuropsychological Screening Test	14-16th %ile

Minnesota Multiphasic Personality Inventory–2

VRIN	T50
TRIN	T50
F	T67
FB	T87
FP	T48
FBS	Raw score = 36
L	T74
K	T47
S	T52
Hs	T90
D	T97
Hy	T114
Pd	T62
Mf	T52
Pa	T79
Pt	T94
Sc	T81
Ma	T38
Si	T67

Note. SS, standardized score.

mental problem due to some other cause or condition, I found no convincing evidence of any acquired cognitive impairment or lasting psychiatric condition that could be reasonably tied to the incident accident. I pointed out that Mr. A.'s self-report concerning the nature of the work accident and his subsequent course was unreliable and should not be used to determine or quantify injury effects. In addition to the prospect of benefiting monetarily from his involvement in litigation (as he already had in the workers' compensation case), I suggested that Mr. A.'s disability status was being reinforced by the considerable amount of help he was receiving with childcare activities, reducing the burden of caring for a young child who had been abandoned by her mother. I asked to review the DCFS records (never provided), pointing out that it would be very helpful to determine whether Mr. A. had also represented himself as seriously mentally compromised in the child custody venue.

As often happens with medical–legal cases, additional relevant data was received after my report was submitted. Surveillance video generated a couple of months after my exam showed Mr. A. engaging in a range of behaviors that patently contradicted his self-report and very poor neuropsychological test performance, solidifying a diagnostic inference of malingering. The video showed Mr. A. placing bets at a dog track and functioning quite independently in a crowded public setting. He was shown shopping in a store with his daughter and capable of "multitasking" (i.e., operating an automated teller machine while simultaneously monitoring his child who was playing with a ball behind him). In contrast to his claim of social avoidance, he was shown smiling at a woman on the street, turning his head as they passed each other. Despite his claim of severe memory impairment and proneness to disorientation, he appeared to have no trouble with navigation across several surveillance dates, both driving and on foot. At one point, he was shown walking ahead of his daughter toward a car. He did not appear to have any problem locating the car in the parking lot and did not fail to remember to open the car door for the girl even though she was behind him.

FRAMES IN EXPERT TESTIMONY

Greiffenstein and Cohen (2005) point out that the experienced expert witness seeks to respond to latent content embedded in an attorney's questions as much as possible. These authors draw the distinction between active versus passive responding on the basis of whether the expert responds only to the overt, literal meaning of a question versus succeeding in crafting a more effective response that addresses both the manifest and latent content of an inquiry. Of course, expert testimony is also full of latent content, which can be discerned in much the same way that a skillful and empathically attuned psychotherapist detects embedded or disguised meanings in the verbiage or manifest communications of a psychotherapy client. Even though affective, prosodic, and other nonverbal cues are missing from deposition and trial transcripts, a careful read of these documents almost always reveals a great deal of insight and information about a given expert's conceptual frames, biases, characteristic beliefs about the neuropsychological assessment process and expectations concerning the range of behaviors typically exhibited by patients/plaintiffs. This information, however, often exists *below the surface* level, requiring the reader to think about the implicit assumptions, logical consequences, and unspoken implications of ideas and statements that underlie the literal content. In other words, this approach involves attending to both the words *and* music of expert testimony.

In the sections that follow, I present and comment on deposition testimony by experts in the case of Mr. A. I organize this presentation according to themes of common recurrent disagreements between neuropsychology experts, which I have observed over the past 20-plus years of active medical–legal practice. These themes pertain to (1) the weight placed on patient/plaintiff self-report, (2) the nature of data relied on for gauging injury severity, (3) magical thinking about the specificity of neuropsychological tests, and (4) consideration of malingering.

The Weight Placed on Patient Self-Report

There is a great deal of empirical evidence showing that patient self-reports cannot and should not be construed as veridical statements about objective reality. This evidence extends but is not limited to self-reports about memory ability (Rohling, Green, Allen, & Iverson, 2002), past academic performance (Greiffenstein, Baker, & Johnson-Greene, 2002), mental health history (Simon & Von Korff, 1995), medical history (Rogler, Malgady, & Tryon, 1992; Shedler, Mayman, & Manis, 1993), family conflicts (Henry, Moffit, Caspi, Langley, & Silva, 1994), and prior trauma exposure (Widom & Morris, 1997).

Testimony in the case of Mr. A. offers a number of examples of the ways in which experts express their relatively uncritical acceptance of verbal self-report. For example, Dr. E. testified that he primarily relied on Mr. A.'s self-report to judge the severity of his alleged head injury.

QUESTION: Tell me how you distinguish when someone acts normal as opposed to mildly head injured or severe head injured; what criteria do you utilize?

DR. E.: I use my clinical experience and compare them to what I know. As I say, I primarily use the symptoms checklist and their ratings on it.

QUESTION: I'm sorry; I didn't hear that.

DR. E.: I primarily use the symptom checklist and their ratings on it.

QUESTION: The ratings, those are the ones that are by way of self-report of the patient?

DR. E.: Yes.

By placing excessive weight on Mr. A.'s self-report to judge the severity of his alleged head injury, Dr. E. has created a confound that distorts the assessment process. As long as Mr. A. endorses symptoms, for whatever reason, he is almost certain to be found to have problems related to head injury. Using this scheme, a determination of exaggerated or noncredible symptom reporting is highly unlikely, if not impossible; even though this type of behavior is understood to be very common in the context of medical–legal head trauma claims, especially those involving mild head injury (e.g., Mittenberg, Patton, Canyock, & Condit, 2002).

When questioned about neuropsychological issues, Dr. C., the clinical psychologist treating Mr. A., also interpreted Mr. A.'s self-report with unwarranted credulity.

QUESTION: Now, what symptoms or what symptomatology or complaints led you to make the referral for the neuropsych evaluation after the initial visit?

DR. C.: He reported significant memory problems. He reported a lot of confusion, he reported that he had on occasion lost his temper, that he was disinhibited. He indicated that at the accident scene he was dazed and confused and that he felt nauseous prior to being released to go home. He indicated that on one occasion when he took his daughter to school, that there was a law enforcement officer directing traffic and was directing him, and he was disinhibited in the sense that he had a rage and he wanted to get out and just choke or punch this law enforcement officer. And fortunately, he didn't—you know he was able to restrict himself and not do that. He indicated on another occasion that he was shopping with his daughter for shoes and that in doing so, you know, he got so frustrated and so upset with the clerk that he began yelling and screaming. Most of the things that he relayed were, were situations I would call disinhibition, he didn't have the ability to curtail his, his id, if you will, or he didn't have the ability to contain these impulses that he had.

QUESTION: And these problems that he was having and these symptoms that he was exhibiting, are they consistent with the history that he presented as to how the accident happened?

DR. C.: They are consistent, actually, from what he had presented, the information that he had presented. To me, it just seemed so clear-cut, it was a classic case.

QUESTION: Did you form a diagnosis after the initial visit?

DR. C.: I did. Of course, the posttraumatic stress disorder, but what we would also call cognitive disorder NOS [not otherwise specified], or post-concussive disorder, as well. After that initial visit, from my perspective it was urgent to get him in for a neuropsych assessment and make a determination. He, you know, was having severe difficulties with his cognitive functioning.

Dr. C.'s testimony implies that he equates Mr. A.'s self-report with his actual behavioral and cognitive functioning. This assumption blurs the important distinction between a person's verbal report (i.e., a statement by an individual about his or her internal state, feelings, beliefs, etc., which is limited by various conditions such as self-awareness, insight, language skills and honesty, etc.) and an actual symptom, defined as a deviation from normal and usually signifying some type of disorder, which exists independent of the person's self-report or perceptual experience. Of course, such confusion has especially disastrous implications for the accuracy of expert opinions in medical–legal cases where patients/plaintiffs are known to frequently misrepresent themselves and exaggerate symptoms for both conscious and unconscious reasons. Notice that based entirely on Mr. A.'s verbal representations at the time of an initial consultation, all of Dr. C.'s diagnostic impressions involved accident-related conditions. Consequently, a true differential diagnosis was never developed. The astute reader will recognize that excessive reliance on the self-report of a patient/plaintiff claiming difficulty due to closed head injury increases the likelihood of misconstruing common, nonspecific problems as symptoms that are ostensibly unique to head trauma (e.g., Gouvier, Cubic, Jones, Brantley, & Cutlip, 1992; Lees-Haley & Brown, 1993).

The Nature of Data Relied on for Gauging Injury Severity

A number of authors have pointed out the importance of assessing head injury severity on the basis of acute injury characteristics, not symptom complaints or neuropsychological test performance (Alexander, 1995; Dikmen & Levin, 1993; Larrabee, 2005b). Yet, as will be seen from the testimony that follows, some practitioners persist in confusing head injury severity with outcome variables.

QUESTION: Do you rely on any positive neurological findings from the medical records in formulating an opinion as to whether someone suffered from a closed head injury or not?

DR. E.: Yes. I rely on a neuropsych exam, which is a medical exam ordered by neurologists—

QUESTION: How about—

DR. E.: —and physiatrists, and chiropractors, and other psychologists.

QUESTION: How about from medical doctors, any neurological deficits or findings?

DR. E.: Do I rely on M.D.'s findings to determine if there was a head injury?

QUESTION: Correct.

DR. E.: Occasionally that happens; with mild head injuries we usually have to use a neuropsych exam.

QUESTION: Tell me on the occasion that you do rely on them what is it that you look for?

DR. E.: Occasionally, very rarely, you'll get a positive MRI early in the history of the illness; then it will usually clear up.

QUESTION: Okay. Anything else similar to an MRI?

DR. E.: Nothing else that commonly documents a mild head injury.

Later, in the same deposition, Dr. E.'s testimony goes beyond confusing judgments about injury severity with outcome variables and suggests that he views acute injury characteristics as essentially irrelevant to outcome.

QUESTION: Did you believe that he suffered a blow to the head?

DR. E.: It don't matter. No, I don't have any documentation of that; it doesn't matter.

QUESTION: I mean I'll explore "it doesn't matter" later, but I'm trying to figure out what you thought in terms of actual impact. Did you have any understanding that there was any impact with the head and any outside object, any external object, any blow to the head?

DR. E.: His brain slammed against the skull. It's not an outside object; it's his skull.

Attorneys/clients involved in the litigation of head trauma claims need to be alert to testimony that blurs the distinction between injury severity and injury outcome, which always need to be understood and assessed independently. The distinction is tantamount to the difference between independent and dependent variables in experimental research.

Misjudgments about the meaning of assessment data often take the form of unwarranted inferences concerning causal relationships. Careful analysis of testimony in neuropsychology reveals commonly occurring examples of one such logical error, referred to as *post hoc ergo propter hoc* ("after this, therefore because of this"). Of course, neuropsychologists are taught that correlations do not imply causation. Many experts, however, come across as predisposed to find causal connections between alleged injuries and abnormal test results, no matter how unlikely or unconvincing (e.g., *confirmatory bias*).

> QUESTION: When you talk about this type of injury, tell me what factors you're taking into account pertaining to his fall to make the impression that you believe it's a type of injury where the decceleration forces at play forced the brain to hit the front of the skull?
>
> PLAINTIFF COUNSEL: Object to the form.
>
> DR. E.: What?
>
> QUESTION: What aspect of the fall?
>
> PLAINTIFF COUNSEL: Object to the form, also asked and answered.
>
> DR. E.: I look at the neuropsych exam. If it's positive and there has been a fall and probable head injury, then I say there's a probable relationship. I don't examine the fall. I mean I get different reports of how many feet they fall from everyone.

Magical Thinking about the Specificity of Neuropsychological Tests

Expert witness testimony in neuropsychology often reflects irrational ideas about the specificity of test instruments, defined here as the unwarranted belief that most neuropsychological tests validly and uniquely assess clearly differentiated, functionally disparate areas of mental ability and behavior. After more than two decades of medical–legal practice and reading countless reports and transcripts of expert witness testimony, I think of this type of magical thinking as the *great concretization* in our field. While it is well beyond the scope of the present chapter to take up a technical discussion of the many reasons why overconfidence in the specificity of neuropsychological tests amounts to magical thinking, the ambitious reader is referred to more appropriate sources and encouraged to investigate this matter for him- or herself (e.g., Dodrill, 1997; Guirguis, 1997; Matarazzo, 1990). For purposes of the commentary that follows, I believe that neuropsychological test scores must always be considered in context and endorse the position of Greiffenstein and Cohen (2005): "The important concluding maxim is this: The nonspecificity of most neuropsychological tests is the main reason for never interpreting scores in isolation from collateral records and history" (p. 56). This advisory is integral to the important distinction that

Matarazzo (1990) drew between psychological *assessment* and psychological *testing*.

In the case of Mr. A. there were numerous examples of what I have termed as *magical thinking* about the specificity of neuropsychological tests.

> QUESTION: Dr. E., when you set out evaluating Mr. A., what is it you were attempting to do by way of your neuropsychological testing?
>
> DR. E.: Just to determine if he had a brain injury.
>
> QUESTION: And how did you seek to make that determination from your testing?
>
> DR. E.: I sample each quadrant of the brain; I also test underneath the cortex by checking memory and then I check the reticular action, attention and concentration. By doing so I'm really checking three parts of the brain. The first one, the cortex—so I test in four areas—in that one then I'm testing memory; then I'm testing attention, concentration, processing speed.
>
> QUESTION: Let's focus on the first, I guess, set of factors you're looking for when you said you're sampling each quadrant of the brain; how is it you go about doing that?
>
> DR. E.: Research has been done long before me on what—if you have a lesion in the right frontal area, what normal functions or behavior are missing or distorted. The same is done for left frontal, left executive; then you look at left posterior and right posterior. So those functions relating to different areas of the brain have been mapped, and I select tests from those.

Underneath the cortex, indeed! Elsewhere in the deposition, Dr. E. was questioned about the pattern of Mr. A.'s alleged brain injury. The following testimony ensued:

> DR. E.: The frontal system, which is the anterior part, had several deficits as I listed. The back of the brain had none; the right had one, mild; the rest is normal. That particular deficit is hard for some people. It's a picture of jigsaw puzzle pieces and you imagine what it would make if you put them together; some people just can't do that.
>
> QUESTION: Was the level of deficits noted by the findings consistent with your impression of still a mild closed head injury?
>
> DR. E.: Yes.

Consideration of Malingering

Base rates of poor effort during assessment procedures and malingering behavior among individuals claiming mental injury due to mild closed head trauma and other conditions are notoriously high (Larrabee, 2003a; Mittenberg et al., 2002). Advances in the detection of poor effort, as well as insights about different forms of symptom exaggeration and malingering behavior, have resulted from massive research efforts over the relatively recent past (e.g., Larrabee, 2005a; Sweet, 1999). Practicing neuropsychologists can now draw on objective criteria for diagnosing malingered neurocognitive dysfunction (Slick, Sherman, & Iverson, 1999). One of our major professional organizations (National Academy of Neuropsychology) has published a formal policy statement on the importance of always assessing effort in individuals who may have an incentive to be perceived as mentally impaired (Bush et al., 2005). This recommendation has been echoed in a number of publications (e.g., Iverson & Binder, 2000; Sweet, 1999). Nevertheless, when called on to frequently review records and testimony from neuropsychology experts practicing in different parts of the country, I am constantly struck by the reluctance or unawareness that persists among many neuropsychologists concerning the importance of assessing effort and seriously considering malingering in a differential diagnosis. I often have the impression that many colleagues are philosophically predisposed to ignore base-rate statistics and operate from the naive assumption that, generally speaking, people cannot and do not feign impairment very often. In addition, I often have the sense that many neuropsychologists tend to overestimate their ability to detect incomplete effort and motivation to perform poorly on the basis of clinical judgment only, even though such beliefs are contradicted by empirical research findings (Heaton, Smith, Lehman, & Vogt, 1978).

From the beginning of my involvement with the case of Mr. A., at the time I was asked to review records, there were a number of elements that raised concerns of significant symptom exaggeration if not frank malingering behavior. For example, inasmuch as Mr. A. did not require emergency medical services at the accident scene and was able to drive himself home a considerable distance without incident, a life-altering traumatic brain injury was very unlikely. He did not develop any type of medical or neurological complication postaccident and there was no reason to anticipate progressive decline of his mental status or an extraordinary outcome scenario. Throughout the record, there was documentation of complaints that are highly atypical of mild closed head injury (e.g., not being able to assist his daughter with her kindergarten homework) and there did not appear to be any trend of cognitive recovery, at least not as measured by Mr. A.'s subjective symptoms or his performance across serial neuropsychological tests.

Exaggeration and gross distortion were suggested by changing accounts of the subject accident, which became increasingly elaborate and dramatic with the passage of time. The presence of multiple incentives (a workers' compensation claim, a personal injury lawsuit, and the provision of child-care assistance) gave Mr. A. reason to feign or exaggerate impairment; a consideration that was strengthened by features of implausible test performance across two evaluations conducted by Dr. E., neither of which included a single symptom validity test. By uncritically accepting Mr. A.'s self-report, however, neither Dr. C. nor Dr. E. seriously considered exaggeration or malingering as a tenable explanation of Mr. A.'s presentation. There was no indication that either of these experts developed a differential diagnosis that included any non-accident-related condition, virtually eliminating malingering (i.e., a high base-rate condition given the fact pattern) from the realm of possible diagnostic outcomes. Not surprisingly, then, a failure to consider malingering was expressed in many ways throughout expert testimony.

> QUESTION: What is the auditory portion; generally describe that to me?
>
> DR. E.: You just say click with this mouse every time you hear the word one, and then the recording says either one or two and he clicks every time he hears one. It's pretty nonverbal; it's pretty simple. There's not a high verbal component to it. The problem with him on that was that his motor speed was really slow and it makes it questionable whether we should interpret it or not. His hand speed was too slow, even for a mouse.
>
> QUESTION: I'm sorry, I'm having trouble maybe because I'm writing, maybe because your voice seems to be . . .
>
> DR. E.: Well, we double-check finger tapping speed, which is somewhat like tapping a mouse. We have formal measures of that and he was slow on that. So that means it's difficult to interpret the attention test. Even though we eliminated everything else, we can't eliminate the motor response. His motor response was too slow to make a good interpretation so I can't do that.

Dr. E. was likely unaware that motor slowing in a context of mild closed head injury is a known correlate of motivation to perform poorly (Greiffenstein, 2007; Heaton et al., 1978; Larrabee, 2003a; Mittenberg, Rotholc, Russell, & Heilbronner, 1996). Whereas he concluded that anomalous motor slowing contaminated the results of an attention task, there was no *frame* for understanding the slowing as a consequence of effort. Notice that in the absence of an explanatory frame, Dr. E. concluded that the results of the attention test could not be interpreted; as stated earlier, facts are adapted to fit frames, not vice versa (Lakoff, 2004).

Later, in response to direct questioning, Dr. E. addressed his views concerning the association of finger tapping and malingering.

"The best check of malingering is to see if their speeds were consistent across the trials . . . If someone is malingering it will take 10 to 15 trials before they—because if you're pretending to look slow, you can't do it consistently. So there was no malingering or pretending on his motor [*sic*]."

Unfortunately, Dr. E. was not asked to cite the research basis for this testimony. It is likely that the foregoing statements represent misinformation masquerading as an expert opinion. Contrary to Dr. E.'s beliefs, the relevant studies have shown that it is overall finger tapping speed, not variable performance across trials, which best discriminates dissimulators from head-injured subjects (Greiffenstein, 2007; Heaton et al., 1978; Larrabee, 2003a; Mittenberg et al., 1996).

Expert testimony in neuropsychology provides frequent examples of convoluted reasoning. Such reasoning is often encountered in the context of an expert's failure or unwillingness to seriously consider noncredible symptom presentations.

QUESTION: You testified on direct examination that based upon his condition you felt that it wouldn't be advisable for him to drive outside the local area.

DR. C.: That is correct.

QUESTION: You felt like that was too challenging for him, too frustrating, too confusing.

DR. C.: Stimulus overload from multiple vehicles coming at him from multiple directions.

QUESTION: That would present more of a challenge to him, in your opinion, than raising a 6-year-old child?

DR. C.: Actually I was rather impressed—his daughter is a very compliant young lady. And that worked into the formula, as well. I was very impressed at her behavior; I observed her playing with the toys here. I've had direct interactions with her one on one. And she is, she is—she's a remarkable young lady and that she's very compliant.

QUESTION: I understand that, but from an emotional standpoint—

DR. C.: Uh huh.

QUESTION: —does parenting present more challenges, in your professional opinion—

DR. C.: Oh—

QUESTION: —as a clinical psychologist than negotiating highways and driving?

DR. C.: You know, it depends on—I mean, it depends on what type of child that you're parenting. I mean, I parent an ADHD [attention-deficit/hyperactivity disorder] child we adopted when he was 4 days old and so I can, you know, I can agree that he is more of a challenge. But I mean, she and her demands wouldn't hold a candle to my son's. You know, she's very docile, she's very—she's very compliant. And also, some of the coping mechanisms we developed when he was here was that when Daddy gets irritable and angry and upset she, you know, she leaves the scene, she goes to her room and she refocuses and redirects and does something else.

So I felt comfortable enough that she was safe, that he was safe and that the, the biological parenting, fatherhood, if you will, you know, would kick in to protect her and would leave him, you know, intact in dealing with her.

In the foregoing exchange, Dr. C. was confronted with aspects of his expert opinion that were seemingly mutually exclusive. On the one hand, Mr. A. was so vulnerable to the effects of sensory *overload* that he was advised to limit his driving to his immediate neighborhood. On the other hand, the demands of being the sole parent to a young child were mollified by the girl's agreeable, compliant nature. By advancing an opinion that depicted Mr. A. as simultaneously disabled and competent, Dr. C. resolved cognitive dissonance. The inherent contradiction of his position was, presumably, not lost on the clever cross-examining attorney, who likely decided to reserve further challenge for trial.

Occasionally, one finds examples of confabulation in expert testimony (Brodsky, 1999). These confabulations occur for many reasons, including lack of knowledge, failure to consider malingering, and intellectual attempts to attribute any and all complaints and test results to a compensable injury, however unlikely or unsupported by the evidence. Responding to questioning about how and why Mr. A. could initially remember making the long drive home after the accident while claiming later he could not recall the drive, Dr. C. testified as follows:

"It could go in either direction. I mean when neural networks combine, when neural networks combine what could result is—you know, I think of a patient I saw last week who said he couldn't believe the accident was a year ago and now he's having seizures. Those may be seizures of different neurons connecting. You can't predict when they connect."

Asked if he believed Mr. A. was experiencing seizures, Dr. C. opined:

"No visible seizures, but—in a classic sense, you know, somebody lying on the floor having a seizure. But anytime the brain isn't doing something it should be doing, I mean, that's—that's professionally seen as seizure activity."

CONCLUSIONS

Testimony in neuropsychology inevitably reflects *frames* or deeply embedded conceptual systems that structure what a given expert thinks and believes about a particular case and the practice of neuropsychology in general. Frames are pervasive throughout expert testimony but must often be discerned or inferred from unspoken assumptions, metaphors, and the logical consequences of statements and ideas. Disagreements between neuropsychology experts often involve clashes of incompatible *worldviews*. These clashes frequently revolve around recurrent professional themes, such as the range of possible outcomes of mild closed head injury, the reliability of self-report data, the specificity of neuropsychological tests, and consideration of malingering. Differences in expert opinions can often be understood as debates about *framing* and the adversarial nature of the American legal system is largely based on a competition to advance one side's frame over the other.

As pointed out by Lakoff (2004), when a strongly held frame is at odds with the facts, the facts are ignored and the frame is maintained. Careful analysis of testimony can clarify the nature of an opposing expert's frames and their idiosyncratic use of language and metaphors, which serve as a *carrier* of ideas and beliefs that one may or may not agree with. Either way, such analysis is a worthwhile epistemological exercise because it can sharpen one's own understanding of a case and improve an expert's ability to directly address what he or she perceives as confusions, conceptual errors, misstatements, and erroneous assumptions lying at the heart of disagreements in expert opinions. Increased awareness about these matters only enhances the highly desirable role of the expert witness as a master teacher (Brodsky, 1999; Bush, 2003).

My involvement in the case of Mr. A. consisted of four principal activities: records review, direct examination, deposition testimony, and trial testimony. Several experts, including Drs. C. and E., appeared at trial on Mr.

A.'s behalf. The case resulted in a defense verdict, however, and, unlike the outcome of the workers' compensation case, Mr. A. did not receive any settlement or award in the personal injury venue.

Effective testimony, like meaningful teaching, necessarily involves active *reframing* of implicit premises and assumptions on which incorrect or unsupported views and ideas about a case rest. For example, at the time of my deposition, plaintiff counsel already knew that damaging surveillance video had been obtained, showing Mr. A. to be quite capable, active, and independent across several environments. He asked a line of questions intended to advance a frame that surveillance video represents a kind of entrapment, thereby attaching a nefarious connotation that would justify its dismissal no matter the content. By rejecting counsel's premise, my response attempted to reframe or reshape the purpose of surveillance and overcome automatically negative connotations that could distort the value of potentially meaningful information about Mr. A.'s behavior.

> QUESTION: You know within the medical–legal aspects of cases that surveillance is performed by defendants to try to catch claimants doing things that they say they can't do; correct?
>
> DR. BUSH: Of course.
>
> QUESTION: I mean, that's the reason for it?
>
> DR. BUSH: Well, no, I don't think that's the reason for it. I think the reason for that is to establish some independent objective information about what the person's capacities are and are not or what the person's behavior is and is not, independent of what the person tells experts and doctors about that, because there's often a discrepancy, as there appears to be—As there doesn't appear to be, but I think there is in this case.

Hypothetical questions commonly provide excellent opportunities to sharpen distinctions between contrasting frames or *models* of a case. These distinctions can help others grasp (i.e., learn) the logical basis for an intellectual commitment to one frame over another.

> QUESTION: Well, let me ask you to assume that Mr. A. did suffer diffuse axonal injury and that he does have such a traumatic brain injury. What would you expect to be his behavioral or cognitive deficits? What would you expect?
>
> DEFENSE COUNSEL: Let me just object to the form in terms of vagueness of severity and degree.
>
> DR. BUSH: I'll preface the question by telling you—

QUESTION: Let me ask you to assume this: That Mr. A. was forced to either jump or fall off of a trestle, that he sustained a fall or jump in deceleration in excess of—from a fall or jump in excess of 10 feet.

DR. BUSH: Uh huh.

QUESTION: And that he did, in fact, suffer some traumatic brain injury there from. What would you expect his deficits to be?

DEFENSE COUNSEL: Same objection.

DR. BUSH: The assumptions built into the question make it unanswerable, and here's what I would need to know: First of all, was he unconscious? Were there any objective signs of neurologic injury or altered mentation close in time to the accident? Were there any focal neurologic deficits? Were there any abnormal brain imaging findings? These are the sorts of things that I would need to know to assess the likelihood of brain injury.

The distance of the fall is not necessarily that germane to my task as a neuropsychologist. It may be of interest to you, but it's not the best way for rendering an accurate discrimination of the injury characteristics of this accident.

Independent of whether one agrees with the factual merits of my opinion, it is offered here as an example of how expert testimony presents an opportunity to communicate a frame that expresses one's most authentic and deeply held professional views while simultaneously rejecting assumptions and ideas that one believes are incorrect and unjustified. Embedded in the question that follows is an implicit assumption that Mr. A.'s self-report about the accident was essentially credible—an assumption that was grossly contradicted by my formulation of the case.

QUESTION: Assuming that he drove that distance, physically performed it, but that he did not recollect the details, didn't recollect that after the fact, would that be an indication to you not of loss of consciousness but of an altered consciousness?

DR. BUSH: Not necessarily. And here again, given the overall fact pattern, one is at terrible risk for gross diagnostic error in this case by putting too much weight on Mr. A.'s self-report. He is not, the data clearly tell me, a reliable informant when it comes to providing history of the accident and the surrounding events and the effects of the accident, so I wouldn't care to base a diagnostic opinion, given this fact pattern and this body of evidence, on what Mr.

A. says about his memory or lack thereof driving home. The fact is he did drive home. That's what's more telling and that's what's most significant to me.

QUESTION: Who would you rely on?

DR. BUSH: For what?

QUESTION: You said you can't rely on Mr. A. Who do you rely on to—

DR. BUSH: That's a good question, and the answer to it is that I rely on the acute injury characteristics as best as they can be inferred and reconstructed independent of what Mr. A. says, independent of him standing in a puddle of gas, independent of his representation that he can't help his daughter color in triangles. I would not look at test scores. I would not look at subjective complaints. I would not look at his self-report. And this is exactly what the relevant research literature directs us to do for purposes of assessing the neuropsychological severity of closed head trauma. We're to look at acute injury characteristics, Glasgow Coma Scale, loss of consciousness, presence or absence of complications, presence or absence of focal neurologic deficits, presence or absence of abnormal brain imaging findings, presence or absence of medical complications that can sometimes arise following closed head trauma. In other words, we have to look at things that can be discerned from sources independent of what the person says and does, particularly in the context of medical legal venues where the person is often subject to a vested interest in appearing more impaired or more disabled than they actually are.

Neuropsychologists, particularly those willing to take on forensic work, usually have excellent verbal skills. Trained as clinical psychologists, people in our field are often very astute at picking up on nuances of communication and encoded meanings that commonly lie beneath the surface of words and statements. Expert testimony is a complex and highly demanding intellectual and psychological task. Under considerable pressure, we are required to succinctly and clearly explain complicated ideas, which often involve sophisticated and arcane technical material, to laypeople who likely have little interest and knowledge about the subject matter of our field. Moreover, expert disagreements often turn on long-standing professional and scientific controversies, which remain largely unresolved after years of debate and study by learned people who are passionate about the issues. Efficacy in this stressful and challenging role requires not only integrity, composure, knowledge, grit, finesse, and communication skill but also an ability to do what the psychoanalyst Theodor Reik (1948) referred to as *listening with the third ear.* Neuropsychology experts who listen carefully and are able to craft measured responses to both the latent and manifest content embedded in questions posed by attorneys will be maximally effective in their travels through *the looking glass* of the forensic arena.

REFERENCES

Alexander, M. P. (1995). Mild traumatic brain injury: Pathophysiology, natural history, and clinical management. *Neurology, 45,* 1253–1260.

Brodsky, S. L. (1999). *The expert expert witness—More maxims and guidelines for testifying in court.* Washington, DC: American Psychological Association.

Bush, D. S. (2003). On the practice of forensic neuropsychology. In G. J. Lamberty, J. C. Courtney, & R. L. Heilbronner (Eds.), *The practice of clinical neuropsychology: A survey of practices and settings* (pp. 197–211). Lisse, The Netherlands: Swets & Zeitlinger.

Bush, S. S., Ruff, R. M., Troster, A. I., Barth, J. T., Koffler, S. P., Pliskin, N. H., et al. (2005). Symptom validity assessment: Practice issues and medical necessity, NAN policy & planning committee. *Archives of Clinical Neuropsychology, 20,* 419–426.

Dikmen, S. S., & Levin, H. S. (1993). Methodological issues in the study of mild head injury. *Journal of Head Trauma Rehabilitation, 8*(3), 30–37.

Dodrill, C. (1997). Myths of neuropsychology. *The Clinical Neuropsychologist, 11,* 1–17.

Fillmore, C. J. (1976). Frame semantics and the nature of language. *Annals of the New York Academy of Sciences: Conference on the Origin and Development of Language and Speech, 280,* 20–32.

Gouvier, W. D., Cubic, B., Jones, G., Brantley, P., & Cutlip, Q. (1992). Postconcussion symptoms and daily stress in normal and head-injured college populations. *Archives of Clinical Neuropsychology, 7,* 193–211.

Green, P. (2003). *Word Memory Test for Windows: User's manual and program.* Edmonton, Alberta, Canada: Author.

Greiffenstein, M. F. (2007). Motor, sensory, and perceptual–motor pseudoabnormalities. In G. J. Larrabee (Ed.), *Assessment of malingered neuropsychological deficits* (pp. 100–130). New York: Oxford University Press.

Greiffenstein, M. F., Baker, W. J., & Johnson-Greene, D. (2002). Actual versus self- reported scholastic achievement of litigating postconcussion and severe closed head injury claimants. *Psychological Assessment, 14,* 202–208.

Greiffenstein, M. F., & Cohen, L. (2005). Neuropsychology and the law: Principles of productive attorney–neuropsychologist relations. In G. J. Larrabee (Ed.), *Forensic neuropsychology: A scientific approach* (pp. 29–92). New York: Oxford University Press.

Guirguis, S. (1997). Neurobehavioral tests as a medical surveillance procedure: Applying evaluative criteria. *Environmental Research, 73,* 63–69.

Heaton, R. K., Smith, H. H., Jr., Lehman, R. A., & Vogt, A. T. (1978). Prospects for faking believable deficits on neuropsychological testing. *Journal of Consulting and Clinical Psychology, 46,* 892–900.

Henry, B., Moffit, T. E., Caspi, A., Langley, J., & Silva, P. A. (1994). On the "Remembrance of Things Past"; a longitudinal evaluation of the retrospective method. *Psychological Assessment, 6,* 92–101.

Iverson, G. L., & Binder, L. M. (2000). Detecting exaggeration and malingering in neuropsychological assessment. *Journal of Head Trauma Rehabilitation, 15,* 829–858.

Lakoff, G. (2004). *Don't think of an elephant!* White River Junction, VT: Chelsea Green.

Larrabee, G. J. (1998). Somatic malingering on the MMPI and MMPI-2 in personal injury litigants. *The Clinical Neuropsychologist, 12,* 179–188.

Larrabee, G. J. (2003a). Detection of malingering using atypical performance patterns on standard neuropsychological tests. *The Clinical Neuropsychologist, 17,* 410–425.

Larrabee, G. J. (2003b). Detection of symptom exaggeration with the MMPI-2 in litigants with malingered neurocognitive dysfunction. *The Clinical Neuropsychologist, 17,* 54–68.

Larrabee, G. J. (2005a). Assessment of malingering. In G. J. Larrabee (Ed.), *Forensic neuropsychology: A scientific approach* (pp. 115–158). New York: Oxford University Press.

Larrabee, G. J. (2005b). Mild traumatic brain injury. In G. J. Larrabee (Ed.), *Forensic neuropsychology: A scientific approach* (pp. 209–236). New York: Oxford University Press.

Lees-Haley, P. R., & Brown, R. S. (1993). Neuropsychological complaint baserates of 170 personal injury claimants. *Archives of Clinical Neuropsychology, 8,* 203–209.

Matarazzo, J. D. (1990). Psychological assessment versus psychological testing: Validation from Binet to the school, clinic and courtroom. *American Psychologist, 45*(9), 999–1017.

Mittenberg, W., Patton, C., Canyock, E. M., & Condit, D. C. (2002). Baserates of malingering and symptom exaggeration. *Journal of Clinical and Experimental Neuropsychology, 24,* 1094–1102.

Mittenberg, W., Rotholc, A., Russell, E., & Heilbronner, R. (1996). Identification of malingered head injury on the Halstead–Reitan Battery. *Archives of Clinical Neuropsychology, 11,* 271–281.

Reik, T. (1948). *Listening with the third ear: The inner experience of a psychoanalyst.* New York: Grove Press.

Rogler, L. H., Malgady, R. G., & Tryon, W. W. (1992). Issues of memory in the Diagnostic Interview Schedule. *Journal of Nervous and Mental Disease, 180,* 215–222.

Rohling, M. L., Green, P., Allen, L. M., & Iverson, G. L. (2002). Depressive symptoms and neurocognitive test scores in patients passing symptom validity tests. *Archives of Clinical Neuropsychology, 17,* 205–222.

Shedler, J., Mayman, M., & Manis, M. (1993). The illusion of mental health. *American Psychologist, 48,* 1117–1131.

Simon, G. E., & Von Korff, M. (1995). Recall of psychiatric history in cross-sectional surveys: Implications for epidemiologic research. *Epidemiologic Reviews, 17,* 221–227.

Slick, D. J., Sherman, E. M. S., & Iverson, G. L. (1999). Diagnostic criteria for malingered neurocognitive dysfunction: Proposed standards for clinical practice and research. *The Clinical Neuropsychologist, 13,* 545–561.

Spreen, O., & Strauss, E. (1998). *A compendium of neuropsychological tests* (2nd ed.). New York: Oxford University Press.

Sweet, J. J. (1999). Malingering: Differential diagnosis. In J. J. Sweet (Ed.), *Forensic neuropsychology* (pp. 255–285). Lisse, The Netherlands: Swets & Zeitlinger.

Sweet, J. J., & Moulthrop, M. A. (1999). Self-examination questions as a means of identifying bias in adversarial assessments. *Journal of Forensic Neuropsychology, 1,* 73–88.

Tombaugh, T. N. (1996). *TOMM: Test of Memory Malingering.* North Tonawanda, NY: Multi-Health Systems.

Widom, C. S., & Morris, S. (1997). Accuracy of adult recollections of childhood victimization: Part 2. Childhood sexual abuse. *Psychological Assessment, 9,* 34–46.

14

Generating Questions for Cross-Examining a Neuropsychologist

A Defense Consultant's Perspective

Robert L. Heilbronner

The practice of forensic neuropsychology includes a number of challenges and pitfalls that require the consultant and expert to consider a multitude of issues and to anticipate unexpected events, even before a referral is accepted. However, there is little doubt that testifying in court is probably one of the most challenging and anxiety-provoking things one can do when serving as an expert. This is especially true of the cross-examination phase of the testimony, when one is not particularly prepared for certain questions, does not really know the opposing attorney's reason(s) for asking a question in that particular way, or simply is subjected to an aggressive attack on one's character. It is also especially true when a competent consultant on the "other side" has prepared the opposing attorney with up-to-date and state-of-the-art questions to ask. If you can manage these kinds of questions in testimony, then you are probably operating at the top of your game.

One of the ways in which attorneys get the most "bang for the buck" is to retain a consultant to assist in the preparation of questions for cross-examination of an expert or treater. In my opinion, this requires experience, remaining current with the literature, and constructing the questions in a way that the deposing attorney can understand. It also provides a mechanism for gaining insight and understanding into the neuropsychologist's thought processes about the case, including any flawed methodology, interpretation of the data, resulting conclusions, and so on. There are those who may feel that it is not the consultant's role to provide information to an attorney so that he or she can "attack" neuropsychology colleagues. On the other hand, there are others who take pride in working behind the scenes and challenging an opposing expert's opinions, approaches to testing, or methods of analyzing the test data. In either case, the consultant acts professionally and courteously, does not engage in underhanded tricks, and simply provides his or her client (the attorney) with useful but factual information that can be used in the best possible manner.

What follows is a report (from a plaintiff expert) describing a case of alleged traumatic brain injury. As you read it, think about the weaknesses and strengths of the report. Do the conclusions follow logically from the test results? Is the author reporting things accurately? Are there any statements that reflect positive or negative bias? Think of questions that you might create if you were serving as a consultant to a defense attorney on this case.

Following the report is a list of questions that were used in cross-examination of the plaintiff expert. Are these some of the same things you thought of? What is missing? Are any of these questions unnecessary or off the mark? How would you respond to these kinds of questions during cross-examination? This kind of exercise should give you some insight into the process of preparing questions to assist in the cross-examination of an expert and help to guide you in your responses to similar questions should they arise in future cases in which you are involved.

DR. PLAINE-TIFF

Neuropsychological Experts Inc.

Name: P.C.S.
Date of birth: 2/10/60
Education: College
Occupation: Mechanic
Dates of evaluation: 7/21, 8/7, 10/22/99
Physician: Dr. Ian Trogenis

Reason for Referral

P.C.S. was referred for neuropsychological evaluation of his cognitive status and needs at this time. He was referred by his primary physician following his involvement in a motorcycle accident on 4/17/99.

History of Present Illness

On 4/17/99, P.C.S. was on a motorcycle that was reportedly struck by a car exiting a store. He said, "I remember the car was coming toward me and the next thing I know I was on the ground." He does not believe that he lost consciousness but describes an altered mentation ("It's kind of dreamy like; I was sort of out of it. I was just dazed."). He added, "I flew way far from the bike" and "I had little holes in the back of my head from the concrete." He was taken by ambulance to the hospital, where his head and neck were X-rayed; the results were negative. He was released after a few hours with a prescription for Motrin and instructed to follow up with his physician if he had any ongoing problems. He reports the experience of severe pain ("I couldn't move for a couple of days") a few days later. He also recalls having other physical/cognitive symptoms ("I was dizzy. I had a really hard time concentrating. It was like being a little drunk."). He continues to complain of pain/stiffness in his back, poor balance and coordination, sensitivity to noise and light, a possible decline in hearing, slowed and effortful thinking, poor concentration, and memory problems. Emotionally, he is more irritable, has less patience, and has had a number of emotional outbursts toward his wife, children, and coworkers.

P.C.S. was examined by a physiatrist, Dr. Ian Trogenis, on 7/2/99. Diagnostic impressions included traumatic brain injury (TBI) secondary to the motorcycle accident. Recommendations included chiropractic management for musculoskeletal dysfunction and neuropsychological testing to get a full evaluation of his condition. Dr. Trogenis noted that P.C.S.'s deficits in memory, attention, and concentration were not unusual after having been in such an accident, but otherwise he appeared to be in good health.

P.C.S. is the second of four siblings raised at home by his married biological parents. He graduated from high school and described herself as a "B student" with no diagnosis of learning difficulties or need for special services. He completed a BA degree in science in 1982. He was doing mechanic work at a local auto shop at the time of the accident. P.C.S. has been married for 22 years, a relationship he describes as positive and supportive; he and his wife have three healthy children. His medical history is remarkable for a 10-year history of migraine headaches (treated with medication as needed) and a history of depression treated first with Paxil and then

Prozac with some reported benefit. He reports no other surgeries, injuries, psychiatric hospitalization, or prior brain trauma.

Interview of Wife

P.C.S.'s wife was interviewed regarding her husband's current level of functioning. She has noted significant physical, cognitive, and emotional changes since the accident, including headaches that were premorbid but are now more frequent, fatigue ("he's tired a lot"), clumsiness, reduced sexual drive, effortful thinking, memory deficits ("He don't remember what he did 5 minutes ago"), confusion, irritability ("he's out of patience quicker"), emotional lability, occasional depression, and lessened tolerance for stress and frustration. She described multiple instances in which "If he's driving, he forgets where he's going, even to places he goes to a lot. He just blanks out and doesn't know where he's at." She said these changes were evident after the trauma and they are very different from how her husband used to be; they have also not gotten better over time.

Behavioral Observations

P.C.S. was neatly groomed and dressed and generally unremarkable in appearance. He appeared somewhat physically uncomfortable, but independently ambulated with functional gross and fine motor skills. He is right-handed. P.C.S. was pleasant and cooperative throughout the evaluation; his social relatedness and social skills were good. He appeared to be putting forth his best effort, although his tolerance for stress and frustration was limited. He was mildly defensive and self-critical regarding his deficits. His affect was mildly agitated and distressed, with mild irritability noted in response to challenge/failure. His expressive language was intelligible and spontaneous although somewhat rambling and vague at times. His thought processes were logical and coherent. Difficulties with impaired concentration, memory deficits, and confusion ("I became lost on the way to a session and did not have the name or phone number of the treatment center") and mild visual perceptual deficits were noted throughout the evaluation.

Tests Administered

The following tests were administered: Rey 15-Item Memory Test, Halstead–Reitan Neuropsychological Battery, Symbol Digit Modalities Test, Wechsler Adult Intelligence Scale–III (WAIS-III), Wechsler Memory Scale–III (WMS-III), California Verbal Learning Test (CVLT), Wide Range Achievement Test—Third Edition (WRAT-3), Beck Depression Inventory–II (BDI-II), Beck Hopelessness Scale (BHS), Beck Anxiety Inventory (BAI),

Minnesota Multiphasic Personality Inventory–2 (MMPI-2), and Sentence Completion.

Neuropsychological Status

The Halstead–Reitan Neuropsychological Battery was administered to assess the presence and extent of organic brain dysfunction. P.C.S.'s performance indicates performance in the "brain damaged" range for three of seven tasks, yielding an Impairment Index of .4; yet, this falls in the "normal" range (at the 37th percentile) when compared to men of similar age and education. His performance was significantly impaired for two of the four most sensitive indicators of brain dysfunction (Trail Making Test B, Tactical Performance Test Localization).

P.C.S. showed performance within the "perfectly normal" range for perceiving speech sounds and perceiving bilateral tactile, auditory, and visual stimulation. Performance was within the "normal" range for complex problem solving and sensory–motor integration time. Performance was "mildly impaired" for maintaining attention/concentration, nonverbal memory, sensory–motor integration, and bilateral psychomotor speed. Performance was "seriously impaired" for cognitive flexibility and simple and complex sensory perceptual functions. Screening of visual fields indicated no restrictions. A simple hearing screening was passed bilaterally. Aphasia screening revealed mild difficulties with pronouncing words, mental computation, and rephrasing concepts. There were significant right–left differences, with the nondominant left hand showing relative deficits in speed and grip strength; he reported subjective weakness of his left hand during testing.

The Symbol Digit Modalities Test was also administered to assess psychomotor speed. For this test, the subject matches and copies digits and symbols. P.C.S.'s performance was around .5 standard deviations below the mean (at the 32nd percentile when compared to peers of similar age and education), and is considered within normal limits.

The Rey 15-Item Memory Test was administered to assess conscious or unconscious desire to appear impaired. For this task, the subject is asked to memorize 15 items that are semantically grouped, making the task harder than it appears. All but the most impaired subjects should be able to recall a minimum of 9 items. P.C.S. was able to correctly recall 12 of the 15 items (with mild misinterpretation noted), indicating good motivation for testing.

In regard to interpretation of these findings, P.C.S.'s neuropsychological functioning is showing deficits in regard to attention/concentration, bilateral psychomotor speed, cognitive flexibility, and sensory perceptual functions, as well as a relative weakness of his nondominant left hand, consistent with a partially resolved TBI.

Intellectual Assessment

The WAIS-III was administered to obtain an overall estimate of intellectual functioning, as well as to obtain separate measures of verbal and nonverbal abilities. P.C.S. is currently functioning in the "average" range of intellectual ability (Full Scale IQ = 103). There was no significant difference between his verbal and performance skills, with both Verbal IQ (VIQ = 102) and Performance IQ (PIQ = 104) in the "average" range. Overall, he showed a significant relative strength in nonverbal reasoning and did not show any significant relative weaknesses in any domain.

A summary of WAIS-III subtest scores is as follows (an average scaled score is 10):

Verbal	Scaled score	Performance	Scaled score
Vocabulary	9	Picture Completion	11
Similarities	12	Digit Symbol	10
Arithmetic	11	Block Design	9
Digit Span	9	Matrix Reasoning	14
Information	9	Picture Arrangement	9
Comprehension	13	Symbol Search	(11)
Letter–Number	(13)		

P.C.S.'s Verbal Comprehension Index score was in the "average" range (100; 50th percentile when compared to same-age peers). Performance was within normal limits for general information and word knowledge and high average for verbal abstraction. His Perceptual Organization Index score was in the "average" range (107; 68th percentile when compared to same-age peers). Ability to discriminate detail and visual–motor integration were within normal limits. Nonverbal reasoning was very good. Working Memory was in the "average" range (106; 66th percentile when compared to same-age peers). Performance was within normal limits for simple attention/concentration and mental computation. Performance was high average for complex concentration. Processing Speed was in the "average" range (103; 58th percentile when compared to same-age peers) and his scores were within normal limits for psychomotor speed and visual information processing speed. Overall, P.C.S.'s IQ and index scores are essentially consistent with his estimated premorbid level of functioning.

Academic Achievement

The WRAT-3 was administered to assess P.C.S.'s academic achievement abilities. Results indicate that reading/decoding skills for single words are at the high school level (87; 19th percentile when compared to a same-age group). He was able to identify and name all letters and read moderately complex words. Spelling skills were at the high school level (standard score = 92; 30th percentile when compared to a same-age group). P.C.S. was able to write his name and spell moderately complex words. Arithmetic skills are also at the high school level (102; 53rd percentile when compared to a same-age group). P.C.S. was able to do calculations, fractions, and decimals, with occasional errors and misinterpretation of mathematical operations. Overall, P.C.S. shows skills in academic achievement that are within normal limits for the population but significantly lower than would be expected given his college-level education.

Learning/Memory

The WMS-III was administered to obtain a current estimate of P.C.S.'s learning and memory skills. He obtained a General Memory Score of 92 (in the "average" range andat the 32nd percentile when compared to same-age peers), significantly lower than his Full Scale IQ of 103. The following subtest scores were obtained (an average standard score is 100 [with a standard deviation of 15]).

Index	Standard score	Percentile
Auditory Immediate Memory	97	42
Visual Immediate Memory	91	27
Immediate Memory	93	32
Auditory Delayed Memory	94	34
Visual Delayed Memory	94	34
Auditory Delayed Recognition	95	37
General Memory	92	30
Working Memory	99	47

Overall, P.C.S. did not show any significant strengths or weaknesses in regard to the different areas of memory assessed. He was alert and fully oriented to person and time; in contrast, he did not know the name of the town. Knowledge of personal information was good.

In regard to immediate memory, his recall of verbally presented passages was within low-normal limits. Learning of verbal paired associates and recognition of faces were within normal limits and recall of pictured scenes was mildly impaired. In regard to delayed memory, recall of verbal paired associates and faces was within normal limits. Recall of story passages was within low-normal limits. Recall of pictured scenes was mildly impaired. Delayed auditory recognition (recognition of information contained in the passages and of presented word pairs) was within normal limits. In regard to General Memory, recall of faces and verbal paired associates and delayed auditory recogniton were within normal limits. Delayed recall of faces and verbal passages was within low-normal limits and delayed recall of pictured scenes was mildly impaired. In regard to Working Memory, nonverbal attention span was mildly impaired; complex concentration was high average.

The California Verbal Learning Test (CVLT) was administered to further assess verbal learning. For this test, the subject learns a list of items through repetition and then recalls this list immediately and after 20 minutes with and without cues. P.C.S.'s performance indicated new learning for rote verbal material that was mildly impaired, with overall learning around the 9th percentile when compared to same-age peers. Immediate verbal memory span ranged from the 16th to the 50th percentile. Short delay, free recall was significantly impaired (at the 2nd percentile); short delay, cued recall was mildly impaired (at the 16th percentile). Long delay, free and cued recall were severely impaired (below the 1st percentile). He tended to recall the words by their order on the list rather than their semantic meaning, which is a less efficient learning strategy. He showed a strong recency effect (recalling mostly words at the end of the list) and a significant number of perseveration (i.e. repeatedly recalling words within the same trial). His recognition and discriminability of the words were within normal limits (in sharp contrast to his severely impaired long delay recall), an indication of significant memory retrieval problems, which are assisted with verbal cues.

Overall, P.C.S.'s performance on tasks measuring learning and memory indicated overall "average" performance that is significantly lower than his intellectual functioning. Significant relative weaknesses were noted in nonverbal attention span and recall of pictured scenes as well as deficits in new learning, consistent with partially resolved TBI.

Clinical/Projective

P.C.S.'s affect was mildly agitated and distressed. Both he and his wife describe consistent physical, cognitive, and emotional symptoms in him since the trauma, including headaches, fatigue, impaired concentration, memory deficits, irritability, and depression. He reports that he is distressed regarding his lingering symptoms and very concerned that these have not resolved to date. He describes becoming increasingly aware of and concerned regarding his memory since the trauma, with severe symptoms noted immediately posttrauma that are slowly fading over time. He describes unusual emotional blunting ("I'm less anxious and more nonchalant. I just don't care as much about anything"), as well as lessened tolerance for fast, complex, or stressful situations ("I get more overwhelmed with day-to-day functional things.") He describes a premorbid history of depression related to "stress and family issues" and has been followed psychiatrically since shortly before the trauma, treated first with Paxil and currently with Prozac.

P.C.S. denied delusions, hallucinations, and current suicidal/homicidal ideation. There was no evidence of a currently active psychotic process. The BDI-II and BHS were administered to assess symptoms of depression and hopelessness. Results of the BDI-II indicate scores in the "mildly depressed" range. He reported difficulties in the areas of sad affect, discouragement, loss of pleasure in familiar activities, feelings of guilt, agitation, social withdrawal, making decisions, reduced energy with fatigue, irritability, concentration, increased sleep and appetite, and lessened sexual interest. Results of the BHS were in the "moderate" range, with significant feelings of hopelessness, pessimism and expectation of failure/disappointment noted. The BAI was also administered to assess symptoms of anxiety. Results were in the "moderately/severely anxious" range. P.C.S. reported moderate subjective symptoms (unable to relax, feeling terrified, nervous and scared, fear of the worst happening), mild/moderate neurophysiological symptoms (numbness or tingling, wobbliness in the legs, dizzy or lightheaded, unsteady, shaky, faint), mild autonomic symptoms (feeling hot, face flushed, sweating), and mild panic symptoms (heart pounding or racing, difficulty breathing, indigestion).

Projective testing revealed consistent themes of motivation for return to work and career advancement, sleep disturbance, restlessness and agitation, depression, positive family relationships, and uncertainty regarding his future.

The MMPI-2 was administered to assess for the presence of significant psychiatric pathology. P.C.S.'s *T*-scores were as follows (an average *T*-score is 50; scores above 65T are considered clinically significant with the exception of Masculinity/Femininity):

Clinical scale	*T*-score	Significant?
Hypochondriasis	83	Yes
Depression	80	Yes
Hysteria	92	Yes
Psychopathic Deviance	78	Yes
Masculinity/Femininity	52	No
Paranoia	63	No
Psychasthenia	79	Yes
Schizophrenia	67	Yes
Hypomania	59	No
Social Introversion	41	No

Analysis of the validity scales indicates a valid profile, with a typical test-taking approach, overemphasis on pathology, and sufficient resources for intervention. There were six clinically significant scale elevations, indicating concern regarding multiple physical symptoms, clinical depression, disinhibition and emotional lability, difficulties with judgment, agitation and anxiety, social withdrawal, and difficulties with concentration and thinking. Analysis of the overall profile indicates physiological distress, weakness and fatigue, passivity and dependence, irritability, and physical symptoms worsened by emotional distress.

Summary

Overall, P.C.S. presents a clear picture diagnostically. Formal testing indicates deficits in neuropsychological functioning, including a relative decline in his nondominant left hand, difficulties with attention/concentration and cognitive flexibility, bilateral psychomotor slowing, and sensory–perceptual deficits. Intellectual functioning is within the "average" range. Learning/memory testing indicates overall performance significantly lower than expected given his intelligence, with specific weaknesses in nonverbal attention span, recalling pictured scenes, and new learning. Academic achievement is within normal limits but lower than would be expected given his college level education. In addition, he is having difficulties with irritabilility, emotional blunting and depression. Consistent symptoms are reported by him and his wife. All data are consistent with a TBI as a result of the motorcycle accident. There are indications of more right-sided brain damage, including relative weakness of his nondominant left hand, difficulties with spatial orientation, sensory–perceptual deficits, deficits in recall of pictured scenes, and impaired nonverbal attention span. Diagnosis is mildly complicated by his premorbid depression. Taking into account the severity of the trauma, he is making a rather good recovery. It is unclear at this time which, if any, of these symptoms will persist following the normal 2-year posttrauma recovery period for TBI.

Diagnostic Impressions

294.1 Dementia, due to closed head trauma
296.32 Major depressive disorder, recurrent, moderate, in partial remission with medication
Closed head trauma, by medical history and current results

Recommendations

1. Psychotherapy is recommended to assist in implementing compensatory strategies, decreasing depression and emotional distress, and increasing insight into his assets and deficits; follow-up services will be offered.

P.C.S. is apparently benefitting from psychiatric follow-up with antidepressant medication, and it is recommended that this continue.

2. In regard to minimizing the impact of P.C.S.'s difficulties with attention, concentration, memory, and new learning:

    a. He will be best able to concentrate alone in a room with limited distractions. More demanding tasks are best planned for early in his day to minimize the impact of physical and mental fatigue.

    b. Extensive use of normal memory aids (such as schedules, calendars, lists of things to do) will be helpful.

    c. Planning on paper will maximize his efficiency.

    d. Focusing on and finishing one task at a time will reduce difficulties with distractibilty.

    e. Immediately writing down what he has committed to do will increase reliability of follow through.

    f. New learning should be structured to encourage early and frequent success.

    g. Repetition is especially helpful in the learning process.

    h. Increasingly structured verbal cues will assist memory retrieval.

    i. P.C.S. is often able to spot and correct his own errors if he takes the time to double-check his work.

    j. P.C.S. greatly benefits from verbal cues to assist in memory retrieval.

    k. "Talking himself through" problem solving is often helpful.

    l. Keeping important items (such as keys and his wallet) in a consistent place will reduce his time searching for these.

    m. Use of visual cues (including demonstration, written notes, etc.) will also be helpful.

    n. P.C.S. does not respond well to time pressure. It is important that he concentrate on accuracy rather than speed.

3. P.C.S. would benefit from increased cognitive challenge; possibilities include increased reading, taking a simple community college course, educational television, and so on. Slowly increasing his endurance for and comprehension of reading will also be beneficial.

4. All symptoms will be reduced when physical and emotional stress, fatigue, pain, hunger, and time pressure are minimized. Adequate rest, good nutrition and regular meals, and a healthy lifestyle will be important in the healing process. Resuming regular exercise would be of great physical and emotional benefit and continued medical follow-up will continue to be essential. Avoidance of glare and noise may be helpful in reducing headaches. Pain management with minimal medication (rest, exercise, use of topical heat or cold, minimizing motions that aggravate the pain) will be impor-

tant. P.C.S. notes a subjective decline in hearing since the trauma and may wish to discuss further evaluation of this with his physician. He describes jaw pain that increases with stress; deliberate efforts to unclench/relax his jaw, especially when stressed, will be helpful. He may at some point benefit from evaluation/treatment for potential temporal mandibular joint (TMJ) pain.

5. P.C.S. notes difficulties with sleep disturbance. Leaving himself adequate time to relax prior to attempting sleep, eliminiating caffeine after early afternoon, a steady waking time, leaving bed if he has not fallen asleep in 15 minutes, and removing the clock from his line of vision may be helpful.

6. In regard to improving his time management, P.C.S. would benefit from leaving himself extra time between commitments and destinations, becoming more aware of how long tasks are taking him and compensating for this by leaving additional time. Wearing and often referring to a watch is also helpful.

7. In regard to reducing irritability, P.C.S. would benefit from time alone to calm himself when he becomes upset. Becoming more aware of the unfolding process of his emotional distress (and the cues signalling this) will assist in increasing his emotional control. Use of relaxation techniques may be helpful in reducing agitation.

8. The most important information in compensating for deficits will come from careful examination of his errors. It is important that P.C.S. minimize anger/self-criticism following errors and instead concentrate on preventing their recurrence.

9. Information regarding TBI will be provided to P.C.S. and his family.

10. A neuropsychological reevaluation in 1 year is recommended to continuously monitor P.C.S.'s cognitive status and needs.

Dr. Plaine-Tiff,
Board Eligible Neuropsychologist

QUESTIONS FOR DR. PLAINE-TIFF'S DEPOSITION

Credentials/Qualifications

This is an area of inquiry that attorneys already know pretty well. However, depending on the experience of the attorney, they may not know about board certification, licensing issues, the importance of publishing in peer reviewed journals, and so on.

In addition to the usual qualifying questions . . .

- In what area of psychology is your doctorate?
- Is your degree from a program approved by the American Psychological Association (APA)?
- Did you complete an internship in a setting approved by the APA?
- Did you receive postdoctoral training in clinical neuropsychology? Where?
- Are you board certified in clinical neuropsychology? If not, why not?
- What does the designation "board eligible" mean?
- Is this a term recognized by your peers?
- Are you a member of any major neuropsychological professional organizations? Which ones?
- Have you published any articles in peer-reviewed scientific journals on head injury or concussion?
- What is the nature of your current work? Are you in private practice? What percentage of your practice is devoted to forensic activities? What percentage of your forensic practice is for defense? For plaintiff?

Issues Related to Mild Head Injury and Postconcussion Syndrome

Most "neurolawyers" have experience with brain injury and its related sequelae. Those who do not specialize in brain injury litigation will be far less prepared to ask these kind of questions, let alone know what is a reasonable response versus one that should be challenged.

- What are some of the ways to define severity of head injury? Are you familiar with the Glasgow Coma Scale score? What does it measure? Are there other methods to define severity of a brain injury? What are they?
- How do you define mild head injury? Is this something that has achieved a consensus in your field? Can you identify a resource of publication that says that?
- How do you define postconcussion syndrome? What kinds of symptoms must be present to satisfy a diagnosis of postconcussion syndrome? Is this something that has achieved a consensus in your field?

• Taking into consideration the current literature in your field, how long do the symptoms of postconcussion syndrome typically last in the majority of patients with mild head trauma (e.g., 1–3 months)? When symptoms persist beyond that period of time, what does the research say about what causes their persistence?

• In those patients who complain of persistent symptoms for many years after a mild head injury/concussion, isn't it generally true that the persistence of symptoms can best be explained by nonneurological factors?

• Do you ever use the DSM-IV diagnosis of postconcussional disorder? Isn't it true that this is really a research diagnosis?

• Is a diagnosis of postconcussional disorder different from a diagnosis of cognitive disorder, not otherwise specified (NOS)?

• Isn't it true that postconcussion symptoms can occur in a whole host of other medical and/or psychiatric conditions? Don't they also occur in normal subjects? In individuals who are under stress?

Evaluation Findings

• When did you see P.C.S.? How long after the accident was this (less than 6 months)? Why did it take you three sessions to complete the testing? Do you typically divide your testing over several days? How might that affect the test results?

• How do you choose the tests you give a patient with a head injury? Do you have a standard battery that you use for all patients? What is the research that supports the use of this battery?

• Did you do your own testing? If no, who trained your technician? How much time did you spend with P.C.S.?

• Who referred P.C.S. to you? Dr. Ian Trogenis saw him about 1 month postinjury didn't he? Didn't he also recommend treatment for musculoskeletal dysfunction? How do you differentiate the effects of concussion from musculoskeletal pain? Can't chronic pain cause impairments in attention, concentration, and memory?

• P.C.S. was still working at the time you evaluated him wasn't he? What is your understanding as to the kinds of duties he was responsible for at work? How did that differ (if at all) from the duties he was doing before the accident?

• Are you aware that he saw a Dr. Sibling for an evaluation? Did you know that he is P.C.S.'s brother? Does that have any importance to you as a treating clinician?

• What records did you have at your disposal when you evaluated P.C.S.? Isn't it important to have records from the accident (i.e., emergency medical service records and emergency room records) and also have access to preinjury medical records? Did you have P.C.S.'s school records?

- What is your understanding of P.C.S.'s injury? Did you assume at the outset that he had sustained a head injury because he was referred to you by Dr. Trogenis?
- Are you aware of the distinction between a mild versus moderate or severe concussion? What are the criteria for each of them? Is there a difference between a head injury and a brain injury? Can somebody injure his or her head and not his or her brain?
- Did you take a preinjury history? What are some of the medical and psychological conditions that P.C.S. had before the accident (migraines, depression, and TMJ)? Aren't these factors important when considering the neuropsychological effects following concussion? Isn't there a lot of overlap between symptoms of concussion and chronic pain? Depression? How do you differentiate between them?
- What is P.C.S.'s recall of the accident? What do you make of the fact that he recalled almost all of the events surrounding the accident? Is it your understanding that he lost consciousness or not? If P.C.S. was simply "dazed" wouldn't that suggest to you that at most he sustained a mild concussion? Isn't it true that the symptoms associated with mild concussion are the briefest?
- P.C.S. had a Glasgow Coma Score of 15 in the emergency room, didn't he? What does that suggest to you?
- What was the course of his treatment after the accident happened?
- He noted pain early on didn't he? What are the neuropsychological effects associated with pain? Didn't P.C.S. have a preaccident history of chronic pain? Didn't he have a history of migraine headaches before the accident?
- Isn't it true that P.C.S. was also prescribed Prozac and Paxil before the accident? Is it your understanding that he was depressed beforehand?
- Do you take patient's self-reports of symptoms as valid? What about patients who are in litigation? In your report on page 2, you list a number of complaints. Are these things that P.C.S. spontaneously told you? Or, are they in response to your questions? Are they answers in response to questionnaires?
- What do you make of the fact that P.C.S. reported problems reading? Is this something that is commonly affected after a mild head injury? Isn't it true that reading skills are one of the most resistant to brain dysfunction?
- What does symptom overreporting mean? What is symptom exaggeration? How do you explain when a patient's complaints exceed his or her impairments on neuropsychological tests? That is, when he or she complains of a prominent number of symptoms but the neuropsychological test results do not show prominent impairments?
- You said that P.C.S. appeared to put forth his best effort. What tests did you give to measure effort? (The Rey 15-Item Memory Task). Is the 15-

Item Test sensitive to feigned memory impairment? Aren't there other more current, standardized, and state-of-the-art tests of effort that should be included in neuropsychological evaluations?

• You said that P.C.S. was "repeatedly late," which he attributed to once becoming lost and losing track of time. Do you know if he had problems getting lost before the accident?

• You interviewed his wife didn't you? Isn't she also a party in the lawsuit? Isn't she also a patient of yours? How do you know that her report of changes in her husband are reliable?

• Re: Neuropsychological status: You said that P.C.S.'s performance on tests from the Halstead–Reitan Neuropsychological Battery was in the "normal" range wasn't it? Yet, you said his scores were "significantly impaired" on two of the four most sensitive indicators of brain dysfunction. Well, which is it . . . were his scores normal or not? What norms did you use for this determination?

• When scores fall in the impaired range on neuropsychological tests, is it automatically assumed that the person has brain damage? Can't other factors besides brain dysfunction cause scores to fall in the impaired range on these tests?

• You said that he shows deficits in nondominant left hand, difficulties with attention/concentration and cognitive flexibility, bilateral psychomotor slowing, and sensory–perceptual deficits and that these results are consistent with partially resolved TBI. Is weakness of the left hand a symptom of TBI? Are impairments in attention and concentration exclusively associated with head trauma?

• Would you agree that P.C.S.'s WAIS-III scores were all average or above? His scores on the WMS-III were all also average weren't they? So, he didn't show any problems with memory, intelligence on these measures did did he?

• You indicate that P.C.S.'s California Verbal Learning Test long delay, free and cued recall were severely impaired and he tended to recall words by their order rather than their semantic meaning. Recognition memory was good, which suggests that memory retrieval problems probably explained his memory difficulties. Is this something that commonly occurs with head injuries? Can depression affect retrieval abilities? How about chronic pain?

• Why didn't you administer the more current version of the CVLT, the CVLT-2?

• How do you explain severe impairment in memory in a case of a mild TBI? Would you expect such severely impaired performance in a case where there was no loss of consciousness or altered mentation?

• You say that his memory indicated overall "average" performance that is significantly lower than his intellectual functioning. What do you mean by "significant"? Aren't his WAIS-III scores solidly in the average range? So, there really isn't a difference between his memory and intellectual functions is there?

• By the way, did you estimate P.C.S.'s preinjury level of intellectual functioning? How did you do that? Is this a reliable and accepted way of assessing preinjury abilities? Just because the preinjury IQ was estimated to be at a certain level, does this mean we can assume that all other preinjury neuropsychological abilities (e.g., memory and visual–spatial skills) were also at this level?

• In terms of his academic skills, you say that they are within normal limits for the population but significantly lower than would be expected given his college education. What do you mean by that? Do you know where he went to college? Do you know what his grades were?

• Why did you do projectives in a head injury case? Is this a standard method of practice? How much of the profile reflects preinjury personality traits? His score on the Beck Depression Scale indicated mild depression. How do you know he wouldn't have scored at this level beforehand? He was taking antidepressants before the accident wasn't he?

• P.C.S.'s scores on the MMPI-2 were elevated on six of the clinical scales right? Scale 2 was the most elevated, followed by Scales 1, 4, 7, and 8. You say that there was an overemphasis on pathology. What did you mean by that? Is this the kind of profile that commonly occurs in head injury patients? Doesn't it also occur in patients with chronic pain and patients with somatoform disorders?

• Did you calculate P.C.S.'s score on the FBS, Fake Bad Scale? Why not? Are you aware of this scale and its use with head-injured patients who are in litigation? What does a raw score of 29 on the FBS suggest to you? Are you familiar with studies that show that FBS scores greater than 26 in men reflect an exaggeration of somatic problems? Some would even say that it may reflect "somatic malingering." Are you familiar with the term *somatic malingering*?

• In your summary, you state that "P.C.S. presents a clear picture diagnostically . . . " What I'm trying to figure out is how it's a "clear picture" if you already agreed that these deficits can also be caused by other psychological or medical conditions?

• If P.C.S. had performed similarly without there having been an accident, how would you then explain the results? Isn't it true that even normals will score in the impaired range on some neuropsychological measures? In fact, isn't it statistically true that the more tests you give, the more likely it is that some scores will fall in the impaired range?

• How appropriate is it to localize in a case of concussion? Do concussions commonly produce localized or lateralized impairments? Can you cite some research to support your claim? Is there any supportive evidence (e.g., computed tomography and magnetic resonance imaging, neurological exam results) in this case that indicates "relatively more right-sided brain trauma?"

• Can't depression cause impairments on tasks that are also felt to be more right-hemisphere oriented?

• You say, taking into account severity of the injury. . . . What do you mean by that? What severity of injury do you think he had?

• Why did you give a diagnosis of dementia, due to closed head trauma? Doesn't DSM-IV state that you have to have "clear evidence" of having sustained a head injury for this definition to even be considered? You also have to have impairments in social or occupational functioning right? Well, P.C.S. was working when you examined him, wasn't he? He was still married?

• Are you familiar with the term *misattribution?* What does that mean as it relates to postconcussion symptoms? Are you familiar with work by some neuropsychologists that you can treat acute symptoms of concussion through education and by correcting whatever misattributions a person may have about the cause of their symptoms?

• You recommend repeat testing in one year. Do you know if that has been done? What kind of results would you expect? Why?

• The fact that you tested P.C.S. within the first 3 months, wouldn't you expect for him to show improvement over time if he had sustained an uncomplicated concussion? How can you make determinations about permanence when he is still in the acute stage of recovery?

• You saw P.C.S. for a single treatment session in April 2000 (6 months after you evaluated him). In your report, you state that the neuropsychological evaluation indicated "significant brain injury." What do you mean by "significant"? He apparently missed two appointments with you didn't he? Then, he canceled the next appointment. What do you make of him not showing up and cancelling appointments? Would that suggest a lack of compliance with treatment?

• Do you know when P.C.S. contacted a lawyer? Did you ask? Wouldn't this be important information for you to know? Aren't the effects of litigation something to consider when you interpret neuropsychological test results? Especially when you're trying to understand the ongoing complaints of someone with a mild concussion who reports a lot of symptoms many months or years following an accident?

15

Misdiagnosis of Cognitive Impairment in Forensic Neuropsychology

Grant L. Iverson
Brian L. Brooks
James A. Holdnack

Clinical science, psychometric research, and psychometric theory have informed and refined the practice of clinical and forensic neuropsychology for decades. Gradually and systematically we have become more psychometrically sophisticated in the identification of cognitive impairment associated with brain injury, illness, and disease. Despite strong evidence that actuarial methods can be, and often are, superior to clinical judgment (Dawes, Faust, & Meehl, 1989; Grove & Lloyd, 2006; Marchese, 1992), clinical judgment remains the *conditio sine qua non* ("without which it could not be") of neuropsychological assessment.

The purpose of this chapter is to discuss, and illustrate with data, the potential to *misdiagnose* cognitive impairment. It is hoped that presenting these psychometric data will help refine clinical judgment pertaining to the identification of cognitive impairment in clinical and forensic neuropsychology. These data are relevant to the entire practice of neuropsychological assessment, but the focus here is on the potential to, and ease with which one can, *misdiagnose* cognitive impairment in patients with a mild traumatic brain injury or other condition(s) that could have a mild impact on cognitive functioning.

This chapter is divided into six sections. The first section introduces and conceptualizes levels of cognitive impairment. It introduces testable criteria for impairment, including mild cognitive diminishment and mild, moderate, severe, and profound cognitive impairment. The second section contains a review of biases and logical fallacies that affect clinical judgment. Clinical reasoning can be adversely affected by confirmatory bias, illusory correlations, clustering illusions, and neglect of base rates. The third section provides detailed information regarding *neuropsychological profile analysis*, which is one method that uses psychometric information to reduce bias. Neuropsychological profile analysis involves the simultaneous clinical and psychometric interpretation of a battery of tests. Most of our clinical reasoning is based on the interpretation of performance on individual tests, or patterns of test results, within a battery. Neuropsychological profile analysis allows the clinician to quantify an individual patient's performance across an entire test battery and to provide a normative classification for the performance across the entire profile of tests. The implications for forensic neuropsychology are obvious: This approach allows us to determine the prevalence of specific numbers of low test scores when a large number of tests are administered. The fourth and fifth sections illustrate neuropsychological profile analysis with the Expanded Halstead–Reitan Neuropsychological Battery (E-HRNB; Heaton, Grant, & Matthews, 1991) and the combined battery of the Wechsler Adult Intelligence Scale–III (WAIS-III; Wechsler, 1997a) and the Wechsler Memory Scale–III (WMS-III; Wechsler, 1997b), respectively. The final section contains conclusions and recommendations for clinical practice and future research.

CONCEPTUALIZING COGNITIVE IMPAIRMENT

There are no universally agreed on, or widely used definitions of, cognitive impairment. Cognitive impairment can be transient, temporary, fulminating, or permanent. The accurate identification and quantification of these cognitive problems can be difficult, and determining the underlying causes of these problems can be extraordinarily difficult. Cognitive impairment can be subjectively experienced, objectively measured, or both. Subjective and objective cognitive impairment can be concordant or discordant. It is commonly seen in clinical practice that patients with the most severe objective cognitive impairment frequently do not report subjectively experienced cognitive impairment or psychological distress regarding their seriously compromised cognitive abilities. For example, this is often seen in patients who have sustained a severe traumatic brain injury or who suffer from Alzheimer's disease. Essentially, these patients are not aware of, are indifferent to, or cannot fully appreciate their cognitive impairments.

In contrast, patients with mild cognitive impairment, or those with no objectively identifiable cognitive impairment, often have the subjective experience that their thinking skills are seriously compromised—and they experience considerable psychological distress relating to their concern about their thinking skills. It is well known in psychiatry, clinical psychology, and neuropsychology that patients with depression (Bassett & Folstein, 1993; Cutler & Grams, 1988), anxiety disorders (Foa, Cashman, Jaycox, & Perry, 1997), sleep disorders or problems (Ohayon & Lemoine, 2004), or chronic pain (Munoz & Esteve, 2005; Schnurr & MacDonald, 1995) frequently report problems with their thinking skills. These subjectively experienced cognitive difficulties might or might not be associated with identifiable cognitive deficits on neuropsychological tests.

It is helpful to conceptualize cognitive impairment on a continuum. Five categories of cognitive impairment, illustrating this continuum, are listed here. Determining the level of cognitive impairment usually requires considering multiple sources of information, including input from family members, review of medical records, review of collateral records (e.g., school or employment), interviews with the patient, observations of the patient's behavior, psychological test results, and neuropsychological test results.

1. *Profound cognitive impairment/severe dementia.* The cognitive impairment would render the person incapable of living outside a nursing home or an institution. If the person lived at home, he or she likely would require 24-hour-a-day supervision.

2. *Severe cognitive impairment/dementia.* The cognitive impairment would have a substantial adverse impact on everyday functioning. This level of impairment would render the individual incapable of competitive employment. The person should not be driving a motor vehicle and would likely have difficulty with activities of daily living.

3. *Moderate cognitive impairment.* This level of cognitive impairment would have a substantial impact on everyday functioning. The impairment would be noticeable to others in regard to the person's social and/or occupational functioning.

4. *Mild cognitive impairment.* This level of cognitive impairment should be identifiable using neuropsychological tests. The impairment has a mild (sometimes moderate) adverse impact on the person's social and/or occupational functioning.

5. *Mild cognitive diminishment.* This is not cognitive "impairment." Instead, it represents a mild diminishment in cognitive functioning that may or may not be identifiable using neuropsychological tests. The diminishment has a mild adverse impact on the person's social

and/or occupational functioning and it may or may not be noticeable by others.

The foregoing categories seem to reflect levels of cognitive impairment in a face-valid manner. However, the *specific* criteria for each level have not been codified or agreed on. We do not have specific psychometric criteria for interpreting neuropsychological tests in accordance with varying levels of cognitive impairment, nor do we have specific behavioral criteria for quantifying impairment or diminishment in everyday functioning. Clearly, more research is needed to establish and empirically test criteria in both domains. Until then, the diagnosis of cognitive impairment, and level of cognitive impairment, is fundamentally dependent on clinical judgment. Unfortunately, a number of factors can bias clinical judgment and decision making.

BIASES IN CLINICAL JUDGMENT

Bias on the part of the expert in medicine, psychiatry, neurology, psychology, or neuropsychology may be deliberate or nondeliberate. An unfortunate situation for both the judicial system and the respective health care profession is when some experts do not enter the courtroom as credible, neutral professionals but, rather, as biased advocates. Under these circumstances, the expert has chosen, with forethought, to advocate impartially. Other experts may be influenced indirectly, perhaps subtly and persistently, by a number of factors that introduce bias into their formulation of opinions. Most of the factors that bias judgment and decision making are ingrained patterns of perceiving and thinking. These more subtle biases, and the insidious way that they can evolve, must be guarded against (see Sweet & Moulthrop, 1999). The National Academy of Neuropsychology (2005), in a position statement relating to independent forensic neuropsychological evaluations, emphasized the need for objectivity and the avoidance of bias when interpreting test results. A quote from the Academy's position statement follows:

> Objectivity: A primary responsibility of neuropsychologists performing independent neuropsychological examinations is to strive to examine neuropsychological status objectively. Interpretation of results should ideally be made without preconceived ideas about the examinee and with proper attention to the potential effects of bias. Attempts to satisfy the examinee or align with the retaining third party have the potential to bias conclusions and recommendations. Care should be taken to consider potential biases and take action to guard against them (Sweet & Moulthrop, 1999). (National Academy of Neuropsychology, 2005, p. 999)

Essentially, bias in human reasoning occurs when a person processes information in a selective manner—that is, when the individual fails to recognize a logically relevant feature of the problem, or focuses on a logically irrelevant feature of a problem (Evans, 1989). *Confirmatory bias* occurs when we seek evidence to support a position previously anticipated and at the expense of disconfirmatory evidence (Wedding & Faust, 1989). For example, the neuropsychologist might have a general professional opinion that it is very likely that a person who sustained a moderate traumatic brain injury will have permanent cognitive impairments identifiable with neuropsychological testing. The neuropsychologist then gives a battery of tests and discovers "abnormal" performance on one or two tests believed to be sensitive to the effects of brain damage. Confirmatory bias occurs when the neuropsychologist differentially weighs this evidence at the expense of plausible, alternative explanations for the test results (e.g., the patient has a history of learning disability or substance abuse that might explain the test scores, or the scores simply reflect *normal* variation in an individual's performance when given a battery of tests).

Experts sometimes erroneously believe that two things that co-occur are causally related, when in fact they are not. For example, a neuropsychologist may assume that poor performance on a measure of information processing speed indicates brain impairment arising from a remote mild traumatic brain injury (MTBI). However, if the information-processing speed problem was related to the patient's history of learning disability, attention-deficit/hyperactivity disorder, or substance abuse, then the co-occurrence of the remote MTBI and the current cognitive problem represents an *illusory correlation* (Chapman & Chapman, 1969). Confirmatory bias and illusory correlation are two of the most common social psychological phenomena that can bias neuropsychological judgment and inferences. Other factors that can bias judgment and decision making are listed in Table 15.1.

It is very easy to diagnose, and misdiagnose, a person as having cognitive impairment. This is partially related to not having universally agreed-upon criteria for what constitutes cognitive impairment. The criteria set out in the ICD-10 (mild cognitive disorder; World Health Organization, 1992) and DSM-IV (cognitive disorder not otherwise specified; American Psychiatric Association, 1994) are rather nonspecific. Moreover, the ICD-10 criteria do not require neuropsychological testing. In the absence of agreed-upon, objective criteria, each clinician is expected to rely solely on clinical judgment. Clinical judgment is vulnerable to all the forms of bias and errors in reasoning listed in Table 15.1.

A sophisticated neuropsychologist, presented with virtually any set of comprehensive data derived from a healthy adult with no psychiatric or neurological problems, could write a reasonably compelling report suggest-

TABLE 15.1. Biases and Logical Fallacies Affecting Judgment and Decision Making

- *Confirmatory/confirmation bias:* The tendency to search for or interpret information in a way that confirms one's preconceptions or beliefs and avoid information that runs counter these beliefs. Many of the other biases, particularly those presented in this table, are related to confirmatory/confirmation bias.

- *Congruence bias:* The tendency to test hypotheses or clinical inferences directly, and to *avoid* testing hypotheses indirectly or testing alternative hypotheses. This type of bias is related to confirmatory bias. Confirmatory and congruence bias can be illustrated by a clinician selectively attending to the relation between a group of symptoms and postconcussion syndrome, and not attending to the relation between that same group of symptoms and depression, chronic pain, or both.

- *Anchoring:* To rely heavily on, or "anchor," a salient piece of information. This salient piece of information has more influence than it should on the opinion. *Anchoring* is a specific form of confirmatory bias that refers to the differential weighting of *initial* information. For example, counsel for an injured person calls the neuropsychologist and tells her that (1) the plaintiff suffered a "terrible" number of injuries, including a brain injury; (2) a prominent neurologist, Dr. X., has diagnosed the plaintiff as suffering from the long-term effects of a brain injury; and (3) the person who caused the accident was intoxicated. If the neuropsychologist is differentially influenced by the initial information and seeks confirmatory evidence at the expense of disconfirmatory evidence for a specific opinion, anchoring has occurred. The forensic expert also may be influenced by anchoring when the plaintiff attorney, upon initial contact, states that the patient cannot work due to personality changes and severe memory problems resulting from a brain injury. Similarly, anchoring may occur when the defense attorney, upon initial contact, states that 2 years prior to the accident in question the patient filed a bogus workers' compensation claim for a back injury.

- *Illusory correlation:* The inaccurate belief that two co-occurring things are causally or conceptually related. Illusory correlation is related to two possible causal attribution errors: *cum hoc ergo propter hoc* [with this, therefore because of this] and *post hoc ergo propter hoc* [after this, therefore because of this]. Things that co-occur or occur in temporal sequence are not necessarily conceptually or causally related. In forensic evaluations, we can erroneously attribute a person's low test scores to the direct effects of a past event (e.g., motor vehicle accident or toxic exposure), when in fact there are other predominant causes for the low test scores.

- *Clustering illusion:* This is a cognitive bias involving the tendency to see patterns where they don't actually exist. There was a long-standing belief in neuropsychology that Verbal IQ–Performance IQ splits could reliably indicate damage to the left or right hemisphere of the brain. This belief was a combination of a clustering illusion and a neglect of prior base rates. Neuropsychologists must guard against clustering illusion when we say that, based on our experience, we usually see this "pattern" of deficits associated with a certain condition. The clustering illusion can in clinical reasoning can result in the Texas sharpshooter fallacy.

- *Neglect of prior base rates:* The tendency to fail to consider prior known probabilities that are pertinent to the clinical inference or opinion. All the base-rate data presented in this chapter relates to this issue. When a neuropsychologist gives 40 tests that yield 60 individual scores, the clinician should, ideally, know the base rates of low scores for that particular battery in healthy adults. This will reduce the likelihood of false-positive diagnoses of cognitive impairment resulting from neglect of prior base rates.

(continued)

TABLE 15.1. (*continued*)

- *Observer–expectancy effect:* When a clinician expects to find something and sub-consciously manipulates the evaluation or misinterprets the data in order to find it. This can be related to, or influenced by, selective perception, attentional bias, clustering illusion, and neglect of prior base rates.

- *Texas sharpshooter fallacy:* Selecting or adjusting a hypothesis, decision, inference, or opinion after the data are collected, making it impossible to test the hypothesis fairly. This fallacy is related to the clustering illusion. This approach is common in forensic neuropsychology. The classic example is to collect all the neuropsychological test results, identify a single unusual finding or pattern, and then draw a causal inference for that pattern. For example, a person has a large difference between his Verbal IQ and Performance IQ, with PIQ > VIQ. Because this difference is statistically uncommon, the neuropsychologist assumes it must be caused by an MTBI. However, the hypothesis (PIQ > VIQ caused by MTBI) is formed after the fact and it cannot be tested empirically. Moreover, in general, the published literature cannot be used to formally test idiosyncratic hypotheses. However, on this particular issue there is a body of literature that would suggest that this particular hypothesis would be incorrect.

Note. More comprehensive information on these biases and logical fallacies can be found in a number of sources (e.g., Baron, 2000; Bishop & Trout, 2004; Gilovich, Griffen, & Kahneman, 2002; Plous, 1993; Turk & Salovey, 1986; Wedding & Faust, 1989).

ing that the person suffers from cognitive impairment. This is because (1) if a large number of tests are administered, most healthy adults will obtain some low scores, and (2) we now have a large number of discrepancy scores that yield "significant" (e.g., $p < .05$) and "uncommon" (e.g., occurs in fewer than 10% of healthy adults) results. Thus, to diagnose cognitive impairment resulting from MTBI, we simply need to say that whichever combination of low scores is obtained, these low scores are "consistent with the effects of a mild traumatic brain injury." Alternatively, we can capitalize on chance findings by saying that whichever particular "significant" and "uncommon" discrepancy is found, that discrepancy must reflect acquired cognitive impairment. The problem, of course, is that we have no information on the base rates of unusual discrepancy scores when *all* discrepancy scores are considered simultaneously. The base rates for the discrepancy scores are based on each individual discrepancy *in isolation*. Therefore, it might be uncommon for a person to have his or her WAIS-III Perceptual Organization Index 20 points greater than their Verbal Comprehension Index (POI > VCI), with a discrepancy of that magnitude or greater found in only 3.2 % of healthy adults (Psychological Corporation, 2002). However, how common is that particular finding in patients with specific diagnoses? Is there research support for that particular pattern occurring in people with MTBI? Moreover, how common is it to have one or more statistically uncommon discrepancy scores when all possible combinations of discrepancy scores across the WAIS-III and WMS-III are considered simultaneously? This is what we do in clinical practice when we examine the printout containing all the discrepancy scores. This is similar to running 50 *t*-tests in a research study without correcting the error rate (i.e., alpha). It is a common mistake in clinical reasoning to assume that the base rates of uncommon discrepancies for isolated findings apply to the simultaneous examination of all the possible discrepancy scores. Both of these classic forms of *post hoc* neuropsychological reasoning (i.e., the number of low scores, and the "patterns" or discrepancy scores) can be an example of the Texas sharpshooter fallacy (see Table 15.1).

The Texas sharpshooter is a fabled marksman who fired his gun randomly at the side of a barn and then painted a bull's-eye around the spot where the most bullet holes clustered. This logical fallacy occurs when the clinician infers or opines that a cluster in some data must be the result of a specific cause (e.g., a remote MTBI or toxic exposure). There are two reasons why this can be fallacious: (1) the cluster (i.e., pattern of test findings or number of low scores) may be the result of chance, or (2) there are other probable reasons for the clustering. The occurrence of a cluster in the data should be *the basis for forming a testable hypothesis, not inferring a causal relationship*. This potentially faulty reasoning is particularly susceptible to confirmatory bias.

To guard against bias and errors in reasoning, Wedding and Faust (1989) recommend starting with the most valid information, listing alternative diagnoses or clinical inferences, and systematically seeking both confirmatory and disconfirmatory evidence. They noted that it is common practice for neuropsychologists to make lists of test findings that support a particular clinical inference or opinion but uncommon (yet recommended) to list test findings and other information that is inconsistent with a particular clinical inference or opinion. Larrabee has emphasized for years that neuropsychologists should adopt a more scientific approach to interpreting evaluation results and that the test results should make "neuropsychological sense" (Larrabee, 1990, 1992, 2005). He has encouraged neuropsychologists to make sure that (1) the data are consistent within and between neuropsychological domains, (2) the profile is consistent with the suspected etiology of the problems, (3) the data are consistent with the severity of the etiology (e.g., an MTBI), and (4) the data are consistent with the examinee's behavioral presentation (Larrabee, 2005). Points 2 and 3 are particularly important—are the test findings consistent with the injury and the severity of the injury? If not, what are the other plausible explanations for the test findings?

As neuropsychology becomes more sophisticated with its methods for testing cognitive abilities and interpreting test data, it is hopeful (and expected) that these methods will help to further guard against bias in clinical judgment. In the next section, we describe a psychometric method for interpreting large amounts of cognitive test information. This method, of course, is only one technique that clinicians can rely on to reduce bias and avoid overinterpreting isolated low scores.

OVERVIEW OF NEUROPSYCHOLOGICAL PROFILE ANALYSIS

In a forensic neuropsychological evaluation, we carefully, systematically, and thoroughly assess patients using dozens of tests spanning several hours to determine if they have deficits or impairments resulting from a condition, injury, or disease. If we set our criterion for a deficit at 1 standard deviation below the mean, we accept *a priori* that 16% of healthy adults will score in this impaired range on any given test, without actually having an acquired deficit. Alternatively, if we set our criteria at the 10th percentile or 5th percentile we expect those percentages of "healthy" adults to score in that range on the test. We accept *a priori* that if we use normative data that are not corrected for education that people with low education are statistically more likely to be labeled as having acquired deficits when they do not (i.e., false positives), and people with university degrees are statistically more likely to be labeled as not having deficits when they do (i.e., false negatives).

Regardless of whether we use age-based or demographically corrected normative data, we accept *a priori* that the more tests we give, the more likely we are to obtain low scores on many of the tests. Although common-sense and clinical experience support the psychometric fact that giving more tests increases the probability of obtaining low scores on some of them, this issue has been infrequently and inadequately studied.

Neuropsychologists do not (or should not) interpret test scores in isolation. In routine clinical assessment, the practitioner considers individual test results, patterns of test results, and the entire profile as it relates to the patient's history and presenting problem(s). As a general rule, however, it is not possible for the clinician to know the base rate of low (i.e., "impaired") scores in healthy adults across any specific battery of tests. This is because most neuropsychologists use flexible neuropsychological test batteries (Rabin, Barr, & Burton, 2005; Sweet & Moberg, 1990; Sweet, Moberg, & Suchy, 2000; Sweet, Moberg, & Westergaard, 1996); the base rates of low scores across these batteries are unknowable unless the same battery is given to a normative sample or a large control sample. However, in those co-normed batteries that do contain a large normative sample—for example, the E-HRNB (Reitan & Wolfson, 1985, 1993), the Neuropsychological Assessment Battery (NAB; Stern & White, 2003), the WAIS-III (Wechsler, 1997a), and the WMS-III (Wechsler, 1997b)—the base rates of low scores are knowable and can be calculated. We have referred to this knowledge of base rates and the use of this information in clinical decision making as neuropsychological profile analysis (Iverson, Brooks, White, & Stern, in press; Iverson, White, & Brooks, 2006). The base rates of low scores across a battery of tests have been calculated by only a few research groups over the years, as illustrated in this section.

A well-appreciated example of concern regarding misdiagnosis involves the assessment of older adults with suspected mild cognitive impairment (MCI) and early Alzheimer's disease. For several years, researchers interested in MCI and early dementia have been concerned about *false-positive* diagnoses (e.g., de Rotrou et al., 2005; Palmer, Boone, Lesser, & Wohl, 1998). Palmer and colleagues (1998) examined a battery of neuropsychological tests in 132 healthy older adults. Twenty-six test scores were considered simultaneously, and low scores were defined as less than or equal to the 10th percentile and less than or equal to 2 standard deviations below the mean. They reported that 73% had one or more scores at or below the 10th percentile and 37% had one or more scores at or below 2 standard deviations from the mean.

Accidental MCI was a term used by de Rotrou and colleagues (2005) to describe older adults who perform poorly on one or two tests of memory or executive functioning at the time of initial testing who then obtain normal scores on these tests at 12-month follow-up. This, of course, is not a trivial issue when the referral question is to identify possible early dementia. These researchers reported that 48% of older adults classified as having MCI at initial testing normalized their test results at 12-month follow-up. The authors concluded that these people represented false-positive diagnoses of MCI.

Brooks, Iverson, and White (2007b) also examined the issue of accidental MCI. They provided the base rates of low memory scores for the Memory Module of the NAB (Stern & White, 2003). Participants were healthy older adults between 55 and 79 years of age ($M = 68.1$ years, $SD = 6.6$ years) obtained from the standardization sample ($N = 742$). The NAB Memory Module consists of four measures (List Learning, Shape Learning, Story Learning, and Daily Living Memory) that provide 10 demographically corrected T scores. When all 10 memory scores were examined simultaneously, 55.5% of older adults had one or more scores below 1 standard deviation and 30.8% had one or more scores ≤ 5th percentile (i.e., 1.5 standard deviations below the mean). When considering scores more than 2 standard deviations below the mean, 16.4% of healthy older adults from the NAB standardization sample obtained one or more frankly impaired memory scores. Brooks and colleagues also reported that the base rates of low memory scores increase substantially as intellectual abilities decrease. For example, 56.5% of older adults with low-average intellectual abilities, as measured by the Reynolds Intellectual Screening Test (RIST; Reynolds &

Kamphaus, 2003), obtained one or more low memory scores (–1.5 SDs) compared to 18.0% with superior to very superior intellectual abilities.

If false-positive diagnoses of MCI are known to occur at fairly high rates, it stands to reason that false-positive diagnoses of cognitive impairment in forensic neuropsychology, when dealing with MTBI or toxic exposure, also might occur frequently. When using numerous tests to evaluate a patient with an injury or condition that has a small adverse effect on cognition, the risk for misdiagnosing cognitive impairment as attributable to that injury or condition is high. This is because most healthy adults have *intraindividual variability* (Matarazzo & Prifitera, 1989; Schretlen, Munro, Anthony, & Pearlson, 2003) and will have some low scores when a large number of tests are administered. Thus, the neuropsychologist might simply assume that any, or most, low scores obtained reflect acquired brain impairment resulting from a specific personal injury when, in fact, these low test scores reflect other factors, such as momentary lapses of attention or effort, or long-standing personal weaknesses. In these circumstances, the risk for a false-positive diagnosis of cognitive impairment due to a personal injury increases.

PROFILE ANALYSIS USING THE HALSTEAD–REITAN NEUROPSYCHOLOGICAL BATTERY

The core Halstead–Reitan Neuropsychological Battery (HRNB) includes the Reitan–Indiana Aphasia Screening Test, Finger Tapping Test, Grip Strength, Sensory–Perceptual Examination, Seashore Rhythm Test, Speech–Sounds Perception Test, Trail Making Test, Tactual Performance Test, and Category Test (Reitan & Wolfson, 1985, 1993). Clinicians using the HRNB have known for many years that healthy adults routinely obtain low scores when given a battery of tests. The Halstead Impairment Index is a composite measure of the number of impaired test scores. That is, it is the proportion of test scores (out of 7 core scores) that fall within the impaired range. Traditionally, a Halstead Impairment Index score of 0.3 or less was considered normal (i.e., 30% or fewer of the seven tests comprising the index could fall in the impaired range) (Reitan & Wolfson, 1993, p. 92). The General Neuropsychological Deficit Scale (GNDS) is derived from 42 scores from the HRNB and the WAIS (Wechsler, 1955, 1981). When the GNDS norms are used then Halstead Impairment Indexes from 0 to 0.4 are considered broadly normal (Reitan & Wolfson, 1993, p. 316).

The manual of normative data for the E-HRNB (Heaton et al., 1991) provides more specific information on the base rate of low scores in healthy adults when a larger battery of tests is administered. These authors defined impairment as a T-score of 39 or less on tests from the E-HRNB. Using this definition, 15% of healthy normal subjects would be classified as impaired on any single test. However, when multiple tests are given, the probability of obtaining "impaired" scores goes up dramatically. For example, in a healthy sample of 455 adults, 90% had one or more impaired scores (the median number of impaired scores was 4). Approximately one-third of the normative subjects (i.e., 32.5%) had 7 or more scores in the impaired classification range, and over half (i.e., 53.3%) had 4 or more impaired scores. Heaton and colleagues (1991) noted that the "important point to recognize is that some poor test results are to be expected in most normal persons, especially when a large battery of tests is administered" (p. 36). The same analyses were completed for the Revised Comprehensive Norms for an Expanded Halstead–Reitan Battery (Heaton, Miller, Taylor, & Grant, 2004) based on 25 scores (see Table 15.2).

The base rates of low scores presented in Table 15.2 are based on demographically corrected normative scores. These scores were corrected for age, sex, and education (Heaton et al., 1991) and age, sex, education, and ethnicity (Heaton et al., 2004). Clinicians using fixed or flexible batteries with age-based normative data should expect the number of low scores to vary by both education and intelligence. Indeed, it has been reported repeatedly in the literature that neuropsychological test performance is correlated with education (e.g., Heaton et al., 1991; Mitrushina, Boone, & D'Elia, 1999; Moses, Pritchard, & Adams, 1999; Pachet & Longman,

TABLE 15.2. Number of "Impaired" Test Scores ($T = 39$ or Less) in Healthy Adults Who Were Given the Expanded Halstead–Reitan Neuropsychological Battery

Number of "impaired" scores	Heaton et al. (1991)		Heaton et al. (2004)	
	Approximate percent—40 scores	Cumulative percent—40 scores	Approximate percent—25 scores	Cumulative percent—25 scores
More than 10	15.8	15.8	7.0	7.0
10	3.9	19.7	2.5	9.5
9	3.9	23.6	3.4	12.9
8	3.9	27.5	4.6	17.5
7	5	32.5	4.2	21.7
6	5.9	38.4	7.0	28.7
5	7	45.4	7.5	36.2
4	7.9	53.3	9.2	45.4
3	9.9	63.2	13.0	58.4
2	15	78.2	13.4	71.8
1	11.9	90.1	15.0	86.8
0	9.9	100.0	13.2	100.0

Note. The values based on 40 scores are derived from the 455 participants from the E-HRNB normative sample presented by Heaton et al. (1991). These values were estimated from their Figure 6, presented on page 37. The values based on 25 scores are derived from the 1,189 participants from the E-HRNB presented by Heaton et al. (2004). These values were estimated from their Figure 9, presented on page 73.

2006; Sherrill-Pattison, Donders, & Thompson, 2000; Wiederholdt et al., 1993) and with intelligence (e.g., Boone, Lesser, Hill-Gutierrez, Berman, & D'Elia, 1993; Brittain, La Marche, Reeder, Roth, & Boll, 1991; Dodrill, 1999; Kane, Parsons, & Goldstein, 1985; Psychological Corporation, 2002). People with below-average intelligence tend to perform worse on many neuropsychological tests than do people with average intelligence (e.g., Dodrill, 1999; Horton, 1999; Reitan, 1985). Thus, people with below-average intelligence are expected to have more low test scores when a large number of tests are administered, and people with high average or superior intelligence are expected to have fewer low scores (Brooks, Iverson, & White, 2007a; Iverson, Brooks, & White, 2006). This is illustrated further in the section of this chapter that provides base rates of low scores on the WAIS-III and WMS-III.

Case Example

One of us (G. L. I.) has been involved in numerous cases in which the E-HRNB has been administered by another neuropsychologist conducting an evaluation at the request of plaintiff counsel. In that context, low scores obtained from the battery frequently are interpreted as illustrating acquired cognitive deficits arising from a remote MTBI. One particular case involved a man who sustained soft tissue injuries and an MTBI (i.e., a concussion) in a motor vehicle accident (MVA) 3 years prior to the neuropsychological evaluation. He reported ongoing chronic pain in his back and symptoms of mild depression. He had preexisting pain in his back arising from other injuries and a back surgery, but he reportedly had a significant worsening in his condition as a result of the MVA. He did not lose consciousness in the accident, and he had no retrograde amnesia, but he was mildly confused after the accident. He had difficulty remembering the first few minutes after the impact, until the ambulance crew arrived. His Glasgow Coma Scale score, 12 minutes after the ambulance crew was called, was 15. He was transported to the hospital because of complaints of back pain.

The plaintiff-retained neuropsychologist administered the E-HRNB, WAIS-III, and WMS-III. This university-educated man obtained a Full Scale IQ in the high-average classification range. The psychologist interpreted the battery of objective test results as illustrating permanent cognitive impairment arising from the MTBI. The neuropsychologist wrote that the patient's cognitive impairment would significantly compromise his ability to work in his small business. Thus, the Trier of Fact (judge alone, in this case) was presented with evidence that the plaintiff sustained a "traumatic brain injury" that resulted in "cognitive impairment" that adversely affected his ability to work. What was not clear, from reading the report, was how well the plaintiff performed on objective testing. Across the entire E-HRNB (1991 norms), he did not obtain a single low score. As seen in Table 15.2, only 9.9% of healthy adults obtain no low scores across this battery of tests. Thus, when considering his performance *as a whole*, he scored in the superior classification range (i.e., top 10% of healthy adults). Moreover, he did not have a single low WAIS-III or WMS-III subtest score. As seen in Table 15.3, 48% of people of high-average intelligence have one or more scaled scores of 7 or less when 20 subtest scores from the WAIS-III and WMS-III are considered simultaneously. Thus, this man did not perform well across the battery of tests—he performed extraordinarily well. It was important to illustrate these points, through careful cross-examination, because the plaintiff was being portrayed as seriously cognitively compromised and unable to do his job.

The neuropsychologist in this case emphasized "variability" in test scores and urged the judge to consider the "big picture." Given the fact that the plaintiff had no low scores across all the tests comprising the E-HRNB, WAIS-III, and WMS-III, it is reasonable to conclude that in this aspect of the big picture, he likely was performing in the top 5% of the healthy adult population when all of his abilities are considered simultaneously. It is common for neuropsychologists to examine variability, either through scatter or thorough strengths and weakness analyses, and then infer cognitive impairment. It is important to keep in mind, however, that variability is common in healthy adults (e.g., Matarazzo & Prifitera, 1989; Schretlen et al., 2003). Moreover, variability increases in relation to the number and types of tests administered. This is illustrated in Figure 15.1. As seen in this figure, when only six verbal subtests of the WAIS-III are considered simultaneously, 31% of healthy adults have a 2-standard-deviation spread between their highest and lowest score. However, when 14 subtests are considered simultaneously, 82% of healthy adults have a 2-standard-deviation spread between their highest and lowest scores. Clearly, as the number of test administered increases, the likelihood of significant variability among the test scores increases.

In this case, the plaintiff had high-average intelligence. The neuropsychologist explained that low scores were not expected because he was well above average in intelligence. This belief, however, has been described as a myth in neuropsychology (Dodrill, 1999). People with high-average or superior intellectual abilities are not expected to have uniformly high scores across a battery of neuropsychological tests. This is illustrated in the next section where the base rates of low scores for the WAIS-III and WMS-III are stratified by intelligence and education.

PROFILE ANALYSIS USING THE WAIS-III AND WMS-III

The WAIS-III (Wechsler, 1997a) and WMS-III (Wechsler, 1997b) are two of the most widely used batteries for measuring cognitive functioning in adults

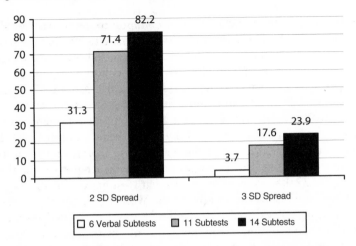

FIGURE 15.1. Percentages of healthy adults who have large spreads between their high and low test scores on the WAIS-III. The average score for a WAIS-III subtest is 10 with a standard deviation of 3 points. Examples of 6-point spreads include 4–10 (2nd percentile to 50th percentile), 6–12 (9th percentile to 75th percentile, and 9–15 (37th percentile to 95th percentile). Examples of 9-point spreads include 3–12 (1st percentile to 75th percentile), 5–14 (5th percentile to 91st percentile), and 7–16 (16th percentile–98th percentile). This figure was derived from data presented on page 211 of the *WAIS-III Administration and Scoring Manual.*

(Rabin et al., 2005). The WAIS-III yields IQ scores, index scores (Verbal Comprehension, Perceptual Organization, Working Memory, and Processing Speed), primary subtest scores, and supplementary subtest scores. The WMS-III is a battery of tests designed to evaluate attention, concentration, working memory, learning, immediate and delayed recall, and recognition of information presented in verbal and nonverbal modalities. This test is comprised of 11 subtests, with 6 primary subtests and 5 optional subtests. Eight index scores are derived from the primary scores. The WAIS-III and WMS-III are appropriate for adults ages 16 to 89 years and were co-normed using a stratified, U.S. representative sample of 2,500 and 1,250 healthy adults, respectively. Age-corrected and demographically corrected norms are available for both the WAIS-III and WMS-III. The demographic norms are corrected for age, education, sex, and ethnicity.

When the WAIS-III and WMS-III are both administered in a neuropsychological evaluation, 20 primary subtest scores and 12 index scores are calculated. Of course, numerous secondary scores also are obtained, but this section focuses on only the 20 primary subtest scores that are used to derive the indexes. Table 15.3 presents the base rates of low primary age-corrected subtest scores on the WAIS-III and WMS-III using two cutoff scores and stratified by age, education, and intelligence (obtained and predicted). It is important to note that it is common to get low scores. In the total sample, 77.5% of healthy adults had at least one low subtest score on the WAIS-III and WMS-III (i.e., a subtest with a scaled score of 7 or less). It is below average for healthy adults to have 7 or more low scores and uncommon to have 12 or more low scores (i.e., scaled score of 7 or less).

It would be a mistake to assume that having a few low scores on the WAIS-III and WMS-III, in the average healthy adult, represents impaired cognitive functioning. As seen in Table 15.3, healthy adults with lower education and lesser intelligence have more low scores, and by virtue of this are more likely to be misdiagnosed as having cognitive impairment. For example, 97.4% of healthy adults with estimated low-average Full Scale IQ have low subtest scores (using the Wechsler Test of Adult Reading [WTAR] Demographics Prediction method to estimate IQ). Whereas having 4 or more low scores is common in adults with estimated low-average Full Scale IQs, this many low scores in adults with estimated superior Full Scale IQ is uncommon (again, using the WTAR–Demographics Prediction method).

Case Examples

The following cases are examples of how neuropsychological profile analysis can be used in clinical and forensic practice. Examples are provided in which base rates of low scores seem to contribute to accurate diagnosis and to misdiagnosis.

Mr. Jones was a 49-year-old Caucasian man at the time of the evaluation. He was seen at the request of his disability insurance company. He had worked as a realtor for 17 years prior to going on disability, and he had been receiving disability benefits for 2 years. He reported a history of depression dating back to adolescence. He had periodic episodes of depression throughout his adult life, and had been on antidepressants on five separate occasions. The insurance company sent him for an independent neuropsychological evaluation. He was administered the Structured Clinical Interview for DSM-IV Axis I Disorders (SCID-I). He met criteria for current major depressive disorder, severe without psychotic features. He also met criteria for panic disorder without agoraphobia. He was taking Mirtazapine (antidepressant), Trazodone (antidepressant), Lorazepam (benzodiazepine), and Zopiclone (a hypnotic for sleep). Mr. Jones was administered the Personality Assessment Inventory and he did not elevate any of the validity scales. His score on the Beck Depression Inventory–II was 32 (severe). He performed in the normal range on all components of three effort tests (Test of Memory Malingering, Victoria Symptom Validity Test, and the 21 Item Test). He was administered a comprehensive battery of neuropsychological tests, including the WAIS-III and WMS-III. His Full

TABLE 15.3. Base Rates of Low WAIS-III and WMS-III Subtest Scores

	N	Scaled score = 7 or less				Scaled score = 6 or less			
		Zero low test scores	Average	Below average (< 25%)	Uncommon (< 10%)	Zero low test scores	Average	Below average (< 25%)	Uncommon (< 10%)
All adults	1,250	22.5%	1–6	7–11	12+	39.2%	0–3	4–7	8+
Age Groups									
16–19	200	21.5%	1–6	7–9	10+	36.0%	0–4	5–6	7+
20–29	199	26.6%	0–6	7–10	11+	41.7%	0–4	5–7	8+
30–44	201	28.4%	0–6	7–11	12+	44.3%	0–3	4–8	9+
45–64	222	24.3%	1–6	7–11	12+	41.9%	0–4	5–7	8+
65–74	178	16.9%	1–6	7–12	13+	29.8%	0–3	4–7	8+
75–89	250	17.6%	1–6	7–11	12+	40.0%	0–4	5–7	8+
Education									
8 or less	154	3.9%	3–11	12–15	16+	22.7%	1–6	7–10	11+
9–11	159	8.8%	3–11	12–14	15+	19.5%	1–7	8–10	11+
12	420	20.5%	1–5	6–9	10+	34.3%	0–3	4–6	7+
13–15	288	28.8%	0–4	5–7	8+	48.6%	0–2	3–4	5+
16+	229	40.2%	0–2	3–6	7+	61.1%	0–2	3–4	5+
Full Scale IQ									
< 80	99	0.0%	11–16	17–18	19+	0.0%	7–12	13–15	16+
80–89	201	0.0%	6–11	12	13+	1.0%	3–6	7–8	9+
90–109	589	13.8%	1–4	5–6	7+	35.1%	0–2	3–4	5+
110–119	234	51.7%	0–1	2	3+	75.2%	0	1–2	3+
120+	127	62.2%	0–1	2	3+	82.7%	0	1	2+
WTAR-Demo. FSIQ									
< 80	63	0.0%	8–16	17	18+	0.0%	4–11	12–15	16+
80–89	155	2.6%	4–12	13–15	16+	8.4%	2–8	9–11	12+
90–109	700	16.9%	1–5	6–8	9+	36.7%	0–3	4–5	6+
110–119	251	53.4%	0–2	3	4+	70.9%	0–1	2	3+
120+	32	50.0%	0–1	2	3+	75.0%	0	1	2+

Note. The percentages of subjects with zero low test scores are provided. The "average" number of low scores stratified by different demographic variables includes zero low scores for well educated adults and adults with above-average intelligence. Note, however, that adults with below-average intelligence are expected to get many low scores. Thus, if they do not, their performance across the entire battery of tests is actually "above average." For example, if a person with a Full Scale IQ of 85 obtains only four scores of 7 or less, this would be *better* than expected (i.e., above average). The range of low scores representing below average performance, or the "low average" classification range (i.e., < 25th percentile), varies considerably based on education and intelligence. The cutoff number of low scores, representing fewer than 10% of each sample, also varies considerably by education and intelligence.

Scale IQ was 110. His lowest subtest score on the WAIS-III was 10. On the WMS-III, he obtained six primary subtest scores of 7 or less, and two subtest scores of 6 or less. As seen in Table 15.3, having three or more scaled scores of 7 or less is uncommon in adults with high-average intelligence (occurring in fewer than 10%). Having two scores of 6 or less is below average for adults with high-average intelligence. The neuropsychologist concluded that the man had "psychological impairments and memory problems that would prevent him from performing the material and substantial duties of his occupation." This opinion was based on the severity of his psychiatric problems and his cognitive difficulties in combination.

Mrs. Smith was a 43-year-old Caucasian woman who was involved in an MVA 3 years before the independent neuropsychological evaluation was conducted at the request of her counsel. Her vehicle was struck from behind while she was at a stop sign. She sustained soft tissue injuries to her neck (whiplash) and an alleged MTBI. There was no apparent loss of consciousness, but she seemed dazed and distressed at the scene. However, she did not appear to have an appreciable period of posttraumatic amnesia. An ambulance attended the scene of the accident, but she was not transported to the hospital. She complained of chronic pain in her neck, depression, and cognitive problems at the time of the evaluation. The neuropsychologist did not administer effort testing. The WAIS-III and WMS-III were given as part of a comprehensive evaluation. Her Full Scale IQ was 91. On the WAIS-III, she obtained two low scores (Arithmetic and Block Design = 7). On the WMS-III, her lowest subtest score was on Spatial Span (SS = 8). Her WMS-III Index scores were all in the high-average to superior classification range, with the exception of her Auditory Immediate Index, which was average. Her WMS-III primary subtest scores ranged from 8 to 16 (Spatial Span and Faces I). The psychologist concluded that she had memory impairment, primarily "in the form of high variability." As seen in Table 15.3, only 14% of adults with average intelligence have zero low scores when considering all the WAIS–WMS primary subtest scores simultaneously. Having two low scores is common. The case settled, so the neuropsychologist did not have to testify and undergo cross-examination on these test findings.

A 24-year-old man was seen 4 months following an MVA; he was seen at the request of his lawyer. There was a high-speed collision in which he was an unrestrained passenger who was propelled into the windshield. He sustained a witnessed loss of consciousness for less than a minute, postinjury combativeness at the scene of the accident, a Glasgow Coma Scale score of 14 at approximately 20 minutes postinjury, and approximately 1.5 hours of posttraumatic amnesia. A day-of-injury CT (computed tomography) scan of his brain revealed a small right frontal contusion. He was administered a comprehensive battery of neuropsychological tests. He performed in the normal range on all of the scores derived from two effort tests (Medical Symptom Validity Test and Test of Memory Malingering). His Full Scale IQ on the WAIS-III was 93. He obtained four low scores on the WAIS-III (Arithmetic = 7, Letter–Number Sequencing = 7, Symbol Search = 7, and Digit Symbol Coding = 6). He obtained three low scores on the WMS-III (Logical Memory I = 7, Logical Memory II = 6, Family Picture II = 6). Having seven low scores is uncommon, occurring in less than 10% of healthy adults with average intelligence. The neuropsychologist concluded that the man was experiencing ongoing neurocognitive problems, at 4 months postinjury, as a result of his complicated MTBI.

It is helpful to know how often healthy adults, with certain demographic characteristics and levels of intellectual ability, obtain low test scores. Understanding the base rates of low scores across a battery of tests can facilitate the accurate interpretation of a few isolated low scores and numerous low scores. This information can help refine clinical judgment and reduce bias.

CONCLUSIONS AND DIRECTIONS
FOR FUTURE RESEARCH

In clinical and forensic practice, we may make assumptions that bias our interpretation of the test results. These assumptions relate to some of the fundamental principles of neuropsychological theory and practice, such as *deficit measurement* (Lezak, 1976, 1983). Most of us were taught that if we give enough tests, and the right tests, we will accurately identify the person's deficits. We typically assume that the person has deficits because, after all, he or she was referred for a neuropsychological evaluation. Thus, if we are a competent neuropsychologist who has conducted a thorough evaluation, we will clearly delineate the examinee's deficits. Many of us were taught to create a summary sheet and to carefully identify any score that seemed low. These low scores become highly salient clinical data, with broadly normal scores or superior scores being deemphasized. In fact, many neuropsychologists were taught to refer to high-average or superior scores as "within normal limits." Of course, a superior score is no more or less "normal" than an unusually low score. Overreliance on salient data, seeking confirmatory evidence, clustering illusions, and overlooking disconfirmatory evidence are a few forms of bias that can affect clinical judgment and reasoning and lead to false-positive diagnoses of cognitive impairment. The very nature of what we do, and how we do it, sets us up to overdiagnose cognitive impairment. Therefore, it is critical that we learn as much as possible about the base rates of low scores in healthy adults, and in specific clinical populations, across different batteries of tests. This will help us guard against overreliance on "salient data" (i.e., isolated low test scores) in formulating our clinical opinions.

Figure 15.2 illustrates the theoretical and methodological relationship between normal functioning and frank neurocognitive impairment. The area between normal functioning and frank impairment, referred to as mild diminishment, is *defined* by the presence of low scores but is *divided* by the clinical reasoning that attributes causation to the low scores. The logic of

the figure relates to the accurate attribution of cause. That is, in a civil forensic evaluation the cause of the cognitive impairment, from the plaintiff's
perspective, is the personal injury. If we adopt the plaintiff's perspective,
then a *false-positive* mild diminishment, defined by the presence of low
scores, involves a clinical judgment that the scores were caused by the personal injury when in fact they were not. In reality, the low scores were actually attributable to normal variability or measurement error, or they may
represent static, long-standing, and/or relative weaknesses that do not impact functioning. *True-positive* mild diminishment, again defined by the
presence of low scores, involves the clinical judgment that the low scores
are beyond normal functioning and are correctly attributed to cognitive impairment due to a particular injury, illness, condition, or event. *False-negative* conclusions occur when low scores are incorrectly attributed to normal
variability or other factors when, in reality, they are caused by the personal
injury. *True-negative* conclusions occur when low scores are correctly attributed to normal variability or other factors (such as preexisting alcohol-
ism, learning disability, and/or attention-deficit/hyperactivity disorder). The
person might actually have mild cognitive impairment but the cause of the
impairment is not the personal injury—thus, from a forensic–causation perspective, the person would be considered a true negative.

   This chapter, by design, focused more on the potential to *misdiagnose*
cognitive impairment. In other words, the chapter focused on the issue of
false positives. We illustrated how easy it is to misinterpret normal cogni-

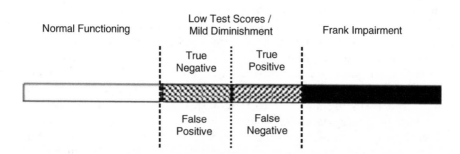

FIGURE 15.2. Theoretical and methodological relationship between normal functioning, mild neurocognitive diminishment, and frank neurocognitive impairment due to a
specific personal injury. False-positive neurocognitive diminishment or impairment is
meant to represent those people who are identified as having a problem due to a personal injury, when in fact the low test scores represent normal functioning, normal human variability in neurocognition, long-standing static cognitive difficulties unrelated to
what is being litigated, or measurement error, broadly defined. False-negative conclusions occur when low scores are incorrectly attributed to normal variability or other factors when, in reality, they are caused by the personal injury.

tive functioning as "abnormal." We also discussed how intentional or unintentional biases increase the likelihood of false-positive diagnoses of cognitive impairment. It is essential, of course, to appreciate that a "missed diagnosis" is equally important. That is, false negatives can occur more easily when psychometric data are viewed in isolation and not combined with other sources of clinical and collateral information. Moreover, intentional and unintentional biases can increase the likelihood of false-negative diagnoses of cognitive impairment.

It is important for clinicians to be aware of the biases that might impact clinical judgment and the ease with which a person can be misdiagnosed as having cognitive impairment, and to become informed about new methods and analyses that are designed to reduce the likelihood of misdiagnosis and increase the accuracy of diagnosis. Neuropsychological profile analysis, which is designed to assist clinicians in their interpretation of large amounts of cognitive data, is sophisticated and is based on a psychometric foundation. In the case examples presented in this chapter, the clinicians did not incorporate neuropsychological profile analysis to help interpret their data from the HRNB or the WAIS-III/WMS-III. Neuropsychological profile analysis creates salient data, previously unavailable to clinicians, which can help address intentional bias and guard against unintentional bias in forensic evaluations. Future research is needed to (1) determine whether specific batteries of tests can differentiate groups, such as those with traumatic brain injuries and lingering cognitive problems, depression, and healthy controls; (2) identify profiles or patterns that occur with a reasonable degree of diagnostic accuracy in specific clinical groups, (3) operationally define cognitive impairment, and (4) link the operationally defined cognitive impairment to problems with real-world functioning.

REFERENCES

American Psychiatric Association. (1994). *Diagnostic and statistical manual of mental disorders* (4th ed.). Washington, DC: Author.

Baron, J. (2000). *Thinking and deciding* (3rd ed.). New York: Cambridge University Press.

Bassett, S. S., & Folstein, M. F. (1993). Memory complaint, memory performance, and psychiatric diagnosis: A community study. *Journal of Geriatric Psychiatry and Neurology, 6*(2), 105–111.

Bishop, M. A., & Trout, J. D. (2004). *Epistemology and the psychology of human judgment.* New York: Oxford University Press.

Boone, K., Lesser, I., Hill-Gutierrez, E., Berman, N., & D'Elia, L. (1993). Rey–Osterrieth Complex Figure performance in healthy, older adults: Relationship to age, education, sex, and IQ. *The Clinical Neuropsychologist, 7*, 22–28.

Brittain, J., La Marche, J., Reeder, K., Roth, D., & Boll, T. (1991). Effects of age and IQ on Paced Auditory Serial Addition Task (PASAT) performance. *The Clinical Neuropsychologist, 5*, 163–175.

Brooks, B. L., Iverson, G. L., & White, T. (2007a). Low neuropsychological test scores are common in healthy older adults. *Journal of the International Neuropsychological Society,* 13(S1), 106.

Brooks, B. L., Iverson, G. L., & White, T. (2007b). Substantial risk of "accidental MCI" in healthy older adults: Base rates of low memory scores in neuropsychological assessment. *Journal of the International Neuropsychological Society,* 13(3), 490–500.

Chapman, L. J., & Chapman, J. P. (1969). Illusory correlation as an obstacle to the use of valid psychodiagnostic signs. *Journal of Abnormal Psychology,* 74, 217–280.

Cutler, S. J., & Grams, A. E. (1988). Correlates of self-reported everyday memory problems. *Journal of Gerontology,* 43(3), S82–90.

Dawes, R. M., Faust, D., & Meehl, P. E. (1989). Clinical versus actuarial judgment. *Science, 243,* 1668–1674.

de Rotrou, J., Wenisch, E., Chausson, C., Dray, F., Faucounau, V., & Rigaud, A. S. (2005). Accidental MCI in healthy subjects: A prospective longitudinal study. *European Journal of Neurology, 12*(11), 879–885.

Dodrill, C. B. (1999). Myths of neuropsychology: Further considerations. *The Clinical Neuropsychologist, 13*(4), 562–572.

Evans, J. (1989). *Bias in human reasoning.* Hillsdale, NJ: Erlbaum.

Foa, E. B., Cashman, L., Jaycox, L., & Perry, K. (1997). The validation of a self-report measure of posttraumatic stress disorder: The Posttraumatic Diagnostic Scale. *Psychological Assessment, 9*(4), 445–451.

Gilovich, T., Griffen, D., & Kahneman, D. (Eds.). (2002). *Heuristics and biases: The psychology of intuitive judgment.* Cambridge, UK: Cambridge University Press.

Grove, W. M., & Lloyd, M. (2006). Meehl's contribution to clinical versus statistical prediction. *Journal of Abnormal Child Psychology, 115*(2), 192–194.

Heaton, R. K., Grant, I., & Matthews, C. G. (1991). *Comprehensive norms for an extended Halstead–Reitan Battery: Demographic corrections, research findings, and clinical applications.* Odessa, FL: Psychological Assessment Resources.

Heaton, R. K., Miller, S. W., Taylor, M. J., & Grant, I. (2004). *Revised comprehensive norms for an expanded Halstead-Reitan Battery: Demographically adjusted neuropsychological norms for African American and Caucasian adults professional manual.* Lutz, FL: Psychological Assessment Resources.

Horton, A. M., Jr. (1999). Above-average intelligence and neuropsychological test score performance. *International Journal of Neuroscience, 99*(1–4), 221–231.

Iverson, G. L., Brooks, B. L., & White, T. (2006). New discrepancy scores for the Neuropsychological Assessment Battery. *Canadian Psychology, 47*(2a), 110.

Iverson, G. L., Brooks, B. L., White, T., & Stern, R. A. (in press). Neuropsychological Assessment Battery (NAB): Introduction and advanced interpretation. In A. M. Horton, Jr., & D. Wedding (Eds.), *The neuropsychology handbook* (3rd ed.). New York: Springer.

Iverson, G. L., White, T., & Brooks, B. L. (2006). Base rates of low scores on the Neuropsychological Assessment Battery (NAB). *Canadian Psychology, 47*(2a), 110.

Kane, R. L., Parsons, O. A., & Goldstein, G. (1985). Statistical relationships and discriminative accuracy of the Halstead–Reitan, Luria–Nebraska, and Wechsler IQ scores in the identification of brain damage. *Journal of Clinical and Experimental Neuropsychology, 7*(3), 211–223.

Larrabee, G. J. (1990). Cautions in the use of neuropsychological evaluation in legal settings. *Neuropsychology, 4,* 239–247.

Larrabee, G. J. (1992). Interpretive strategies for evaluation of neuropsychological data in legal settings. *Forensic Reports, 5,* 257–264.

Larrabee, G. J. (2005). A scientific approach to forensic neuropsychology. In G. J. Larrabee (Ed.), *Forensic neuropsychology: A scientific approach* (pp. 3–28). New York: Oxford University Press.

Lezak, M. D. (1976). *Neuropsychological assessment.* New York: Oxford University Press.

Lezak, M. D. (1983). *Neuropsychological assessment* (2nd ed.). New York: Oxford University Press.

Marchese, M. C. (1992). Clinical versus actuarial prediction: A review of the literature. *Perceptual and Motor Skills, 75*(2), 583–594.

Matarazzo, J. D., & Prifitera, A. (1989). Subtest scatter and pre-morbid intelligence: Lessons from the WAIS-R standardization sample. *Psychological Assessment, 1*(3), 186–191.

Mitrushina, M. N., Boone, K. B., & D'Elia, L. F. (1999). *Handbook for normative data for neuropsychological assessment.* New York: Oxford University Press.

Moses, J. A., Jr., Pritchard, D. A., & Adams, R. L. (1999). Normative corrections for the Halstead Reitan Neuropsychological Battery. *Archives of Clinical Neuropsychology, 14*(5), 445–454.

Munoz, M., & Esteve, R. (2005). Reports of memory functioning by patients with chronic pain. *Clinical Journal of Pain, 21*(4), 287–291.

National Academy of Neuropsychology. (2005). Independent and court-ordered forensic neuropsychological examinations: Official statement of the National Academy of Neuropsychology. *Archives of Clinical Neuropsychology, 20*(8), 997–1007.

Ohayon, M. M., & Lemoine, P. (2004). [Daytime consequences of insomnia complaints in the French general population]. *Encephale, 30*(3), 222–227.

Pachet, A., & Longman, R. S. (2006). Challenging Reitan & Wolfson: Demographic corrections are necessary. *Archives of Clinical Neuropsychology, 22*(6), 559.

Palmer, B. W., Boone, K. B., Lesser, I. M., & Wohl, M. A. (1998). Base rates of "impaired" neuropsychological test performance among healthy older adults. *Archives of Clinical Neuropsychology, 13*(6), 503–511.

Plous, S. (1993). *The psychology of judgment and decision making.* New York: McGraw-Hill.

Psychological Corporation. (2002). *Updated WAIS-III/WMS-III technical manual.* San Antonio, TX: Author.

Rabin, L. A., Barr, W. B., & Burton, L. A. (2005). Assessment practices of clinical neuropsychologists in the United States and Canada: A survey of INS, NAN, and APA Division 40 members. *Archives of Clinical Neuropsychology, 20*(1), 33–65.

Reitan, R. M. (1985). Relationships between measures of brain functions and general intelligence. *Journal of Clinical Psychology, 41*(2), 245–253.

Reitan, R. M., & Wolfson, D. (1985). *The Halstead–Reitan Neuropsychological Test Battery: Theory and clinical interpretation.* Tucson, AZ: Neuropsychology Press.

Reitan, R. M., & Wolfson, D. (1993). *The Halstead–Reitan Neuropsychological Test Battery: Theory and clinical interpretation* (2nd ed.). Tucson, AZ: Neuropsychology Press.

Reynolds, C. R., & Kamphaus, R. W. (2003). *Reynolds Intellectual Assessment Scales and Reynolds Intellectual Screening Test professional manual.* Lutz, FL: Psychological Assessment Resources.

Schnurr, R. F., & MacDonald, M. R. (1995). Memory complaints in chronic pain. *Clinical Journal of Pain, 11*(2), 103–111.

Schretlen, D. J., Munro, C. A., Anthony, J. C., & Pearlson, G. D. (2003). Examining the range of normal intraindividual variability in neuropsychological test performance. *Journal of the International Neuropsychological Society, 9*(6), 864–870.

Sherrill-Pattison, S., Donders, J., & Thompson, E. (2000). Influence of demographic variables on neuropsychological test performance after traumatic brain injury. *The Clinical Neuropsychologist, 14*(4), 496–503.

Stern, R. A., & White, T. (2003). *Neuropsychological Assessment Battery.* Lutz, FL: Psychological Assessment Resources.

Sweet, J. J., & Moberg, P. J. (1990). A survey of practices and beliefs among ABPP and non-ABPP clinical neuropsychologists. *The Clinical Neuropsychologist, 4*, 101–120.

Sweet, J. J., Moberg, P. J., & Suchy, Y. (2000). Ten-year follow-up survey of clinical neuropsy-chologists: part I. Practices and beliefs. *The Clinical Neuropsychologist, 14*(1), 18–37.

Sweet, J. J., Moberg, P. J., & Westergaard, C. K. (1996). Five-year follow-up survey of practices and beliefs of clinical neuropsychologists. *The Clinical Neuropsychologist, 10*, 202–221.

Sweet, J. J., & Moulthrop, M. A. (1999). Self-examination questions as a means of identifying bias in adversarial assessments. *Journal of Forensic Neuropsychology, 1*(1), 73–88.

Turk, D., & Salovey, P. (1986). Clinical information processing: Bias inoculation. In R. Ingram (Ed.), *Information processing approaches to clinical psychology* (pp. 305–323). San Diego, CA: Academic Press.

Wechsler, D. (1955). *Manual for the Wechsler Adult Intelligence Scale.* New York: Psychological Corporation.

Wechsler, D. (1981). *Wechsler Adult Intelligence Scale—Revised manual.* San Antonio, TX: Psychological Corporation.

Wechsler, D. (1997a). *Wechsler Adult Intelligence Scale—Third edition.* San Antonio, TX: Psychological Corporation.

Wechsler, D. (1997b). *Wechsler Memory Scale—Third edition.* San Antonio, TX: Psychological Corporation.

Wedding, D., & Faust, D. (1989). Clinical judgment and decision making in neuropsychology. *Archives of Clinical Neuropsychology, 4*(3), 233–265.

Wiederholdt, W. C., Cahn, D., Butters, N. M., Salmon, D. P., Kritz-Silverstein, D., & Barrett-Connor, E. (1993). Effects of age, gender and education on selected neuropsychological tests in an elderly community cohort. *Journal of the American Geriatrics Society, 41*(6), 639–647.

World Health Organization. (1992). *International statistical classification of diseases and related health problems—10th edition.* Geneva, Switzerland: Author.

Index

267